Screening the Past

In this important new book, Pam Cook explores film culture's obsession with the past through searching and provocative analyses of a wide range of films, from *Mildred Pierce* and *Brief Encounter* to *Raging Bull* and *Dance With a Stranger*. She engages with current debates about the role of cinema in mediating history through memory and nostalgia through a discussion of *In the Mood for Love* and *Far From Heaven*, suggesting that many films use strategies of memory to challenge established ideas of history, and the traditional role of historians.

Cook discusses the various ways in which films by contemporary directors such as Martin Scorsese, Kathryn Bigelow, Todd Haynes and Wong Kar-wai deploy creative processes of memory, arguing that these movies can tell us much about our complex relationship to the past, and about history and identity. She also investigates the recent history of film studies, reviewing the developments that have culminated in the exciting, if daunting, present moment. This is a rich and stimulating volume that will appeal to anyone with an interest in cinema, memory and identity.

Pam Cook is Professor of European Film and Media at the University of Southampton. She is co-editor of *The Cinema Book* (revised edition, 1999), and her many publications on film include *Fashioning the Nation: Costume and Identity in British Cinema* (1996) and *I Know Where I'm Going!* (2002) in the British Film Institute's *Film Classics* series.

Screening the Past

Memory and Nostalgia in Cinema

Pam Cook

Routledge
Taylor & Francis Group

LONDON AND NEW YORK

First published 2005
by Routledge
2 Park Square, Milton Park, Abingdon, Oxon, OX14 4RN

Simultaneously published in the USA and Canada
by Taylor & Francis Inc
270 Madison Avenue, New York, NY 10016

Routledge is an imprint of the Taylor & Francis Group

© 2005 Pam Cook   *1005284333* T

Typeset in Perpetua and Bell Gothic by Bookcraft Ltd, Stroud, Gloucestershire
Printed and bound in Great Britain by The Cromwell Press, Trowbridge, Wiltshire

British Library Cataloguing in Publication Data
A catalogue record for this book is available from the British Library

Library of Congress Cataloging in Publication Data
Cook, Pam.
    Screening the past: memory and nostalgia in cinema / Pam Cook.
        p. cm.
    Includes bibliographical references and index.
    1. Nostalgia in motion pictures. 2. Memory in motion pictures.
    3. Motion pictures – Psychological aspects. I. Title.
    PN1995.9.N67C66 2004
    791.43'653—dc22   2004006798

ISBN 0-415-18374-X (hbk)
ISBN 0-415-18375-8 (pbk)

Contents

Figures

LIST OF FIGURES

Acknowledgements

Warm thanks to Charlotte Brunsdon and Rachel Moseley for invaluable help and support in the early stages. I am also indebted to Rebecca Barden and Lesley Riddle at Routledge for their patience and encouragement. Thanks are due to those who invited me to give talks on my research, and offered useful feedback: Carla Despineux, Ed Gallifant, Christine Geraghty, Jayne Morgan, Laura Mulvey, Verena Mund, Sarah Street and Mary Wood. I am also grateful to the University of Southampton for granting me leave to complete the book. As always, love and thanks to Sam Cook for pearls of wisdom and moral support.

The following articles have been previously published and are reproduced here with the kind permission of the copyright holders:

Cook, Pam, 'The Age of Innocence', Sight and Sound 4(2) (February 1994), pp. 45–6. Courtesy of Sight and Sound.

Cook, Pam, 'Duplicity in Mildred Pierce', from E. Ann Kaplan (ed.), Women in Film Noir (London: British Film Institute, 1998), pp. 69–90. Courtesy of BFI Publishing.

Cook, Pam, 'The Gold Diggers', Framework 24 (1984), pp. 12–30. Courtesy of Framework.

Cook, Pam, 'The Last Temptation of Christ', Monthly Film Bulletin 55(657) (October 1988), pp. 287–8. Courtesy of Sight and Sound.

Cook, Pam, 'Mandy: daughter of transition', from Charles Barr (ed.), All Our Yesterdays: Ninety Years of British Cinema (London: British Film Institute, 1985), pp. 355–61. Courtesy of BFI Publishing.

Cook, Pam, 'Masculinity in crisis?', Screen 23(3/4) (1982), pp. 39–46. Courtesy of Screen.

Cook, Pam, 'Melodrama and the women's picture', from Sue Aspinall and Robert Murphy (eds), BFI Dossier No. 18: Gainsborough Melodrama (London: British Film Institute, 1983), pp. 14–28. Courtesy of BFI Publishing.

Cook, Pam, 'No fixed address: the women's picture from *Outrage* to *Blue Steel*', from Steve Neale and Murray Smith (eds), *Contemporary Hollywood Cinema* (London and New York: Routledge, 1998), pp. 229–46. Courtesy of Routledge.

Cook, Pam, 'Scorsese's masquerade', *Sight and Sound* 1(12) (April 1992), pp. 14–15. Courtesy of *Sight and Sound*.

Cook, Pam, 'Stars and politics', from Christine Gledhill (ed.), *Star Signs: Papers from a Weekend Workshop* (London: BFI Education, 1982), pp. 23–31. Courtesy of BFI Publishing.

Cook, Pam, 'Women and the western', from Edward Buscombe (ed.), *BFI Companion to the Western* (London: British Film Institute/Andre Deutsch, 1988), pp. 240–3. Courtesy of BFI Publishing.

'The pleasures and perils of exploitation films' was first delivered at the Feminale Film Festival conference *Girls, Gangs, Guns* in 1999.

'Memory in British cinema: brief encounters' was first delivered at the University of Bristol in 2001.

'Fashion and sexual display in 1950s Hollywood' was first delivered to the BFI/Birkbeck MA seminar in 1995.

'Replicating the past: memory and history in *Dance With a Stranger*' was first delivered at the Museum of the Moving Image Education Department conference *Past Pleasures* in 1997.

'Fictions of identity: style, mimicry and gender in the films of Kathryn Bigelow' was first delivered at the Norwich Cinewomen Film Festival in 1996.

Every effort has been made to trace copyright holders of photographs, and any omissions brought to our attention will be remedied in future editions.

INTRODUCTION

The past today

The essays collected in this volume represent a personal voyage through 25 years of cultural history. They begin with the present, looking back on significant intellectual and ideological developments from the perspective of lived experience rather than academic distance – a timely enterprise in the light of current debates about the relationship between private memory and history. Many of them bear the hallmarks of this lived experience. They straddle the borders of the academic and the journalistic, the objective and the personal. Most of them were delivered as talks, in particular cultural contexts, and are discursive in tone. They have an immediacy (and, I hope, a freshness) born of a direct engagement with ideas and issues in circulation at the time they were written, and in that sense they are historical documents in their own right, evidence of an intellectual and cultural journey. For that reason they appear in more or less virgin state, subject to minimal revision. This applies to the previously published pieces too, which were selected on the basis of their contribution to key debates in the evolution of film studies. Many of those articles have themselves been part of a process of rewriting history that has transformed them many times over. It is not my intention to 'set the record straight' or to construct a definitive account of past events. Instead, I offer a personal perspective on some of the most exciting and challenging developments in film culture, in which I have been intimately and passionately engaged.

Since the 1970s, film studies has undergone some dramatic periods of revision, often in direct response to wider cultural forces – indeed, to me it is the most dynamic of all academic disciplines in that respect, constantly reinventing itself. Because it is closely tied to industrial, technological and economic developments, cinema is at the centre of cultural activity and change. To my mind, we have not yet begun to understand its power, not only in everyday life, but in the history of ideas. These larger issues will no doubt continue to be addressed by scholars and historians as we navigate a path through the jungle of global media and new technologies. Looking to the future inevitably involves a reassessment of the past, and an opportunity to take stock in the present. That is the spirit behind this book, which looks back at a particular intellectual history from the perspective of the current moment.

The arrival of that moment has seen the proliferation of terms such as 'postmodernism', 'postcolonialism' and 'postfeminism', all of which suggest the end of one era and the beginning of another. These words designate a transitional period in which many of the tenets of earlier phases of cultural theory have been challenged and destabilised. They also indicate a shift away from 1970s identity politics to a more nuanced understanding of political and cultural intervention. This is a complex issue, which can be perceived either negatively or positively. There are some who argue, for instance, that the age of postfeminism has seen the erosion of the gains made by the 1970s wave of feminism, and the erasure and relegation of women's cultural activity and achievements. My feeling is that history proceeds by fits and starts, and that it is salutary (as well as frustrating) to be made to realise that nothing can be taken for granted. The challenge to feminism may well take the form of a conservative backlash, but it can also provide an opportunity to rethink, and to regroup. It has often been remarked that postmodernism is characterised by nostalgia, perceived as a longing for the past that stands in the way of historical analysis. I prefer to think of my own encounters with the past in these pages as part of a process of critical reassessment, and although a touch of nostalgia may surface from time to time, my main interest is in tracing the dynamic transformation of thinking about cinema and film culture over the past 25 years.

In order to facilitate that process, the essays are organised into themed sections, each with a short introduction that contextualises them within contemporary debates, while suggesting ways of reassessing their significance for the current moment. This has the advantage of allowing a historical engagement with the past that acknowledges the input of changing agendas. The different sections indicate cultural shifts and transformations that nevertheless reflect a consistent set of preoccupations – with history and memory, gender and national identities, and the significance of visual technologies and the image in understanding the impact of global media on everyday lives. Perhaps most important, the essays form part of the wider history of ideas with which Anglo-American film culture has been engaged since the 1970s. In the wake of the revolutionary events of May '68 in France, those ideas were rooted in a widespread desire to democratise the media so that marginalised voices could be heard. In retrospect, many of those aspirations that oppositional theories and film-making practices could in themselves radically transform the power relations between media industries, producers and consumers were idealistic. The process of democratisation delivered by technological developments within the entertainment industries themselves, driven by ideologies of individual freedom and choice, have more or less taken over the arena of resistance, with the result that the aims and outcomes of oppositional strategies are less easily identifiable.

The current conjuncture is both daunting and exciting, demanding a wholesale revision of established ways of thinking about, and producing, valid cultural analysis. It is the aim of this book to contribute to those debates, and to help create a cultural history that both respects the past and is sensitive to the present, recognising that they are intimately linked. The past exists to be reinvented; the challenge is to reinvent it in a way that allows for creativity and imagination as well as analysis and exposition, and furthers our under- standing of the complex processes involved in historical reconstructions.

Chapter 1

RETHINKING NOSTALGIA
In The Mood for Love and *Far From Heaven*

History, memory, nostalgia

One of the most significant developments in film studies over the last fifteen years or so has been the growing preoccupation with memory and nostalgia. The recourse to history and the archive in the wake of the revision of 1970s film theory, together with the dramatic impact of global technologies on thinking about personal experience and identity, have focused attention on the dismantling of traditional power relations between producers and audiences. The authority assumed to reside in the text as the location of official meanings and ideologies has shifted to the viewer, perceived as a kind of scavenger, engaged in a process of appropriating the text and rewriting it to suit their own purposes. So-called 'dominant' ideologies, whether of patriarchy, capitalism or colonialism, have been overturned, or at least challenged, as consumers have disassembled and reassembled them, producing new configurations and interpretations that emerge from localised sites often far removed from the source texts and their producers. This has resulted in a startling proliferation of discursive intertexts and textual commentaries, whose origins and validity are not always clear, which have the potential to transform the way history is traditionally written and perceived. At the same time, the master narratives of major events focused on the activities of public figures have shifted to include the experience and perspective of the 'ordinary person'. This situation has been dramatised in films such as *Forrest Gump* (1994), whose use of special visual effects to place its naive, fictional hero at the centre of recorded American history has been much discussed. Television has produced series such as *People's Century* (1998–9), which tells the history

1

of the twentieth century through the eyewitness accounts of ordinary folk, and dramas of reconstruction such as *The Trench* (2002), which invited viewers to participate in the re-enactment of traumatic battlefield experiences of the First World War.

While they emerge from very different production circumstances, these examples share a number of features. *Forrest Gump* foregrounds the processes of reconstruction, creating an amalgamation of past and present, documentary footage and fiction, which acknowledges the way history and myth are elided in national memory. *People's Century* also manipulates archive footage and contemporary interview material, but it effaces the process of fabrication, presenting both as documentary evidence and thereby authorising itself as history, albeit unofficial. While both *Forrest Gump* and *People's Century* superimpose the present on the past, *The Trench* goes one step further, recreating the past as theatre to be performed and re-lived in the present. This was a controversial move, provoking criticism that to submit the participants to such harrowing experiences for the purposes of media spectacle was exploitative and in poor taste. History, it seems, requires a proper distance.

One of the effects of such media experiments is to bring spectators closer to the past, to produce a kind of second-hand testimony that includes the audience as witnesses to reconstructed events. These postmodern histories, which are events in themselves, rely on empathy and identification to create memories that are not based on first-hand experiences, but which nevertheless have a powerful emotional affect. Our access to history, via memory, is by way of imaginative encounters in which viewers figure, often heroically (the Forrest Gump syndrome) and sometimes ironically (as with the theme park masquerade), as performers in a pageant. The term 'prosthetic memory' has been used to describe the process whereby reconstructions of the past produce replacement memories that simulate first-hand experience. Such enterprises lay themselves open to charges of lack of authenticity, of substituting a degraded popular version for the 'real' event, and to accusations that by presenting history as dramatic spectacle they obscure our understanding of social, political and cultural forces. The pessimistic view assumes that the images and stories of the past fed to us by the global media networks produce 'false' memories, or at least memory scenarios whose veracity, or relationship to the real, are impossible to determine. Yet, in the very act of addressing audiences as nostalgic spectators and encouraging them to become involved in re-presenting the past, the media invites exploration and interrogation of the limits of its engagement with history. Where authentic histories claim to educate us about the past itself, imposing narrative order on chaotic reality, these modern-day reconstructions tell us more about our relationship to the past, about the connections between past and present, and our affective responses. They can also inspire viewers to seek further knowledge and understanding.

There is often a sense of melancholy about critiques of media attempts to memorialise history through dramatic reconstruction. A sense of despair prevails, as though something has been lost that is now irrecoverable. What is mourned is not so much the loss of 'reality' itself – although that is certainly an element in some writing, where manipulated media images are said to take the place of actual events in the minds of spectators, completely circumscribing their understanding of what has taken place. Rather, what is assumed to be lost is an ethical dimension, in that audiences are deemed to have been duped into accepting inauthentic versions and forgetting the 'truth'. What has been lost, it seems, is the authority of history itself, and its ability to produce convincing and objectifiable accounts of the past which will achieve a consensus. This has been accompanied by the erosion of the traditional status of historians, and their role as impartial analysts who possess the necessary skills and knowledge to provide credible histories for the rest of us. Whereas history still has recourse to notions of objectivity in order to define itself, memory is perceived as a more unpredictable affair, coloured by the vagaries of subjective response and amnesia. While the boundary between 'objective' history and 'subjective' memory is no longer clear cut, such distinctions still prevail in critical debates on the topic.

These debates are themselves suffused with nostalgia, which can be defined as a state of longing for something that is known to be irretrievable, but is sought anyway. In so far as it is rooted in disavowal, or suspension of disbelief, nostalgia is generally associated with fantasy and regarded as even more inauthentic than memory. Even though memory is tinged with subjectivity, it can still be regarded as authentic, especially when it comes to eyewitness accounts that provide a record of the impact of momentous events on the lives of individuals – the enormous increase in studies of personal testimony and cultural memory testifies to this. The fact that the eyewitness was actually present at the time invests their recollections with an aura that transcends the knowledge that their experience is reconstructed for the purpose of current agendas, and endows it with authority and emotional power. Once again, the distinction between nostalgia, memory and history has become blurred. The mechanisms of fantasy and suspension of disbelief associated with memory and nostalgia are present in history as well, to a degree. Where traditional approaches prefer to emphasise the differences between them, in order to sanction the legitimacy of history as a means of explaining the world, it is equally possible to see them as a continuum, with history at one end, nostalgia at the other and memory as a bridge or transition between them. The advantage of this formulation is that it avoids the common hierarchy in which nostalgia and some 'inauthentic' forms of memory are relegated and devalued in order to shore up notions of history 'proper'. Instead, it recognises that the three terms are connected: where history suppresses the element of disavowal or fantasy in its re-presentation of the past, nostalgia foregrounds those elements, and in effect lays bare the processes at the heart of remembrance. In that sense, it produces knowledge and insight, even though these may be of a different order from those produced by conventional historical analysis, and may be experienced in different ways.

This gives nostalgia a more interesting and challenging dimension. Rather than being seen as a reactionary, regressive condition imbued with sentimentality, it can be perceived as a way of coming to terms with the past, as enabling it to be exorcised in order that society, and individuals, can move on. In other words, while not necessarily progressive in itself, nostalgia can form part of a transition to progress and modernity. The suspension of disbelief is central to this transition, as nostalgia is predicated on a dialectic between longing for something idealised that has been lost, and an acknowledgement that this idealised something can never be retrieved in actuality, and can only be accessed through images. This process can be seen as an activity of 'let's pretend', or role-play: past events can be recreated so that the audience can experience them in the present, imagine what it was like then, and connect emotionally with representations of the past. Although this is an imaginative, and performative, operation, it also depends on a cognitive response, on the viewers' perception that the representation is not the same as the real thing, and on their critical assessment of the authenticity of the reconstruction. Audiences can consciously enjoy a playful or affecting engagement with history at the same time as exercising their aesthetic judgement. The sense of loss in nostalgic encounters is all the more powerful because it is predicated on the acknowledgement that the past is gone forever. Nostalgia plays on the gap between representations of the past and actual past events, and the desire to overcome that gap and recover what has been lost.

The critiques of memory and nostalgia in film studies are part of a more general engagement in the humanities with issues of history and identity, ranging across disciplines. But they are also partly a response to the emergence of the nostalgic memory film itself, which reconstructs an idealised past as a site of pleasurable contemplation and yearning. This is a very broad category, incorporating heritage cinema, period melodramas and westerns, as well as remakes and pastiches. While there have always been nostalgic memory films, the past 30 years have seen a substantial increase in their production. In the postmodern electronic era, as reality becomes increasingly virtual, the desire to find some form of authenticity has intensified. At the same time, consumer capitalism has taken full advantage of nostalgia to market commodities, including films and television programmes. Neverthe-less, modern memory films have not simply exploited nostalgia; in many cases, they have engaged with the process, exploring its limits and questioning traditional notions of history and representation. I have argued that nostalgia cannot be regarded as a simple device for idealising and de-historicising the past, as has frequently been claimed. Similarly, the nostalgic memory film, even in its most apparently innocent manifestations, has the potential to reflect upon its own mechanisms, and to encourage reflection in audiences. The more self-reflexive nostalgic films can employ cinematic strategies to actively comment on issues of memory, history and identity, and it is to such examples that I now turn. I shall explore two recent films that can be regarded as overtly nostalgic, but which also set out to reveal the complexities of the relationship between history and memory. The first is Wong Kar-wai's *In the Mood for Love* (2000), which has been hailed as a masterpiece of new Asian cinema, but has also been criticised for aestheticising and effacing history. The second is Todd Haynes' acclaimed tribute to Douglas Sirk melo-dramas of the 1950s, *Far From Heaven* (2002), which sparked a debate about the value of cinematic pastiche. It is no coincidence that both films foreground costume, performance and masquerade to illuminate issues of authenticity, memory and identity. They take full advantage of the nostalgic gaze at exqui-sitely designed period clothes and sets characteristic of historical fiction, but they use cinematic strategies of nostalgia in different ways to question the relationship between past and present, then and now. In both cases, costume, set design and performance play a crucial role in the films' investigation of history, memory and time.

In the Mood for Love: a dress tells the time

In the Mood for Love is set in Hong Kong in the 1960s. This was a key period for Wong Kar-wai himself, who moved from Shanghai to Hong Kong in 1963, at the age of five. In interviews he has declared that he wanted to recreate that time and place through his own recollections, and although *In the Mood for Love* is not strictly autobiographical it is littered with memories of personal signifi-cance to the director. Iconographic memorabilia and period styles blend with snatches of music and other cultural references to produce a kind of medita tion on the passage of time, viewed as a fusion of past and present encapsu-lated in a single, apocryphal moment. Wong's trademark stylistic flourishes are evident in the ironic use of clocks to evoke a relentless forward momentum, and the dream-like slow-motion and step-motion effects that imply the reverse, a slowing-down of cinematic time that seems to resist the inevitability of history. The *mélange* of cultural allusions contributes to this sense of nostalgic reverie: the film reconstructs 1960s Hong Kong through a promiscuous blend of references to popular cultural forms such as songs, films, novels and fashions from the 1930s, 1940s and 1950s, spanning traditional and modern manifestations. All this suggests that *In the Mood for Love* is less concerned with exploring colonial history than in taking a self-indulgent, backward look at an idealised, lost culture and way of life.

Indeed, even those who admire the film find it conservative in some respects. As well as those who criticise it for ignoring the sociopolitical context, others see in its romance of frustrated desire a regressive celebration of traditional Chinese melodramas that seem to endorse self-sacrifice and moral restraint as social imperatives. One of the key reference points for *In the Mood for Love* has been identified as Fei Mu's celebrated 1948 melodrama *Spring in a Small City* (recently remade by Zhuangzhuang Tian as *Springtime in a Small Town* [2002]), in which a married woman forgoes her own desire for a former lover and decides to stay with her ailing husband, whom she no longer loves. There are resonances here with the theme of quaint, old-fashioned morality that prevents Maggie Cheung as Su Li-zhen and Tony Leung as Chow Mo-wan from consummating their adulterous passion in Wong's film. Another reference point, not remarked upon to the same extent, is the similarity between *In the Mood for Love* and David Lean's 1946 film *Brief Encounter*, which is discussed in detail later in this volume. While the debt to Chinese melodrama, and to *Spring in a Small City* in particular, is not in dispute, Wong's film actually corresponds closely to *Brief Encounter* in its formal structure, themes and visual iconography. Without suggesting an intentional connection or tribute, in the light of the British contribution to Hong Kong's colonial past, it seems relevant to acknowledge those correspondences, while respecting the differences between the two films.

Like *In the Mood for Love*, *Brief Encounter* tells the story of an unconsummated romance between two married people, a middle-class housewife and the young doctor with whom she falls in love. It is a memory film, looking back from the perspective of Britain after the Second World War to the 1930s, perceived as a more innocent time. The complex structure, told in flashback through the heroine's reminiscences, plays on coincidence, delay and the postponement of gratification, while the pressures of time, and the forward drive to modernity are indicated by the prominence of the railway station clock, and the trains coming and going with ferocious speed through the station where the lovers meet. The dialectic between forward momentum and delay creates a sense of stasis, as though the characters are on the brink of change, yet trapped in the past and unable to move forward. As with *In the Mood for Love*, cinema is a significant reference point, providing a vehicle for the heroine's romantic fantasy as well as a metaphor for the processes of memory itself. *Brief Encounter* alludes only obliquely to sociopolitical forces, hinting ironically at Britain's imperial history. The tension between tradition, personified by the respectable heroine, and modernity, embodied in the progressive young doctor, is worked out through the romance scenario, whose potentially tragic consequences and ambivalently happy ending project a profound unease with the way forces of change affect individual lives. On its release in 1946, *Brief Encounter* was hailed as a masterpiece of new British cinema by critics, while postwar audiences were not so sure — many apparently found its outdated morality and middle-class values risibly anachronistic. Yet despite its conservatism, it remains a powerful exploration of the role of memory and nostalgia in mourning the loss of an imagined national past.

Brief Encounter employs ritual to explore time and memory. The characters engage in regular everyday activities such as shopping, eating and going to the cinema, and it is through these familiar routines that their paths cross accidentally, leading to their romantic liaison. The use of ritualised time creates one of the film's more interesting ruminations on memory: despite the repetitive (and carefully signposted) plot structure, the complicated sequence of events is difficult to grasp. The effect is to create confusion about what happened when, not only expressed by the heroine as she narrates her story, but also in the minds of the audience. Fantasy, forgetfulness and the distortion of linear time are thus built in to the memory narration, and form part of the viewers' experience, encouraging spectators to perceive memory as a transformative process rather than an accurate retrieval of the past. In *Brief Encounter*, time and place are both depicted as imaginary; the markers of authenticity, which are in fact often anachronistic, are ironic reminders of the fabricated nature of real time. This underlines the sense of arrested motion, as the characters find themselves caught between opposing forces of tradition and progress.

In the Mood for Love is also governed by ritual and repetition, as the protagonists, engaged in mundane pursuits, weave their way around one another in the confined spaces of their apartment block or local noodle bar. Some scenes are replayed, with minor variations, several times. While this contributes to an illusion of time passing, it also produces an impression of the same event being rehearsed over and over again. Indeed, this is made explicit by the lovers practising fantasy scenarios of confrontation with Li-zhen's errant husband, or acting out their unfaithful spouses' imaginary seduction routines. Time appears frozen, and the huge clock that dominates Li-zhen's office, which is superfluous to the narrative exposition, is a symbolic reminder of the arbitrary nature of time itself.

It has often been remarked that Wong's reconstruction of Hong Kong is impressionistic rather than strictly authentic — the film was shot in Bangkok,

Figure 1.1   Time stands still: Tony Leung and Maggie Cheung in *In the Mood for Love* (2000). Courtesy Block 2 Pictures/Jet Tone and the Kobal Collection.

where the narrow streets and run-down buildings were able to suggest the 1960s ambience more effectively than present-day Hong Kong. Wong employs a kind of shorthand to sketch in a mood or feeling rather than an actual location. At the same time, titles provide details about specific times and places, which sit rather oddly with the deliberate fusion of different periods and regions. It is as though history is being viewed through the filter of nostalgic memory – and, indeed, Wong makes liberal use of screens, mirrors, windows and extremely tight framing to imply a perspective coloured by distance and obstructed vision. Towards the end of the film, Mo-wan returns to his Hong Kong apartment from Singapore, ostensibly to visit his former landlord, pausing to gaze longingly at the door of Li-zhen's old room. An intertitle – quoting from the short story 'Intersection' by Liu Yi-chang, the inspiration for *In the Mood for Love* – appears on screen: 'That era has passed. Nothing that belonged to it exists any more.' Following the final sequence in the ruins of Angkor Wat in Cambodia, a closing title states: 'He remembers those vanished years. As though looking through a dusty window-pane, the past is something he could see but not touch. And everything he sees is blurred and indistinct.'[1]

The melancholy that pervades *In the Mood for Love*, enhanced by the music, especially the haunting, repetitive love theme, is explicitly linked to memory and nostalgia. The obsessive desire to recapture the past, accompanied by the knowledge that it cannot be retrieved, is at the heart of Wong's evocation of the diasporic experience of the displaced Chinese communities. *In the Mood for Love* is on one level a celebration of the hybrid and cosmopolitan character of Hong Kong Chinese cultures, presented as elegant and exotic. On another level, it sees the upheavals caused by historical change as a negative force, bringing about the dispersal of an authentic national identity, as individuals and families find themselves thrown together and driven apart by historical necessity. Wong uses nostalgic memory to express this tension between tradition and modernity, showing his protagonists almost literally unable to move on. When Li-zhen hurries to meet Mo-wan in his hotel room, her ascent of the staircase is manipulated through fast editing so that she appears to move backwards and forwards at the same time, expressing her ambivalence about the situation, but also conjuring up a sense of indecision, and a hesitation about taking the next step. Together with the number 2046 on his door, an ironic reminder of the year that Hong Kong will be reabsorbed into the Chinese mainland, and the back-tracking camera as Li-zhen walks away down the corridor, culminating in the slowing down and freezing of the image, this produces an impression of hiatus, a pause for reflection on past and future developments. In the final scene set in 1966 Cambodia, when Mo-wan whispers his secret into the archaic stones of the temple in Angkor Wat, he draws on an ancient tradition that seems to connect him to a precolonial, even pre-historic era — an imagined national past that is unlikely ever to have existed. The scene is preceded by archive documentary footage from French television coverage of President de Gaulle's visit to Cambodia, heralding a period of momentous change and upheaval, and renewed colonial activity on the part of the Western powers. In re-enacting this traditional ritual, Mo-wan seems to confirm his alienation from modernity, and his desire to escape the inevitable. At the same time, his actions and demeanour suggest a Zen-like acceptance that he is at the mercy of events, an instrument rather than agent of history. There could hardly be a more affecting evocation of the passing of an era and the concomitant loss of identity for those individuals caught up in it.

It would be misleading to see the Cambodia sequence as the moment when the film opens out to embrace history, since history is woven into the very texture of the film. As already discussed, the *mise-en-scène* and soundtrack are laden with mementoes from bygone eras, celebrating a rich and diverse cultural heritage. Despite the claustrophobic settings, the daily routines and habits of the characters communicate a wealth of information about a wider context of social and cultural change. One of the most telling indicators of change is the costume, with Mo-wan's dapper suits and ties and Li-zhen's elegant array of cheongsams, handbags and high-heeled court shoes conveying not only their prosperous status, but also the Westernisation of traditional Chinese dress under the influence of global consumer capitalism. Clothing plays an important, symbolic role in Chinese history — who can forget the worldwide impact of the uniform adopted to signify the Cultural Revolution, itself a modern variation on the traditional tunic? The cheongsam, an icon of fashionable Chinese womanhood, was appropriated by Western designers in the 1950s and 1960s. The figure-hugging tunic dress, with its high mandarin collar and slit skirt, is a hybrid of traditional Chinese design and Western style, both exotic and erotic in its connotations. On one hand, it designates sexual emancipation, social status and financial independence; on the other, because of its association with prostitution and Western decadence, it suggests poverty and oppression. The cheongsam encapsulates opposing forces of tradition and modernity, revealing a femininity at once sexualised and constricted, and it is no coincidence that it features prominently in popular culture as an emblem of the personal and social dilemmas faced by women.

In *In the Mood for Love*, Li-zhen's breathtakingly beautiful cheongsams express her predicament, as she is torn between old and new. In harmony with the set designs, the stylised flowers that adorn many of her dresses evoke the changing seasons and the transitory nature of life, drawing on traditional Chinese cultural themes. More than half the patterns are abstract, denoting a contemporary Western style that is also evident in her beehive hair-do, and her expensive jewellery, handbags and shoes. All her dresses have excessively high, stiff mandarin collars, projecting more than a hint of slavery and subjugation. Most of the other female characters also wear cheongsams – with two important exceptions: Amah, the servant of Li-zhen's landlady Mrs Suen, sports a traditional tunic and trousers, befitting her lowly status, while Mo-wan's wife, who is having an affair with Li-zhen's husband, consistently wears Western clothes, as indeed does Mo-wan himself.

In addition to its symbolic role as signifier of historical change, the cheongsam is a central device in the film's evocation of suspended time. In the course of the film, Li-zhen flaunts 22 different versions, half of which she wears only once, while the other half make more than one appearance.[2] The number of dresses puts her prosperity on display, but each dress also functions as a marker of continuity in the scene changes and the linear progression of the narrative. Sometimes this is a straightforward matter, with her costume indicating a narrative time shift, or guaranteeing the internal coherence of sequences containing more than one scene. However, as already discussed, while the film does have a linear narrative, it is made up of short, episodic scenes and sequences whose repetitive structure suggests the arbitrary nature of time. When Li-zhen's cheongsams recur in different scenes, the effect is to create confusion about the sequence of events, and the editing process itself, as some of those scenes could easily have been inserted elsewhere without sacrificing comprehension. The cheongsam is thus established not only as a monumental cultural icon, but also as a central figure in Wong's meditation on history, memory and time. Its power lies in the way it encapsulates past, present and future in a single image, resolving irreconcilable social tensions and contradictions in much the same way as myth. Yet it is tinged with melancholy, its sensuous, fragile beauty underlining the sense of loss at the heart of Wong's profoundly nostalgic film.

Far From Heaven: sampling and remixing the past

The nostalgic memory film conjures up a golden age, which is both celebrated and mourned, providing an opportunity to reflect upon and interrogate the present. Past and present are conflated, as contemporary concerns are superimposed on earlier historical periods in the process of reconstruction. Despite all their claims to authenticity, nostalgic fictions depend upon a slippage between current styles and period fashion in order to draw audiences in to the experience. The past is presented as a site for a complex imaginative encounter, combining fantasy, emotion and critical judgement, to which the knowledge that it can never be fully retrieved is essential. Memory films allow the slippage

11

between past and present to be consciously addressed, since memory itself reorders the past from the perspective of today. In the process of looking back, the past is explored, mourned, and exorcised to enable characters (and audience members) to come to terms with the present. Some memory films use the conflation of past and present characteristic of nostalgia to question ideas of progress. They create a time-warp effect in order to suggest that historical change has not necessarily moved society forward. Others foreground the mechanisms of reconstruction to reveal both disjunctures and similarities between then and now. While some may re-present a golden age that is stable and timeless, many reconstruct a past era as turbulent and unsettled, as a liminal realm that provides an outlet for escapist fantasy.

Far From Heaven pays tribute to Douglas Sirk melodramas of the 1950s, celebrating their capacity to examine social issues of gender, sexuality and race through bitter-sweet romantic themes and extravagant use of *mise-en-scène* that produce a kind of critical commentary on American society. Sirk's melodramas were themselves nostalgic, harking back to a pastoral idyll uncontaminated by consumer capitalism and social conflict, a myth at the heart of the American Dream. Many of Sirk's characters yearn for a state of lost innocence, free from social constraints, only to find that it cannot be regained. They flout convention in their search for happiness, usually with tragic consequences. Todd Haynes' film is not exactly a remake; rather it samples several of the Sirk melodramas, updating them by making explicit meanings submerged in the source texts, producing parallels between the 1950s and now.[3] The activity of pastiche is foregrounded, and used to full effect as the film-makers lovingly reconstruct the Sirk 'look' through set design, costume and cinematography, and meticulously reproduce the image of 1950s small-town America projected by those melodramas. This results in a compelling emotional appeal to audiences via memories of those films, which were themselves calculated to produce a powerful affective response in viewers. Where many remakes mimic the original, *Far From Heaven* mirrors its source material (appropriately enough, given Sirk's predilection for mirror shots). The result is an intensification of nostalgia, as the sense of loss engendered by Sirk films is doubled by that produced by their reconstruction. The mirror image, like the cinematic image, inevitably reflects a distorted view of its subject, and Haynes' retrospective lens produces a reverse likeness in which aspects of the original films – in particular, themes they were unable to address openly – are made explicit. Much of the emotional intensity of the Sirk melodramas derives from a sense of repression, as the overblown *mise-en-scène* is used to articulate what cannot be directly expressed. The process of reconstruction thus results in a further loss of innocence, as the dark undercurrents of middle-class 1950s America are brought to the surface.

While *Far From Heaven* employs strategies of pastiche to induce nostalgia, it refrains from becoming pastiche itself. Rather, it is a revised version, rewriting the earlier texts with the benefit of hindsight. The new version has its own authenticity, deriving principally from the performances of the lead actors, who completely avoid parody, investing their characters with dignity and emotional integrity. Julianne Moore as suburban housewife and mother Cathy Whitaker, Dennis Quaid as her sexually confused husband Frank, and Dennis Haysbert as Raymond, the gardener with whom Cathy falls in love, are convincing in their own right, as well as reminding viewers of Jane Wyman, Lana Turner, Dorothy Malone, Lauren Bacall, Robert Stack and Rock Hudson. The carefully crafted dialogue, poignant in its polite formality, even in intimate scenes, evokes the 1950s without tipping over into camp, and the irony inherent in some scenes — for example, when Cathy naively expresses her liberal views on race — is not at the expense of the protagonists, but directed at the society they inhabit. The actors do not mimic Sirk's characters, even though they remind us of them, nor do they represent modern translations of those characters, as in conventional remakes. Their performances are part of the process of creating a new slant, not just on Sirk's melodramas, but on the social context in which they were made. The effect is of a 1950s America in the grip of social upheaval, despite attempts to produce an impression of stability. Haynes' film sets out to revise accepted versions of the 1950s, a period which has often been projected as a time of social and economic security.

Like *In the Mood for Love*, *Far From Heaven* produces a nostalgic vision of a moment in the national past when the fabric of society was tearing at the seams, and the emerging contradictions put pressure on prevailing ideologies of social harmony based on economic stability. *Far From Heaven* digs beneath the surface to uncover the fractures in the 1950s vision of the happy heterosexual couple and the white, middle-class family that formed the basis of the burgeoning consumer economy. Like the Sirk melodramas, it approaches those contradictions primarily through the perspective of its middle-class heroine, but in its inventive remix, it brings into clearer focus the stories that the Sirk films could not fully tell — the marginalised histories of African-American experience and resistance, presaging the Civil Rights movement, and of homosexual lives confined and pathologised by compulsory heterosexuality, precursors of the modern Gay Rights movement. As with Wong's film, the characters are largely helpless in the face of the social forces affecting their lives — even Cathy's liberal views on racial equality do not really connect with the lived experience of black African-Americans. The protagonists are at the mercy of events, unable to change society for the better; social prejudice prevents Cathy and Raymond from living together as a mixed-race couple, while Frank is condemned to an underground existence with his homosexual lover.

With the break-up of her marriage and Raymond's departure to Baltimore, Cathy becomes a single mother, and presumably the primary breadwinner, since Frank's executive job at Magnatech is now on the line. She is thus, despite herself, caught up in profound changes affecting the monogamous family unit and the economic and sexual position of women. *Far From Heaven*'s tragic scenario depicts characters caught up in history who try to resist what is happening to them as the result of social pressures, but are powerless to do so, and must accept their destiny. Their ingenuousness in the face of change invests the film with a deep sense of melancholy, as they inhabit sets shrouded in blue light, or windswept landscapes apparently perpetually in the grip of autumn, despite the changing seasons. Sandy Powell's dramatic costumes, with their rich hues of red, orange and green, enhance the autumnal ambience created by the intensely coloured falling leaves, flowers and foliage. In its sheer extravagance, the array of sophisticated New Look designer dresses worn by Cathy and her friends suggests conspicuous consumption and cultural capital,[4] while Raymond's check shirts, jackets and chinos indicate his upward mobility, and Frank's uniform grey suit, white shirt and tie, not to mention his trilby hat, connote an element of disguise, a desire to blend, chameleon-like, into the background, which is consonant with his double existence.

Whereas the lavish *mise-en-scène* of Sirk's melodramas is so over-the-top that it is said to produce an ironic distance that encourages the audience to criticise consumer culture, the costume and production design of *Far From Heaven* is used to comment on the process of reconstruction itself, giving rise to a different sort of irony, one that recognises the gap between the source material and its re-presentation with the knowledge of hindsight – Sirk's imitation of life becomes Haynes' imitation of art. This knowingness tempers the nostalgia of Haynes' film, increasing the distance between then and now by fixing the Sirk films as symptomatic of their time, despite all their self-conscious irony. The film's 'smart' quality has been seen as camp, as draining it of emotion, with Julianne Moore's moving performance its saving grace. Yet this response is in itself nostalgic, harking back to the Sirk original, perceived as more authentic, behind the pastiche and obscuring the depth of feeling in *Far From Heaven* itself. In one of the film's most affecting sequences, Cathy tells Raymond that because of town gossip she cannot continue their friendship, provoking an impassioned outburst from him about the need to look beyond surfaces to the truth. With tears running down her face, Cathy admits that she is bound by convention, and pleads with Raymond not to make a scene. The sense of missed opportunity is palpable, and the heart-rending emotion of this sequence is mirrored later, when Cathy, her marriage in shreds despite her efforts to save it, offers to move with Raymond to Baltimore to

Figure 1.2 Sampling the past: Julianne Moore in *Far From Heaven* (2002). Courtesy Killer Films and the Kobal Collection.

start a new life. Tragically, happiness is still beyond their reach, as he rejects her suggestion, realising that social prejudice will continue to tear them apart. These scenes are charged with an overwhelming sense of loss that matches anything in the Sirk melodramas. After Cathy, dressed for the first and only time in a business-like tailored suit, waves goodbye to Raymond at the railway station and returns to her children in the car, a high crane shot pulls back to reveal the town framed by early spring blossom – a fragile, delicate emblem of hope which is not without irony, since the future is already known.

Todd Haynes' probing beneath the surfaces of Sirk's melodramas reveals a hidden American history. While the Sirk films challenged the success ethic of the American Dream, many of the painful contradictions faced by people in the 1950s remained under wraps. Haynes sets out to discover what lies beneath Sirk's images, acknowledging that our access to the past is via such images, and using melodrama's capacity to visualise fantasy and desire. Melodrama expresses regret at opportunities lost, and while it depends on a melancholy resignation in the face of destiny, it also imagines what might have been ('if only things could have been different'). *Far From Heaven*'s retrospective look at the 1950s imagines a scenario in which the lives of its characters could have been very different, and it is all the more poignant in light of the knowledge that while some things may have changed, many remain the same.

15

Conclusion: the value of nostalgia

As memory films, *In the Mood for Love* and *Far From Heaven* echo one another in many respects. Both mobilise nostalgia to celebrate the past, while using it to challenge history and notions of progress. Both depict characters trapped in time, unable to affect the course of events, and both view social change pessimistically through the perspective of doomed romance. The connections between the two films extend beyond their melodramatic scenarios of frustrated desire, to the deployment of costume, set design, music and performance as key players in the process of period reconstruction, as well as emotional stimuli and vehicles for symbolic expression, geared to intensifying nostalgia. *In the Mood for Love*'s repetitive use of the Nat King Cole song, 'Perhaps, Perhaps, Perhaps', resonates with the 'if only' theme of *Far From Heaven*, emphasising the melancholy at the heart of both films. The references to Western styles and the relentless drive to modernity noted in Wong's reconstruction of 1960s Hong Kong are mirrored in the orientalism evident in the 1950s sets of Haynes' film, where the passage of time and the fleeting nature of life is similarly marked by the passing of the seasons. This orientalism, which is also present in the delicate paintings on the credit sequences, perhaps hints at the renewed colonial activities of the USA in South East Asia and its devastating consequences, creating further interesting connections between the two films.

Critiques of nostalgia films condemn them for de-historicising the past, for creating a timeless zone outside social change and historical analysis. This implies a particular view of history and social change, as though they are themselves free from subjective emotion and the processes of representation. In both the cases I have considered here, past, present and future have been conflated, in a process of superimposition and elision that reflects the activity of memory itself. This has produced an impression of suspended time, which is not outside history, but expresses a desire to question linear progression, and the way we think of social progress and history. The nostalgic celebration of popular culture and its material artefacts in such films enables us to view commodities, including historical fictions, in a different way, as indicators of desires and aspirations, much like diaries or family photographs. The status of these mementoes as historical evidence is complex, since they are inevitably subject to reinterpretation in the present. While the activity of reinterpretation is acknowledged by modern historians, it is rarely included in their analyses. In analysing nostalgic films, the role of the cultural historian is transformed. It is no longer a straightforward matter of decoding and deconstructing the social meanings, or of locating the texts in their contemporary context – although these remain an important part of the historian's task. Rather, it is a question of analysing the complex, transformative relationship of the texts to history itself, of reading and interpreting what they have to tell us about that relationship, so that our knowledge of historical representation is advanced. This may involve a redrafting of the techniques and conventions of historical analysis to take on board the dialectic between memory and history, holding together objective analysis and subjective response in a productive tension. As I hope to have demonstrated in the above discussion, nostalgia can provide the means to realise such new forms of history.

Notes

1 In the booklet accompanying the Criterion Collection DVD, Liu Yi-chang's story is reproduced in English translation by Nancy Li. The quotations inserted into *In the Mood for Love* are translated in the booklet as follows. 'Nothing from that period survived. He could only look for his lost happiness in his memories. Yet, the memory of happiness was like a faded photograph, blurred and unreal. When he heard Yao Surong sing, he remembered those vanished years. Those bygone days were something he could only look at through a dusty windowpane; something he could see, but couldn't touch. And everything he saw was blurred and indistinct.'

2 Li-zhen has around 50 costume changes in *In the Mood for Love* – a high number even for a period costume drama.

3 *Far From Heaven* samples *Magnificent Obsession* (1954), *All that Heaven Allows* (1955), *Written on the Wind* (1956) and *Imitation of Life* (1959), as well as Rainer Werner Fassbinder's 1973 Sirk homage *Fear Eats the Soul*, to produce a composite 'Sirk melodrama' that is a remix of the source texts. This is an interesting development of the remake, which is also evident in *Down with Love* (2003), the pastiche of Rock Hudson and Doris Day films starring Ewan McGregor and Renée Zellweger.

4 The significance of the New Look in redefining 1950s femininity is discussed in detail elsewhere in this volume (see especially Part 5).

Further reading

Birmingham Feminist History Group, 'Feminism as femininity in the nineteen-fifties?', *Feminist Review* 3 (1979).

Boym, Svetlana, *The Future of Nostalgia* (New York: Basic Books, 2001).

Burgoyne, Robert, 'Prosthetic memory/traumatic memory: *Forrest Gump*', *Screening the Past* 6 (16 April 1999). Available online at www.latrobe. edu.au/www/screeningthepast/firstrelease/fr0499/rbfr6a.htm (accessed 29 June 2004).

Cook, Pam, *I Know Where I'm Going!* (London: BFI Film Classics, 2002).

Elsaesser, Thomas, '"One train may be hiding another": private history, memory and national identity', *Screening the Past* 6 (16 April 1999). Available online at www.latrobe.edu.au/www/screeningthepast/reruns/ rr0499/terr6b.htm (accessed 20 July 2004).

Higson, Andrew, 'Re-presenting the national past: nostalgia and pastiche in the heritage film', in Lester Friedman (ed.), *British Cinema and Thatcherism: Fires Were Started* (London: University College London Press, 1993).

—— , *English Heritage, English Cinema: Costume Drama Since 1980* (Oxford: Oxford University Press, 2003).

Hoesterey, Ingeborg, *Pastiche: Cultural Memory in Art, Film and Literature* (Bloomington: Indiana University Press, 2001).

Hutcheon, Linda, *The Politics of Postmodernism* (London: Routledge, 1989).

Jameson, Fredric, *Postmodernism, Or the Logic of Late Capitalism* (Durham: Duke University Press, 1991).

Klinger, Barbara, 'Selling melodrama', in *Melodrama and Meaning: History, Culture and the Films of Douglas Sirk* (Bloomington: Indiana University Press, 1994).

—— , 'The new media aristocrats: home theater and the domestic film experience', *Velvet Light Trap* 42 (fall 1998).

Knapp, Steven, 'Collective memory and the actual past', *Representations* 26 (spring 1989).

Kuhn, Annette, *An Everyday Magic: Cinema and Cultural Memory* (London: IB Tauris, 2002).

Marchetti, Gina, 'Hong Kong: 1960s introduction', The Criterion Collection DVD *In the Mood for Love*, 2002.

Rosenstone, Robert (ed.), *Revisioning History: Film and the Construction of a New Past* (Princeton: Princeton University Press, 1995).

—— , *Visions of the Past: The Challenge of Film to Our Idea of History* (Cambridge: Harvard University Press, 1995).

Screen 12(2) (summer 1971): *Special Number: Douglas Sirk.*

Sobchack, Vivian (ed.), *The Persistence of History: Cinema, Television and the Modern Event* (London: Routledge, 1996).

Stacey, Jackie, 'Hollywood memories', in Annette Kuhn and Jackie Stacey (eds), *Screen Histories: A Screen Reader* (Oxford: Oxford University Press, 1998).

Teo, Stephen, 'Wong Kar-wai's *In the Mood for Love*: like a ritual in transfigured time', *Senses of Cinema* (March–April 2001). Available online at www.sensesofcinema.com/contents/01/13/mood.html (accessed 29 June 2004).

Turim, Maureen, *Flashbacks in Film: Memory and History* (London: Routledge, 1989).

Further viewing

Brief Encounter (David Lean, UK, 1946)

Far From Heaven (Todd Haynes, USA, 2002)

Forrest Gump (Robert Zemeckis, USA, 1994)

In the Mood for Love (Wong Kar-wai, Hong Kong, 2000)

People's Century (WGBH/BBC, USA/UK, 1998 99). www.pbs.org/wgbh/peoplescentury/about/index.html (accessed 29 June 2004).

Springtime in a Small Town (Zhuangzhuang Tian, China/Hong Kong/France, 2002)

The Trench (BBC, UK, 2002). www.bbc.co.uk/history/programmes/trench/index.shtml (accessed 29 June 2004).

Reviewing the past

History, gender and genre

INTRODUCTION

It is fashionable these days to dismiss most 1970s film theory as irrelevant. The movement towards historicism and the archive has productively challenged the abstractions and unsubstantiated assertions generated by text-based theory, particularly in the area of spectatorship, provoking an intensification of debates about history itself. The reinvention of history as an academic discipline has in its turn produced renewed argument about the limits of historical enquiry, and its ability to provide objective evidence and definitive accounts of the past. This process of revision has led to an increasing preoccupation with memory, as a means of exploring the conjunction of personal experience and public events in historical reconstruction. It has become almost a truism that the past is produced by the present, and that the result is a hybrid fabrication, a reinterpretation and recombination of primary and secondary materials from the perspective of current concerns and agendas.

Despite this widespread acknowledgement, it is still rare to find histories that demonstrate an awareness of the multiple, complex factors that impact on their own analysis, let alone on the texts and other objects they study – perhaps because this would be a difficult and time-consuming task, and one that would risk allowing questions of representation to cloud the linear narrative of events to which so many historians are wedded. The drive to contextualise, to position the text within its social background, is most often realised in terms of providing a credible account of what was happening at the time, effacing the activity of reconstruction in the present. This is an interesting situation, given the fact that modern historians are required to display sensitivity to conjuncture, and to be accountable for their methods and sources. The impatience with theory has sometimes resulted in the wholesale rejection of its usefulness in provoking reflection and debate beyond the issue of who knows the truth about what happened when. In one fell swoop, 1970s theory, usually characterised in negative terms as obsessed with ahistorical psychoanalysis, is relegated to the past, as though it has nothing to do with today. Similarly, the questions of ideology, representation and textual analysis with which it is associated are dismissed as outmoded.

All this is understandable in the light of the need for the new historicism to displace what had gone before, and to forge a different trajectory. However, one would expect today's historians to adopt a more subtle approach to the past. The problem with the outright refusal of 1970s theory is that it severs the connections between then and now, and hinders our understanding of the development of ideas in film studies. The perception that 1970s film theorists were unconcerned with history and memory is in any case misleading, since the period was characterised by intense debate about the compatibility of diverse intellectual strands such as Marxism, psychoanalysis, structuralism, anthropology and history. Those debates paved the way for the extensive revision of theory and history that contributed to the current conjuncture. Part of that revision was the acknowledgement that no single methodological approach is sufficient in itself to provide an analysis of social and cultural change, and that multidisciplinary work could provide a way forward. Another aspect was the recognition that it was no longer adequate to produce accounts that homogenise the object of study, effacing contradiction. Above all, these debates were characterised by a passionate desire to produce analyses that would adequately represent the experience of those marginalised or under-represented in traditional histories.

The articles in this section connect with these developments in different ways, tracing a shift away from textual analysis towards historical exposition. Taken together, they reveal connections as well as disparities between theory and history, and between the 1970s and now. They also trace a shift in thinking about ways of writing women into history, and with the issues of representation that emerge as a result. The focus is on genre, and how women feature in films that are assumed to be primarily addressed to men, such as film noir, the western, and low-budget exploitation. The context for the earliest piece, 'Duplicity in *Mildred Pierce*' (1978), was a renewed feminist interest in 1940s film noir, which had been extensively written about in terms of the role of the *femme fatale* as a male fantasy figure, who existed solely to exorcise the fears of men returning home in postwar America. The fate of these strong, transgressive heroines, who were desired, feared, and punished in the course of the narrative, seemed to reflect the position of women in postwar American society, as they were divested of their economic and sexual independence and returned to a domestic role within the family. The situation of the 1940s *femme fatale* had even wider ramifications, as it was perceived as a paradigm for the unequal power relations between men and women in male-dominated society as a whole, underpinned by patriarchal attitudes and ideologies. Those ideologies were identified as 'dominant', as shoring up the ruling patriarchal order. It was argued that they were sustained by deep-seated, often unconscious structures, which governed our culture and its artefacts, and held us all in place as social subjects. An important tool in transforming the dominant, patriarchal social order was the deconstruction of the representational structures that sustained it, including those of the classic Hollywood narrative, perceived as a primary instrument of capitalism and patriarchy. Feminist writers took on the task of making visible and critiquing ideologies embedded in popular Hollywood films, with a view to changing the way women were represented, and by extension their position in society.

With the benefit of hindsight, the flaws in this approach are obvious. 'Duplicity in *Mildred Pierce*' is a prime example of textual analysis inspired by 1970s feminist agendas, which reconstructs the object of study in its own image, neglecting its historical context. Central to the analysis is a notion of a patriarchal order that is also outside history, and is discussed in terms of myth. The analysis refers only briefly to the social position of women in the 1940s, since it is primarily concerned with issues of representation and ideology. It employs psychoanalysis as a method of reading the text without justifying its use, and it makes assumptions about genre and audience expectations that remain unexamined. Despite these shortcomings, the article raises some interesting questions, which continue to be relevant and could be explored further. One is the issue of memory, history and repression: the essay presents the ideological arena as fraught with conflict and struggle. As one social order (in this case, patriarchy) gains ascendancy over others, it does so by virtue of a violent repression that is never secure, since the forces it represses threaten to re-emerge. This could almost be a description of history itself, and the process of contestation whereby one version of events gains ascendancy over others, and achieves consensus. The narrative of *Mildred Pierce* can be perceived as a model for the activity of historical repression, as one version of events (Mildred's) is contested and relegated by another (the detective's), which is endowed with authority. *Mildred Pierce* is a memory film, narrated through the reminiscences of its heroine, and it provides an interesting example of reflection on the processes of memory and history, and the role of ideology in those processes. These issues are ripe for further discussion, as the question of who writes history, and for whom, is of equal concern today as it was in the 1970s. Another important topic raised by the article is the relationship of myth to history, since it asks where our narrative models come from, and how they are structured, an increasingly significant subject in the context of current debates about the role of popular media in producing history and memory.

The relationship of myth to history is the starting point for 'Women and the western' (1988), which begins with the feminist argument that women's actual role in building the West is effaced by the classic Hollywood western. While accepting that the western is dominated by a white, male perspective, and offers an impoverished range of stereotypes to represent women's contribution, it argues that the genre is predicated on myth rather than reality, and should be regarded as such. Rather than looking for authentic histories of women's experiences, the analysis returns to the basic structural oppositions that govern the myths of the West. It then surveys a range of films, exploring the ways in which each deals with and transforms those structures. A consistent pattern emerges whereby, in order to re-draw sexual and racial boundaries, the western features strong, independent heroines only to domesticate or eliminate them in the final scenes (with some notable exceptions). This approach has much in common with that taken towards *Mildred Pierce* – perhaps the most glaring similarity is the recourse to formal structures rather than a historical perspective. This could be put down to lack of space; however, it would have been feasible to produce a schematic, chronological account of the western, tracing changes in the representation of women. Yet this would have resulted in a linear, teleological history, which the article deliberately sets out to avoid. 'Women and the western' attempts to account for the contradictions that characterise the role of women in what has been perceived as the most masculine of all genres: on one hand, its focus on powerful heroines; on the other, its subordination of those heroines to the desires of the white, male hero. It demonstrates that these contradictions are not entirely contained by all the films, with the result that there is space in the western for criticism of the masculine ethos from a feminine point of view. This position has been endorsed by the recent film directed by Maggie Greenwald, *The Ballad of Little Jo* (1993), which rewrites the history of the West from a feminist perspective, skilfully appropriating the devices of the western genre, and overturning many of its hallowed principles.

The rewriting of genre conventions is also the subject of 'The pleasures and perils of xploitation 'films (1999), which considers the role of women in low-budget exploitation cinema, traditionally regarded as mere fodder for sadistic male fantasies. Strangely enough, in the light of its dependence on (mostly female) nudity and sexual violence, many women film-makers – some of whom, such as Stephanie Rothman, were declared feminists – started their careers in exploitation. The article takes a historical approach, tracing the emergence of exploitation cinema by looking at the growth of independent companies such as Roger Corman's New World, which employed film-school graduates in order to keep costs down, offering them the opportunity to direct their first features. The piece assesses the constraints and opportunities available to women exploitation directors, many of whom have not crossed over into the mainstream, unlike their male counterparts. Despite this, the work produced by women working in exploitation is perceived to be among the most sophisticated in the genre, demonstrating a witty and subversive intelligence as well as political acuity. These films turn the tables on the more misogynist aspects of exploitation cinema, challenging preconceptions about the young males assumed to be its primary audience. The article revises an earlier essay, written in 1976, and it echoes debates in feminist circles about women and low-budget pornography in the late 1980s. While it validates the work of women exploitation directors, it questions the wisdom of writing the history of women film-makers via a focus on directors alone, arguing that a more complex map of women's historical contribution to cinema emerges when the full range of their work as designers, scriptwriters, musicians, stars, producers and so forth is taken into account. 'The pleasures and perils of exploitation films' attempts to set a new agenda for historical enquiry that challenges the auteurist bias of so many film histories.

Further reading

Bordwell, David, *Making Meaning: Inference and Rhetoric in the Interpretation of Cinema* (Harvard: Harvard University Press, 1991).

Clover, Carol J., *Men, Women and Chainsaws* (London: BFI Publishing, 1992).

Kaplan, E. Ann (ed.), *Women in Film Noir* (London: BFI Publishing, 1978, rev. ed. 1998).

Kitses, Jim and Rickman, Gregg (eds), *The Western Reader* (New York: Limelight Editions, 1998).

Landy, Marcia, 'Introduction', in *Cinematic Uses of the Past* (Minneapolis and London: University of Minnesota Press, 1996).

Modleski, Tania, 'A woman's gotta do ... what a man's gotta do? Cross-dressing in the western', *Signs: Journal of Women in Culture and Society* 22(3) (1997).

Williams, Linda, 'Feminist film theory: *Mildred Pierce* and the Second World War', in E. Deirdre Pibraim (ed.), *Female Spectators: Looking at Film and Television* (Bloomington: Indiana University Press, 1987).

——— , *Hard Core: Power, Pleasure and the Frenzy of the Visible* (London: Pandora, 1990).

PART ONE

Further viewing

The Ballad of Little Jo (Maggie Greenwald, USA, 1993)
Mildred Pierce (Michael Curtiz, USA, 1945)
Student Nurses (Stephanie Rothman, USA, 1970)

Chapter 2

DUPLICITY IN *MILDRED PIERCE*

> We live in a society ruled by the father, in which the place of the mother is suppressed. Motherhood and how to live it, or not to live it, lies at the roots of the dilemma.
>
> Laura Mulvey[1]

To write about *Mildred Pierce* (Michael Curtiz, 1945) as an example of film noir poses more problems than are immediately apparent. In spite of the fact that several articles about the film[2] place it as typical of the 1940s genre characterised by a prevailing mood of pessimism and paranoia, a visual style dependent upon 'expressionist' lighting and décor, systematic use of geometric patterns of light and shadow, distortion produced through camera angles and wide-angle lenses and a convoluted organisation of narrative, *Mildred Pierce* does not fit easily into the self-contained, homogeneous world created by those formal strategies now accepted as characteristic of film noir.[3]

The difficulties of establishing and maintaining the boundaries of genre are obvious. Elements of film noir can be found in films as far removed in time and place as *Pursued* (Raoul Walsh, 1947), *Vampyr* (Carl Dreyer, 1932) and *Nostalgia* (Hollis Frampton, 1971). It is not the intention of this article to discuss *Mildred Pierce* in terms of the representation of women in film noir, nor to try to prove that the film is not a good example of film noir. I would claim instead that the film deals explicitly with questions of genre as part of its project, that the ideological work of the film is to articulate the necessity for the drawing of boundaries and to encourage the acceptance of the repression that the establishment of such an order entails. *Mildred Pierce* is interesting for the ways in which it signifies its problematic: the historical need to reconstruct an economy based on a division of labour by which men command the means of production and women remain within the family, in other words the need to reconstruct a failing patriarchal order. This reconstruction work is problematic precisely because it is based on the brutal and enforced repression of female sexuality, and the institutionalisation of a social place for both men (as fathers and husbands) and women (as mothers and wives) that rests uneasily on this repression, aware of the continual possibility of the eruption into the present of the submerged past.

On one level this work of repression is signified through an explicit manipulation of genre conventions, by which a hierarchy of discourses is established, suppressing the female discourse in favour of the male; on another level, by the organisation of the narrative around complicated 'snares' and 'equivocations' to increase the desire for a resolution that represents the Truth, whatever the cost. On every level the film works on audience expectation and response in order to produce audience subject positions based on defence, and elements of these positions are necessarily retained, even in the face of the re-establishment of Order and Truth, thus emphasising the need for work, sacrifice and suffering in the process of reconstruction. The aim of this article is to suggest some of the ways in which *Mildred Pierce* articulates this problematic, avoiding if possible the idea that the film simply reflects the historical needs of postwar America. The drama of the institution of the patriarchal order, the familiar Oedipal story, is enacted and re-enacted throughout history in many and various forms; in the context of the transition to a postwar economy, an impaired masculine population, the disintegration of the family unit and the increased economic and sexual independence of women, the Oedipal structure is threatened: the system that gives men and women their place in society must be reconstructed by a more explicit work of repression, and the necessity for this repression must be established unequivocally, by resolving equivocation. The ideological work of the film then is the way in which it articulates its project, encouraging certain subject positions rather than others, signifying a problem that is not only specific to *Mildred Pierce* itself, and the conditions in which it was produced, but also general in so far as the institution of patriarchy is a historical problem.

The extent of the problem of the institution of patriarchy is indicated in the work of J.J. Bachofen,[4] who, in his scholarly and imaginative study of ancient myths and symbolism, traces the historical transition from mother-right to father-right, a transition articulated by a number of myths of which the Oedipus story is only one. From his studies Bachofen insists that there is universal evidence for the historical existence of a matriarchal society that preceded our patriarchal system, a claim that has brought his ideas into question.[5] Nevertheless, his work remains fascinating for its revelation of the extent to which the idea of a society based on mother-right persists in mythology, a society which was forcibly overturned in the transition to a 'higher' form of civilisation: patriarchy. I would argue that *Mildred Pierce* draws extensively on this mythology, and on the symbolism Bachofen identifies as specific to the myth: that the project of the film is to re-present the

Figure 2.1   Past imperfect: Joan Crawford and Zachary Scott in *Mildred Pierce* (1945). Courtesy Warner Bros and the Kobal Collection.

violent overthrow of mother-right in favour of father-right[6] through the symbolic use of film lighting and the organisation of its narrative structure.

In an interesting article on *Mildred Pierce*,[7] Joyce Nelson discusses the film in terms of its narrative structure, drawing attention to the device of the 'false suture'[8] used to structure audience response, to lead the audience to concentrate on the need to resolve the enigma rather than to speculate on the possibility of alternative readings. The 'false suture' involves the masking, through the work of other filmic and cinematic codes, of the exclusion of a reverse-shot in order to create an enigma that the film will answer for the viewer, later, in the final flashback, when the missing shot is reinserted and the truth about the murder is revealed.

Nelson points out an apparently obvious fact, which is nevertheless not always mentioned in discussions of the film as film noir: the scenes that take place in the present are significantly more suggestive of film noir than are the two segments comprising Mildred's version of her own story. She goes on to show that Mildred's discourse is markedly different from the framing discourse of the detective, in that he is simply concerned with establishing the Truth, with resolving the enigma, while Mildred's story contains complexity

31

and ambiguity, showing a concern for feelings rather than facts. The detective's discourse is directed towards cleaning up the past, and this involves the invalidation of Mildred's version of the story, in terms of form *and* content. At the end of the second flashback the detective reveals that he knew the truth all the time, that Mildred was 'only the key'. This initiates the final flashback in which the enigma is resolved, shot almost entirely in noir style.

Nelson goes on to discuss the representation in the film of the relationship of similarity between Veda and Mildred, suggesting that the film asks us, through the device of metaphorical substitution, to confuse the wicked Veda with the honest Mildred, thus establishing Mildred's innate guilt, even though she is not guilty of the actual murder.

I find Joyce Nelson's reading of *Mildred Pierce* interesting because it uses a theoretical approach which assumes that the ideological work of the film lies in its structure, and in the structures in which it engages its audience. Although I disagree with some of her conclusions, this reading offers some useful insights into *Mildred Pierce*, which I should like to use as a starting point for my own discussion of the film and develop a little further. I shall draw on the structure of the film itself, its use of narrative and filmic codes of lighting, but also on those non-cinematic elements already indicated: the mythology outlined by Bachofen, and the sexual structure of the Oedipus complex appropriated from mythology by Freud. What follows is not intended to be a textual analysis; rather, I am trying to suggest a way of reading the film that opens up the question of the working of patriarchal ideology and the place it holds for women and men, and the implications of this question for sexual politics as well as for feminist film criticism.

Mildred Pierce and genre

As I indicated in my opening paragraph, the film does not fit easily into the category of film noir. Although the opening and closing sequences, and two short interruptions during the film, are shot in 'classic' noir style, the first two long flashback sequences in which Mildred tells the story of her past are significantly different – more evenly lit, few variations in camera angle, and so on – except towards the end of the second flashback when Mildred realises that Monte has betrayed her and she 'confesses' to the murder, when noir *mise-en-scène* takes over Mildred's discourse as well. The first flashback sequences are also concerned with different subject matter: the family, sexual and emotional relationships, property, work and investment. Mildred's discourse is the discourse of melodrama, her story is the stuff of which the 'women's picture' was made in the prewar and war years when women were seen to have an active part to play in society, and the problems of passion, desire and emotional excess articulated by melodrama[9] could be tolerated. The difference between the two forms of discourse (Mildred's story and the framing noir discourse) is marked enough for some account of the function of this marking to be necessary.

It seems that a basic split is created in the film between melodrama and film noir, between 'women's picture' and 'man's film', a split that indicates the presence of two 'voices', female and male, which in itself is a mark of excess since 'classic' film is generally characterised by the dominance of a metadiscourse, which represents the Truth. *Mildred Pierce* is constituted as a sexually ambiguous film, an ambiguity founded on duplicity which is eventually resolved by the reassertion of the patriarchal metadiscourse. In the process of resolution, melodrama, Mildred's point of view, is displaced by film noir (in which female discourse is suppressed but remains in the form of threatening shadows and man-killing Amazonian women), when in the final flashback narrative and lighting codes combine with extreme camera angles and music to connote imminent chaos, and the truth about Monte's murder is revealed. The consequences of the retreat from patriarchy are represented as the complete upheaval of social order leading to betrayal and death, in the face of which the reconstitution of the patriarchal order is seen to be a necessary defence.

The question of the retreat from patriarchy brings me to Bachofen's theory of the relationship between mother-right and father-right. From his study of myth he establishes two basic cultural levels. The first of these is a primitive level of swamp generation where the union of water and land brings about birth, which swiftly becomes death and returns to the land. This level is telluric, associated with sexual promiscuity and characterised as female. The second level is luminous and transcendent, associated with light and the sun, a higher intellectual and spiritual level, characterised as male. The second (patriarchal) level is the one to which all human life aspires, and therefore the more primitive level (called hetaerism by Bachofen) must constantly be overcome. The schema is more complex than this, taking in various stages between the two levels. Demetrian matriarchy, for instance, occupies a position midway between hetaerism and patriarchy, and is therefore an area of struggle since it stands in opposition both to the excesses of hetaerism and to the institution of patriarchy, which signals the loss of matriarchal rights and privileges. In the transition from mother-right to father-right there is a further stage: the Dionysian, which heralds the founding of patriarchy, undermining the Demetrian principle by an alliance with hetaerism and a return to the sensual frenzy of a more primitive era, characterised as an era of sexual freedom in which women are held in common by men. Against the abuse of women's bodies implied by hetaerism the man-killing Amazon arises, yet another stage in the transition to patriarchy.

Bachofen isolates a symbolic grid that supports the basic division between female (matriarchal) and male (patriarchal), a shortened version of which could be set out as follows:

Female	Male
Tellurian	Uranian
Material/Corporeal	Spiritual/Intellectual
Night	Day
Dark	Light
Passive	Active
Left	Right
Mass solidarity	Individuality
Womb	Phallus

It is not arbitrary to apply Bachofen's schema of the struggle between mother-right and father-right to *Mildred Pierce*. Apart from the film's thematic concern with a mother who attempts to gain control of family and business, the classic struggle between Mother and Father, and its 'inevitable' resolution, are multiply coded in the film in the narrative organisation and the symbolic use of film lighting.

Film noir

In accordance with Bachofen's schema the dark–light contrast in the film noir sections of *Mildred Pierce* is taken to connote sexual ambiguity: the presence of male and female in the text, the struggle between two symbolic orders. In film noir generally, the protagonist, usually male, moves unhappily through this world of sexual ambiguity (against which his paranoia is a defence) until it is resolved, either by his own death at the hands of the Father, or by his taking over from the Father as the agent of death. Although there are exceptions, women who are represented as the agents of death usually turn out to be only instruments when the duplicity is resolved by the narrative. It is unusual for film noir to have a female protagonist narrating her own story; in *Mildred Pierce* Mildred's story is revealed as duplicitous, thus foregrounding the work of repression involved in narrative resolution.

As already indicated, the noir sections of the film are situated in the present, a present therefore characterised by violence and death, uncertainty and duplicity. Duplicity is underlined in the text of the film by the use of contrasting light and shadow and by the use of a 'snare' in the narrative: the exclusion of the reverse-shot that would reveal the true murderer encourages the audience to believe that Mildred is the murderer/agent of death, especially when, in true noir-heroine style, she proceeds to set Wally Fay up as the murderer, apparently to protect herself, using her sexuality as bait. 'You make me shiver, Mildred,' says Wally, reinforcing the belief that it is Mildred who is the location of duplicity.

Later, at the police station, the brisk, orderly atmosphere makes Mildred nervous as she waits to be questioned: again she is seen as the location of uncertainty, this time in the face of the Law, which will tolerate no uncertainty or ambiguity.

The first flashback ends at the point where Mildred is at the height of her economic success and Bert gives her the divorce she wanted. We return to the present in the police station, and the lighting (shadows) on Mildred's face suggests her guilt in the present when she has just been seen as successful in her own right in the past. The function of this interruption seems to be to encourage the audience to anticipate the fate of independent, successful career women, and to force a separation or distance between the audience and any sympathy or identification with Mildred's success. Towards the end of the second flashback, when Mildred's story draws to its (false) conclusion and closer to present time (when the murder takes place), deceit and betrayal, represented by Wally, Veda and Monte, are rife, and Mildred has lost everything that was dear to her. Film noir conventions invade Mildred's discourse and she confesses to the murder.

Mildred's confession does not introduce any contradiction into her discourse. On the contrary, it allows her to insert herself into the present as a woman still in control of her destiny, with the power of death over the men who betray her. In the face of this assertion of power, based on duplicity, since Mildred is not the real murderer, the detective's response is to remove all possibility of duplicity by invalidating Mildred's confession. He reveals the truth, which he knew all the time anyway, confronting Mildred with Veda, who confesses, believing that Mildred has betrayed her, and is taken away from Mildred into the custody of the Law.

In this final cleaning-up process all power is seen to return into the hands of the Law. The paternalistic detective, who has secretly always controlled the progress of the narrative because of his foreknowledge of the truth, dispels duplicity by throwing light upon the scene: his assertion of the Truth is supported symbolically when he opens the blinds to let in the dawn – light is the masculine principle that heralds the dawn of patriarchal culture and the defeat of matriarchy. This defeat is accomplished by the forcible and final separation of Mildred and Veda, thus making it possible for Mildred to live with Bert in a 'normal' couple relationship. She is returned to point zero, completely stripped, rehabilitated. To understand why such violent repression had to be seen to be necessary it is important to look at the use of melodrama in the film.

Melodrama

The melodramatic sections of the film are set in the past, Mildred's own account of her history in terms of her rejection of her class (represented by Bert, who is critical of Mildred's petit bourgeois aspirations, but is down on his luck, unemployed, his masculinity impaired) and her rejection of the patriarchal symbolic order (she expels Bert from the family and rejects Wally Fay as a substitute, taking over the place of father/provider herself). The crucial question posed at this point is, of course, 'Has Mildred the right to rule the family?' At first the answer seems to be positive: she is strong, hard-working, honest and single-minded, not to mention ambitious. She seems to possess precisely those characteristics lacking in the men. Mildred attempts to return to the Demetrian stage of matriarchy in which women command home and state, represented here by her family and her restaurant business. However, her retreat from patriarchy leads 'inevitably' through the cause and effect of narrative to the primitive stage of hetaerism and the deterioration of all social order, represented by Veda and Monte, whose relationship implies the Dionysian stage characterised by Bachofen as heralding the coming of patriarchy.

The first sign of deterioration comes when Mildred's one night of illicit passion with Monte is followed by Kay's death. The loss of one daughter strengthens Mildred's obsession with Veda, and with making a success of her business, in the course of which she forms a relationship of mutual solidarity with her friend Ida, who helps her to run the business, while men (Wally and Monte) are relegated to the secondary status of instruments.

In the second flashback deterioration sets in, revolving around Veda's problem with finding a sexual identity, since she has no father, and a mother who is also a father. Sexual ambiguity is compounded by Veda's sexual blackmail of the Forrester family (aided by Wally), and the implication of a sexual relationship between Veda and Monte. Veda and Mildred separate after a confrontation, but Mildred cannot live without Veda, and finally marries Monte in order to get her back. While Veda and Monte enjoy themselves at a party, Mildred discovers that she has lost her business because Monte and Wally have done a deal without telling her. When she discovers that Veda and Monte have gone to the beach house together she follows them with the gun. At this point Mildred confesses to the murder of Monte.

Mildred's take-over of the place of the father has brought about the collapse of all social and moral order in her world: Monte and Veda are on the point of breaking the ultimate taboo: that against father incest. In the face of impending chaos and confusion the patriarchal order is called upon to reassert itself and take the Law back into its own hands, divesting women completely of any power they may have gained while the patriarchal order was temporarily impaired. This involves establishing the truth without a doubt, restoring 'normal' sexual relationships and reconstituting the family unit, in spite of the pain and suffering such repressive action must cause. Pain and suffering are a necessary part of the work of reconstruction (represented by Bert, who has earned his right to take the place of the father again through suffering and self-sacrifice).

The split between melodrama and film noir is overcome by the force of the Law, and Bert and Mildred walk into the dawn together, reconstituted as a couple, the image bearing the marks of repression in the form of another couple from the past: two women who work together, this time to support the patriarchal institution by scrubbing the steps of the police station. They remain as a reminder of the consequences that would ensue should 'illicit' or ambiguous couplings become a possibility again.

The 'snare'

Barthes has emphasised the importance of *delay* to the unfolding of narrative.[10] In *S/Z* he isolates several forms of 'reticence' that are used to hold back the resolution of the enigma. The 'snare' is identified as a deliberate evasion of the Truth.

The act of involvement in 'classic' narrative is for the reader/viewer an act based on misrecognition. The reader suspends knowledge of the Truth for the required length of time: 'I know, but … '. Pleasure is generated by the possibility of the return of infantile wishes and phantasies repressed by the passing through the Oedipus complex. In the 'classic' narrative knowledge is suspended for a limited amount of time and Truth is re-established at the end through the resolution of the enigma. Thus 'classic' narrative re-enacts the Oedipal drama itself: the passage from misrecognition (the pre-Oedipal stage of bisexuality when both male and female are thought to possess a penis and the mother is the love-object of both male and female children) to knowledge (the discovery of the fact of castration through sight of the mother's body without a penis), at which point boys must identify with the father, who has the power of castration, and give up (temporarily) their desire for the mother, and girls must identify with the mother in her (already) castrated

37

state, also giving up their desire for her. Thus boys and girls become 'sexed' human beings, relinquishing bisexuality in favour of the choice of a love-object from the opposite sex. 'Classic' narrative affirms this heterosexual structure, the mainstay of the family unit and of social reproduction, again and again.

Bachofen's description of the transition from mother-right to father-right corresponds in many ways to Freud's Oedipus complex, since the transition rests on the suppression of motherhood and the constant struggle of patriarchy to resist the return of an earlier matriarchal symbolic order characterised by greater sexual freedom and democracy.

In *Mildred Pierce* the Oedipal drama is re-enacted in an explicitly repressive form, since the 'snare', the deliberate withholding of the reverse-shot, which is the basis for the audience's 'misrecognition' of Mildred as an agent of death, is reinforced on several levels in the film, and the knowledge that Mildred is not the murderer is withheld from the viewer, so that the resolution of the enigma, the progress to 'knowledge', rests entirely with the detective as the representative of the Law.

As Monte dies, whispering 'Mildred', the next shot shows a car drawing away from the beach house, in long-shot so that we cannot see who is driving. A dissolve leads us into a shot of Mildred walking on the pier in a suicidal state. Film noir lighting suggests duplicity: an unknown threat might emerge from the shadows. Joan Crawford, who plays Mildred, is an ambiguous sexual figure as a star with a history of playing 'independent women' roles, emphasised in this scene by the broad shoulders of her coat. The fundamental misrecognition has been established as we are led to believe that Mildred is the murderer, that she has exercised the power of life and death which only the Father holds.

The 'snare' is compounded further when, in the following sequence, Mildred attempts to set Wally up for the murder, since we assume from what we 'know' so far that she is protecting herself from discovery. It is probable that she is the uncastrated mother, and the spectator is invited to enter into a pre-Oedipal phantasy, a recollection of a repressed, but not forgotten, time when much more sexual freedom was possible. At the same time, the phantasy is represented as increasingly threatening, encouraging the spectator to take up a defensive position and to wish for the resolution of ambiguity, to put an end to feelings of anxiety.[11]

The function of the first flashback is to articulate the phantasy by recreating the circumstances in which Mildred denies her own castration by taking over as head of the family, and building up her own business. She invades the territory of men: that of property and investment, and after Kay's death rejects men as sexual partners, becoming obsessed with Veda and her work. Her relationship with Veda,[12] coupled with her close friendship with Ida (played by Eve Arden, another actress who is an ambiguous sexual figure), represents an attempt to return to the pre-Oedipal bisexual state, a regression from patriarchy. This regression includes the men too, who are represented as weak and dissipated, untrustworthy, except for Bert, who grows to maturity during the film.

Veda represents the consequences of this retreat from patriarchy. Her close physical resemblance to Mildred emphasises her function as a 'double', created by Mildred as a defence against castration.[13] She is, however, all the things that Mildred is not: deceitful, promiscuous, greedy and hysterical; she represents the threat of chaos, the excess which Mildred's discourse calls into being and which it cannot resolve.

The threat of chaos extends to the world of business as well. The evasion of the patriarchal law produces a situation in which nothing is stable, since business relationships are closely tied to sexual relationships in the film, and Mildred's business rests on the goodwill of her two partners, Wally and Monte, both less than reliable. These are hardly the best circumstances in which to rebuild an economy; in order to create a stable economic situation suitable for investment, sexual order must be re-established; excess and ambiguity must be resolved through a 'necessary' repression.

In her false confession Mildred claims to have resolved the excess herself by killing Monte. As I have already suggested, however, if Mildred had killed Monte this would perpetuate the situation in which the mother is seen to have the power of life and death, in this case explicitly the power to enforce the taboo against incest. The situation of unresolved excess would remain, since Veda would go free.

The resolution of excess is achieved when the detective invalidates Mildred's confession, revealing that he knew the true murderer all the time. The existence of the 'snare' is made explicit, thus putting Mildred *and* the audience in the same position, at the mercy of the Law.[14] The resolution is articulated by the scene in which Veda confesses, believing that Mildred has betrayed her, and mother and daughter are separated for ever – Veda, the representative of excess, being removed for imprisonment or death. The final flashback, the 'true' story of the murder, confirms the resolution: when Mildred comes to the point of killing Monte she is incapable of doing so. Veda, however, is not, and kills Monte (surrogate father) in a frenzy of libidinal excess. The final flashback is shot in 'classic' noir style: it is not until Mildred and Bert are finally reunited under the aegis of the Law that ambiguity is resolved and the shadows dispersed by the light of the new day.

The body of the film[15]

I have tried to show that the problematic articulated by the film *Mildred Pierce* is one of uncertainty and duplicity, centred on Mildred's body as the location of sexual ambiguity, and the return of an infantile phantasy about the body of the mother, a phantasy which allows for a potentially more democratic structure of sexual relationships based on bisexuality, a structure repressed by the heterosexual division the Oedipus complex attempts to enforce. The problematic is signified on one level by the relationship between Veda and Mildred: Veda is seen as a part of Mildred's body, an extension of herself, the phallus she will not relinquish. 'Veda is a part of me', Mildred says to Ida at one point, and publicity photographs of the film inevitably show Mildred holding Veda (and sometimes Kay as well) close to her.

I have tried to indicate that this phantasy of the mother's body, with its connotations of sexual excess and the erosion of the patriarchal order, cannot be tolerated by the film, and is resolved by a brutal act of repression in which Mildred is castrated, not only through the invalidation of her discourse, but by her enforced separation from Veda (which allows for no possibility of emotional reconciliation), which amounts to an act of mutilation perpetrated by the police on Mildred's body.

I should like to suggest some ways in which I think an analogy is drawn between the 'body' of the film, its material structure, and Mildred's body as the location of duplicity.

The 'snare' utilised in the opening section serves a double function: it omits something (a reverse-shot), and then proceeds to mask the omission by the use of a long-shot of the car driving off, and a dissolve to Mildred on the pier. There is an absence, or lack, in the film that the film itself masks in the same way as Mildred masks her own 'lack'.

Masking also takes place on the level of *mise-en-scène*, in the use of film noir conventions of lighting: sharp contrasts of light and shadow suggest partial truth; something is missing, but whatever it is remains hidden. Since the enjoyment of the phantasy rests on the temporary masking of the truth, the insertion of the film noir segments into the structure of the film both reinforces the phantasy and reminds the spectator that something is to be revealed.

The use of even lighting and more classic shot compositions in Mildred's discourse indicate a plenitude, a situation in which nothing is missing and which belongs to the past, as the mother's body represented plenitude for the child in the pre-Oedipal situation. Again, the interruptions by the film noir segments serve both to confirm the ambiguity upon which the phantasy of plenitude is based, and to remind us that something is hidden. The presence of two markedly different styles of film genre underlines the sexual ambiguity in the structure of the film itself, since each genre is specifically associated with a different audience and market: melodrama with women and film noir with men.

What is hidden in the body of the film is eventually revealed as the presence of the father as agent of the Law, represented by the detective, who was actually in control of the structure of the film all the time, who unmasks the gap and then proceeds to fill it with the missing reverse-shot, thus revealing the 'lack' in the mother's body (the body of the film), into which he inserts his own discourse, the Truth. The enigma is resolved by dispelling ambiguity in favour of the heterosexual symbolic order implied by patriarchy, explicitly suppressing matriarchy and reconstituting Bert and Mildred as a 'normal' heterosexual couple.

As Mildred and Bert walk off into the light of the new dawn from which all shadow and duplicity have been erased, they turn their backs on another couple, two women in the classic position of oppression, on their knees: an image of sacrifice that closes the film with a reminder of what women must give up for the sake of the patriarchal order.[16]

Notes

1 Laura Mulvey, '*Riddles of the Sphinx*: a film by Laura Mulvey and Peter Wollen', *Screen* 18(2) (summer 1977), pp. 61–77.

2 See, for instance, Stephen Farber, 'Violence and the bitch goddess', *Film Comment* 10(6) (November/December 1974), p. 8; and John Davis, 'The tragedy of Mildred Pierce', *Velvet Light Trap* 6 (fall 1972), pp. 27–30.

3 Described in J.A. Place and L.S. Peterson, 'Some visual motifs of film noir', *Film Comment* 10(1) (January 1974), pp. 30–2; and Paul Schrader, 'Notes on film noir', *Film Comment* 8(1) (spring 1972), p. 8.

4 J.J. Bachofen, *Myth, Religion and Mother Right* (New Jersey: Princeton University Press / Bollingen Foundation, 1973 [1861]).

5 See, for instance, Frederick Engels in *The Origin of the Family, Private Property, and the State* (New York: Pathfinder Press, 1973 [1884]).

6 James Cain's novel *Mildred Pierce*, which appeared in 1941, is significantly different from the film in that it presents Mildred's story in terms of her economic, emotional and sexual problems after the break-up of her marriage to Bert. The film draws more on myth and less on naturalistic detail than the novel.

7 Joyce Nelson, '*Mildred Pierce* reconsidered', *Film Reader* 2 (1977), pp. 65–70.

8 Nelson takes the term 'suture' from the influential article by Daniel Dayan: 'The tutor-code of classical cinema', in *Film Quarterly* (fall 1974), pp. 22–31. The concept has been the subject of much debate (see 'Notes on suture' by Stephen Heath in *Screen* 18(4), pp. 48–76), but can be briefly defined as the system by which, in classic cinema, the spectator is bound into the image-frame and narrative.

9 Interesting attempts to define melodrama in terms of excess have been made by Laura Mulvey in 'Notes on Sirk and melodrama', *Movie* 25 (winter 1977/78), pp. 53–6, and by Geoffrey Nowell-Smith in 'Minnelli and melodrama', *Screen* 18(2) (summer 1977), pp. 113–18.

10 Roland Barthes, 'Delay', in *S/Z* (London: Jonathan Cape, 1975), p. 75.

11 These are anxiety feelings similar to those that cause us to wake up when a dream threatens to go beyond the pleasure principle. The detective's action in opening the blinds could be interpreted as a metaphor for waking up.

12 In the novel, Mildred's relationship with Veda is represented as explicitly sexual, in the physical and emotional sense.

13 The relationship of physical similarity between Mildred and Veda represents in Freudian terms Mildred's choice of a love-object based on narcissism, the dyadic relationship that the Oedipus complex attempts to resolve. The 'wicked' side of Veda seems to represent the underside of Demetrian matriarchy, the unregulated excesses of hetaerism.

14 When the 'snare' is made explicit, the meaning of Monte's dying whisper, 'Mildred ...', changes: Mildred now becomes the 'lost object', relegated to the past, a memory (compare this with 'Rosebud' in *Citizen Kane*), rather than the agent of death.

15 Two articles that discuss the concept of film as 'body' are Nowell-Smith, 'Minnelli and Melodrama' and Mark Nash, 'Notes on the Dreyer-text', in *Dreyer* (London: British Film Institute, 1977), pp. 5–35.

16 It is worth noting that Bachofen associates the number 2 with the feminine principle of justice in the section on Egypt in *Myth, Religion, and Mother Right*. The two women on the steps of the police station could be said to represent the subjugation of matriarchal Law.

Chapter 3

WOMEN AND THE WESTERN

Recently, the American West has once again become disputed territory. Historians have turned their attention to women's participation in the westward trek and have discovered, to no great surprise, that their real contribution was far more extensive and diverse than traditional histories and literature have led us to believe.[1] When it comes to movies, the picture is much the same: the impoverished range of female stereotypes on offer (mother, schoolteacher, prostitute, saloon girl, rancher, Indian squaw, bandit) never matches up to reality. In the epic battle between heroes to tame the wilderness, the heroines who fought to change the course of history (the suffragettes, farmers, professional women) fare badly – even the maligned American Indian has been afforded the dubious luxury of liberal reassessment.

It's tempting to put this down, as many critics have,[2] to the male Oedipal bias of the western, a narrative based on a masculine quest for sexual and national identity which marginalises women. Fruitful though this approach may be, it has not really come to terms with the dual, contradictory role of women. On the one hand, she is peripheral (Budd Boetticher: 'What counts is what the heroine provokes, or rather what she represents. She is the one ... who makes him act the way he does. In herself the woman has not the slightest importance.'). On the other hand, she is central (Anthony Mann: 'In fact, a woman is always added to the story because without a woman the Western wouldn't work.'). By the same token, the demand for more realistic images of women does not account for the fact that what lingers in the memory, refusing to be dismissed, is a series of extraordinary heroines, from Mae West's Klondike Annie and Doris Day's Calamity Jane, to Joan Crawford's Vienna and Barbara Stanwyck's Jessica Drummond. The search for realism is perhaps rather self-defeating in a genre that is more concerned with myth than historical accuracy. It might be more illuminating to shuffle the deck (bearing in mind that female card-sharps in the western are few and far between) and see what permutations emerge.

Following Henry Nash Smith, the frontier has often been seen in symbolic terms as a boundary or barrier between opposing ideas: the Garden/Wilderness dichotomy translating into Culture/Nature, and so on. This formulation has both a relationship to actual events (the breaking down of the barrier between East and West under pressure from eastern expansion), and also a link with psychic and social reality (the loss of boundaries of sexual difference, as eastern 'feminine' values came into contact with the 'masculine' Wild West). Not surprisingly, then, many westerns work away at the problem of re-establishing sexual boundaries: it's unusual for the woman who starts out wearing pants, carrying a gun and riding a horse to be still doing so at the end of the movie. Suitably re-clad in dress or skirt, she prepares to take her place in the family, leaving adventure to the men.

Of course, the hero's destiny is also circumscribed: rather than remain a nomad, he has to become civilised and participate in building a new society inside rather than outside the law. In both cases, the rehabilitation can be ambivalent, but the results are different. Over and over again, the woman relinquishes her desire to be active and independent, ceding power to the hero and accepting secondary status as mother figure, educator and social mediator. If she is allowed to be active, it is in the hero's cause rather than her own; for example, in *High Noon* (1952) the young Quaker wife puts aside her pacifist principles to support her husband's heroic stand.

This pattern is remarkably consistent, but the most interesting westerns explore its inherent tensions. *Stagecoach* (1939) – directed by John Ford, whose reverence for motherhood and family is legendary – produced some significant reverberations: the East/West conflict is centred on two women, the respectable Lucy Mallory and the prostitute Dallas, and is played out at the point of life and death as the stagecoach and its motley group of passengers come under attack from savage Apaches. The hope for future civilisation (revolving around who is a 'good mother': Mrs Mallory, who gives birth during the journey, or Dallas) lies not with the effete, class-conscious visitors from the East, but with the westerners, who in spite of their 'illegality' have an instinctive compassion and sense of right and wrong. Dallas herself, reviled by the snobbish easterners, is presented as a more 'natural' mother than Lucy Mallory: shots of her cradling Lucy's baby while the stage is under attack are quite transgressive, since prostitutes are outside the family and the law. It's true that the resolution is entirely conventional: Dallas is the civilising force that brings the outlaw Ringo back into society. Nevertheless, she remains an ambiguous figure, half prostitute, half wife, partly because of the positive value attached by Ford to renegades and social outcasts.

Similar tensions are worked through in *My Darling Clementine* (1946), where East meets West in the confrontation between schoolteacher Clementine and westerner Wyatt Earp. Clementine is a civilising influence on Earp, but he makes the passage from Nature to Culture unwillingly, as though resisting the colonising impetus of the East; and while the wild saloon girl Chihuahua is banished from the scene, her memory lurks in the shadows as a reminder of what civilisation represses.

Male ambivalence towards home and family is also at the centre of *The Lusty Men* (1952), but here Louise Merritt's resistance to the virile, itinerant world of the rodeo to which her husband Wes becomes attached is given a positive critical force. Jeff, Wes's friend, wants to quit that world, and is attracted to Louise; tragically, he is unable to escape either the rodeo's competitive ethos or the male alliances on which it is based. The film's focus on its heroes' crisis of identity paradoxically allows space in the masculine western scenario for Louise's own problems with her wife/mother role.

A mother who resists her secondary status is Ma Callum in *Pursued* (1947), a film-noirish western that approaches its subject in an unusually introspective way. The hero, Jeb, is prevented from achieving proper manhood by Ma Callum's refusal to give him essential knowledge about his past. Only when she tells him the truth, in effect relinquishing the control she has guarded so jealously, can he pass into adult masculinity. Simultaneously powerful and powerless, mothers in the western do indeed reflect the two sides of the Mann/Boetticher coin.

If the good mother represents the feminine ideal in the western, what then of the 'bad girls', the law-breakers against which the ideal is measured? These shady ladies threaten to upset the applecart by challenging men on their own ground; adventurers all, they demand equal status and refuse to take second place, at first, anyway; they wear pants and brandish guns, own land, property and business, demand sexual independence. It's true that this is usually only temporary – if the tomboy has not abandoned her transvestite garb for the arms of the hero by the end of the movie, then she comes to a sticky end. (In *Arizona* [1940], for example, Phoebe Titus' independence is revealed as masquerade and she cedes the struggle to laconic westerner Peter Hunsey.) Nevertheless, the passage to femininity is not always smooth; the bad girl's vacillation between tomboy and wife, with its attendant cross-dressing games, offers some interesting possibilities.

Calamity Jane (1953) contains some extraordinary gender confusions, which its somewhat arbitrary double wedding finale does not entirely iron out. Calamity's feminisation is not quite complete – at the end of the movie she is back in buckskins as gun-toting guard of the Deadwood Stage, while her marriage to hero Wild Bill Hickok is haunted by the spectre of the scene in

Figure 3.1 Gender games: Doris Day in *Calamity Jane* (1953). Courtesy Warner Bros and the Kobal Collection.

which, for the slightest of narrative excuses, he dresses as an Indian squaw. The combination of a comedy-of-errors with the utopian structure of the musical and western conventions enables an egalitarian fantasy (one which the traditional western mobilises in order to undermine) to prevail.[3] In a different way, Marlon Brando's dressing up as a pioneer woman in *The Missouri Breaks*

(1976) also brings to the surface some of the unspoken contradictions in the Western's privileging of masculine desires.

Both these films exploit and expose a potential perversity at the heart of the genre, its regressive drive to elude the law of the father, to play forbidden games. The tomboy offers a different sort of erotic pleasure from the mother, one focused on her bottom, and which provokes the desire of the hero to spank her. This sexual tussle, usually played for laughs, is a kind of parody of the father/daughter, father/mother power relations that will eventually put the tomboy in her place. In *Dodge City* (1939), Errol Flynn offers to spank Olivia De Havilland when she has the temerity to want to work on the town newspaper and contribute actively to the town's political development. Their rough and tumble is a playful prelude to a more serious confrontation, apparently a reversal of roles, in which De Havilland lays out for Flynn the moral necessity of his defending the burgeoning community against the villain. De Havilland's passage to mother figure is played out against two other feminine stereotypes, seen as less than ideal: the saloon girl, who sides with the villain, and the comically ineffectual, repressive temperance league women. The heroine's successful putting aside of her tomboy identity brings the errant hero back into society, and so ushers in progress.

There are women whose status as good or bad western heroines is less easily defined, sisters to the *femmes fatales* of film noir. These duplicitous creatures often inhabit revenge westerns, which focus on the hero's obsessive drive to seek out and kill his *alter ego* for a crime committed against his family. The woman takes on a sphinx-like quality: she both represents, and holds the key to, the enigma he must resolve. In *Winchester '73* (1950) the neurotic hero, Lin McAdam, is matched by an ambivalent heroine, Lola Manners, who may or may not be a prostitute, may or may not be complicit with villain Waco Johnnie Dean, but is indirectly responsible for the latter's death at the hands of McAdam. Her ambivalent status is maintained until the end: as she and McAdam embrace, his long-time buddy High Spade looks on with a quizzical expression as if to question his friend's judgement.

Occasionally, the duplicitous heroine takes on a more sympathetic, tragic hue. In Fritz Lang's extraordinary Brechtian western, *Rancho Notorious* (1952), the hero Vern's obsession with avenging the death of his wife turns him into a ruthless, inhuman monster whose sadistic attitude towards the woman, Altar Keane, who he believes holds the secret to his wife's murder, turns out to be an error of judgement with dire consequences. Believing Altar to be complicit with the murderer, Vern realises his mistake too late, after Altar dies saving his buddy Frenchy's life. Partly because of distancing techniques used in image, sound and narrative, this is one of a few westerns in which the overriding male perspective is brought into question: Altar is explicitly seen as a victim of Vern's need to project on to an external image his own violent, destructive urges. In *Rancho Notorious*, women are finally evacuated from the scene completely, as Vern and Frenchy ride off together.

Hannie Caulder (1971) puts its heroine in the vengeful hero's place. Hannie sets out to avenge her own rape and her husband's murder, acquiring sharp-shooter skills and much-abbreviated masculine garb (a hat, boots and man-with-no-name-style poncho, but no pants). In spite of an obvious intention to titillate, *Hannie Caulder* also manages to produce some interesting reflections on male heroism. Hannie learns from her mentor (who later dies – no easy romantic transition here) the practical and emotional skills required to be a westerner. No room for compassion or love – Hannie must stand alone in the wilderness. She succeeds in killing the villains, satisfying justice, and at the end she is not returned immediately to home and family. But in an elegiac conclusion, she comes face to face with a mysterious man in black who has haunted her progress, and whose presence is a reminder of a final boundary Hannie can never cross. For women can never really be heroes in the western: that would mean the end of the genre.

The western is haunted by the fear of miscegenation, the myth of the rapa-cious Indian bent on capturing and breeding with white women. When white women mate with Indians, the results are generally catastrophic: the woman is seen to be contaminated by the primitive (polygamous) laws of the wilder-ness and henceforth unfit for monogamous family life. It's different when a civilised white man mates with an Indian woman. Surprisingly, perhaps, Indian women are often quite positively portrayed as noble, brave, intelligent and self-sacrificing. But this is merely a variation on the mother figure, whose function is to smooth the way for the male transition to maturity. In *The Big Sky* (1952), Teal Eye enables the relationship between Jim and Boone to move beyond the latently homosexual to a mature friendship, also allowing the younger Boone to overcome his hatred of Indians, while in *Run of the Arrow* (1957) Yellow Moccasin supports O'Meara through his crisis of national iden-tity, even to the extent of giving up her Sioux nationhood to return with him to the States when the crisis is over.

Sometimes, however, the race/sex/nation conflict is less easily resolved. Ethan Edwards, the hero of *The Searchers* (1956), is a classic westerner. Soli-tary, asexual and taciturn, he is driven to seek out and destroy his *alter ego*, the Comanche chief Scar, epitome of the primitive sexuality Ethan's culture represses. Ethan and his quest are imbued with epic overtones: nevertheless, his rescue of his niece Debbie from Scar's clutches is seen as a highly ambig-uous act on a par with Scar's original act of abduction, since Debbie makes it clear she wants to remain with the Indians. Debbie's refusal to see herself as a victim, or to accept a position as object of exchange between the two cultures, doesn't affect her final destiny; but it does allow a criticism of Ethan's racist puritan code to surface, a criticism not entirely erased by the elegiac overtones of the hero's final act of walking out alone into the desert. Five years later, in *Two Rode Together* (1961), Ford's criticism becomes more explicit. Marshal McCabe (James Stewart) rejects the racist attitudes of cavalry and white settlers by leaving for California with Elena, a kidnapped white girl turned Indian squaw.

King Vidor's magnificently melodramatic *Duel in the Sun* (1946) unusually focuses on a woman's crisis of identity. Its racially ambiguous heroine, Pearl Chavez (daughter of a white father and Mexican Indian mother) vacillates between two lovers (the 'good' brother Jesse, epitome of civilised eastern values, and the 'bad' brother Lewt, barbaric and brutal), who represent the struggle within herself between good and evil, wife and tomboy. Pearl is unable to accept her feminine role as Jesse's wife and pursues her transgressive desire for Lewt. On one level, the struggle is between the 'primitive' Indian and 'civilised' white in Pearl – her inability to control her sexual desire is partly responsible for her death. But melodrama's characteristic focus on female desire turns the normal moral order on its head: the forces of civilisation become forces of repression, which lead precisely to the excess that brings about Pearl's and Lewt's deaths. Pearl Chavez's tragedy is that of all the western's tomboys, writ large.

One reason for the western's decline could be its resistance to the impact of social change. One attempt to capitalise on an emerging women's movement was *The Ballad of Josie* (1967), a comedy western starring Doris Day as Josie Minick, the wife of a violent alcoholic in nineteenth-century Wyoming territory, forced to become an independent woman after his death. After a succession of menial jobs, she uses her savings to set up a sheep farm in what has traditionally been cattle country, provoking a range war. The film attempts a blending of contemporary feminist issues (wife battering, child custody, job discrimination) with historical material such as prostitution and women's suffrage, set against the characteristic trajectory of the western heroine from tomboy to wife; but the feminist influence sits uneasily with the western narrative.

Perhaps the nearest Hollywood has come to a feminist western, *Johnny Guitar* (1954), predates the modern women's movement by more than a decade and does not deal directly with social issues at all. Set in a timeless desert wasteland with only the most perfunctory signs of civilisation in evidence, *Johnny Guitar* is overtly presented as myth. Vienna, the film's extraordinary heroine and one of the most compelling female images the western has produced, has often been seen as a feminist ideal, a woman who survives on equal terms with men (though reservations have been expressed

Figure 3.2 More than a woman: Joan Crawford in *Johnny Guitar* (1954). Courtesy Republic and the Kobal Collection.

about the misogynist representation of Vienna's opponent, Emma Small, and the disappointing shoot-out between the two women).[4] Vienna is certainly unusual: a powerful combination of several western heroines in one (a gunslinger, a musician and a successful entrepreneur who outwits everyone by buying up land to capitalise on the coming of the railroad, she is sexually

independent but also mother to the disillusioned Johnny and the Dancin'
Kid's gang). Feminine in her white dress, masculine in black shooting gear,
she moves between tomboy and mother figure with ease, demonstrating and
maintaining a level of control allowed to very few women. But the film's
feminism goes deeper than this, extending to a criticism of the western's male
values. Destructive masculine drives have gone out of control, creating a
world dominated by death, betrayal and revenge. Emma Small is complicit in
this process, while Vienna keeps a distance, speaking out against moral disintegration, expressing perhaps director Nicholas Ray's own disillusionment
with the USA in the grip of McCarthyism. It is in this light, rather than as a
failure of her positive qualities, that Vienna's half-hearted shoot-out with
Emma Small can be seen. Vienna has had enough of death and revenge; she
and Johnny leave the ranchers, bankers and outlaws to their own devices. At
the end of *Johnny Guitar*, still in trousers, still more than equal to any man,
having successfully resisted all attempts to bring her down, Vienna bids farewell to the western.

Notes

1 Sandra L. Myres, *Westering Women and the Frontier Experience 1800–1915* (Albuquerque:
   University of New Mexico Press, 1982). Julie Roy Jeffrey, *Frontier Women: The Trans-
   Mississippi West* (New York: Hill and Wang, 1979).
2 For example, John Cawelti, *The Six-Gun Mystique* (Bowling Green: Bowling Green
   Popular Press, 1971).
3 Mandy Merck, 'Travesty on the Old Frontier', in *Move Over Misconceptions: Doris Day
   Reappraised* (London: British Film Institute, 1980).
4 Jacqueline Levitin, 'The Western: any good roles for feminists?', *Film Reader* 5
   (1982), pp. 95–108.

Chapter 4

THE PLEASURES AND PERILS OF EXPLOITATION FILMS

When I first wrote about low-budget exploitation films in 1976,[1] it was in a particular context. On the crest of the wave of 1970s feminism, I was looking for evidence of the contribution of women to the film-making process, and for ways of writing that contribution into history, as well as ways to account for the apparent exclusion of women from the mainstream industries and from traditional histories. From this perspective, those female directors who had been successful in the mainstream could be counted on the fingers of one hand, and pioneers such as Alice Guy Blaché, Dorothy Arzner and Ida Lupino were perceived as totems for the marginalisation of women film-makers. In 1971, art historian Linda Nochlin posed an ironic question, 'Why Have there Been no Great Women Artists?', which became emblematic of the era. One way of challenging this situation was to foreground women directors who were active in areas that fell outside the mainstream, such as documentary and the avant-garde, and who were better able, it seemed, to produce work that would combat the stereotypes and patriarchal ideologies of the mainstream industries.

This critical and theoretical activity was part of a huge expansion in independent film-making and the creation of alternative production, distribution and exhibition networks, whose value in the 1970s and since in re-energising the mainstream is rarely recognised. Despite the fragmentation of these networks in the 1980s and 1990s, and the erosion of the 1970s political context, there is no doubt that feminist film theory and practice during this period left a legacy and provided a context for subsequent feminist work (the influx of women directors into mainstream production in the mid-1980s is a good example). However, there were certain limitations in taking the director as a model for women's contribution to mainstream film-making. This was a position that ignored the significance, in terms of control and influence, of women scriptwriters, producers, musicians, editors, designers, actors and audiences, to mention but a few of those who collaborate in making films.

The focus on directors persists today, and continues to obscure the broader picture of women's contribution to cinema and film culture. It also reinforces a sense of women's exclusion and marginalisation, which may not be entirely justified, or at least needs to be substantiated by more historical analysis and evidence. Nevertheless, the debates around female authorship, the question of critical recognition, and the problems of retaining a distinctive feminist 'voice' in the context of mainstream production remain current today, when there appear to be greater numbers of women directing in the mainstream. There are still very few books about female directors, let alone all those other women working in cinema. The careers of those directors who do make successful mainstream features are often uneven, with long periods between productions, and those films that do get made are sometimes judged to be flawed by critics who measure them against those of male directors. Female directors working in Hollywood rarely make the 'A' list, and their films generally do not receive Academy Awards or feature in critical pantheons. It would seem, then, that women do not make good auteur material.

To look at the problem another way, it may be that the tenets of auteur criticism are too limited to allow for the difference of women's films. This argument has its attractions, but it does not really hold up under scrutiny. Anyone, male or female, who makes films within a mainstream industrial context such as Hollywood has to negotiate the constraints of that system and the vocabulary it employs, as well as the demands of international markets. Irrespective of gender, a director, to qualify as an auteur, must be seen as successfully manipulating those constraints to put across their personal agenda and style, which are perceived as going against the grain of the system itself and its ideologies. This seems to me to provide an accurate description of what women directors, like any others, have to do if they choose to work in the mainstream, and it offers a valid way of assessing the value of the end results. However, those involved in the process of critical assessment and evaluation clearly do use gender criteria to judge the success or otherwise of those results. Partly due to the cultural impact of feminism, the doors of the male canon have opened to include contemporary directors such as Chantal Akerman, Sally Potter, Jane Campion and Kathryn Bigelow, all of whom offer a very different, often critical slant on mainstream cinema. And new histories are slowly emerging that challenge the ascendancy of Great Male Innovators such as D.W. Griffith, Alfred Hitchcock or Orson Welles.[2]

It could be the material or subject matter that women directors deal with that precludes their being granted first-rank status. It is sometimes argued that women film-makers – and not just directors – are often confined to 'women's pictures' and to material that deals primarily with interior, personal and emotional issues, though this claim remains to be substantiated. Today, women work across the board in a variety of genres from action to comedy, from westerns to melodrama, and it is likely that they always have. The problem is one of visibility. While the director can be one of the more visible roles in film production, female directors are not necessarily accorded the same visibility as their male counterparts. Those women directors working in Hollywood who are singled out for the status of auteur are generally those who are perceived to take risks with form and subject matter, and who are therefore regarded as swashbuckling adventurers in the mould of male auteurs. The auteur, male or female, is a maverick figure, a hero battling to overcome the monsters of the system.

The idea of the woman director as hero has its attractions, though we might ask why we need such heroes, and why we need to identify with exceptional figures at the expense of the group. This brings me neatly back to 1970s exploitation films, since one of my earliest heroes, Stephanie Rothman, fought to produce feminist work within the hostile environment of low-budget exploitation cinema, with amazing results. During the 1970s, exploitation films directed by Stephanie Rothman were at the centre of Anglo-American feminist debates about what might constitute a new language of cinema capable of countering the patriarchal myths and stereotypes of mainstream Hollywood. The experience of working within exploitation film-making can only be verified by the testimony of those women who have made films in that context.[3] Although I shall discuss that film-making context here, I am primarily concerned with the historical significance of low-budget exploitation cinema, and of Stephanie Rothman's work in particular, to feminist film culture.

Debate in the 1970s centred on the relative value of working inside or outside mainstream Hollywood. Working inside was perceived by many as selling out, and as giving over control to the male-dominated studios, who were seen as imposing constraints in the form of negative stereotypes of women, particularly in highly sexualised images that put the female body on display. Such images were perceived as reinforcing the patriarchal division that characterised femininity as passive and masculinity as active. By working outside the mainstream, it was argued, women had more control over the film-making process and were in a better position to forge new images that would depict women as active participants in history and society without using them for erotic display. An opposing view suggested that stereotypes were not retrograde in themselves; they could be dismantled or deconstructed and reassembled to create new meanings, and to reveal the contradictions that they attempted to suppress. Thus the dominant codes could be subverted from within, and the tables turned in favour of women's interests. Those of us who took this last position were concerned to challenge the view that there was an unproblematic 'feminist cinema' or 'feminist film culture' that was already there, available to be mobilised. We contested the idea of a women's viewpoint as pure feminist discourse, or coherent world view, arguing that a feminist film should be 'part of a process of learning and struggle towards feminist conscious-ness rather than assuming the feminist position as given, a "truth" which can simply be set against the "falsity" of the dominant ideology'.[4]

Stephanie Rothman's work was part of this polemic, since her films could be seen as a prime example of feminist subversion from within, using the generic formulae of exploitation cinema in the interest of her own agenda as a woman director. However, exploitation films were problematic for feminists in a number of ways. Not only were the films' use of sexualised images of women a bone of contention, the highly charged subject matter, in particular the relatively graphic depiction of rape and sexual assault, were viewed by many as pandering to sadistic male fantasies, and encouraging incidence of actual sexual abuse. A 1981 retrospective of Roger Corman's New World Productions at the National Film Theatre in London, which included the films Rothman made for Corman, was picketed by women's groups expressing anger and concern on behalf of victims of rape and sexual violence that such films should be shown. This was a valid response to some of the excesses of exploitation genres, and I do not intend to rehabilitate or redeem low-budget exploitation. Rather, I shall attempt to reassess its historical contribution to feminist film culture.

One of the problems in assessing that contribution is that low-budget exploitation films generally receive little serious critical attention from either journalists or academics. Carol Clover's groundbreaking book *Men, Women and Chainsaws* (1992) is one of the few academic texts to address low-budget horror and rape-revenge from a feminist perspective, but its particular focus on the horror film seems to have precluded a history of exploitation cinema itself. There have been other attempts to give low-budget exploitation films cultural respectability, but these have concentrated on specific areas that can be reclaimed according to traditional critical canons of authorship and genre – by tracing a consistent set of preoccupations through Roger Corman's cycle of Edgar Allan Poe adaptations, for example, or in the work of those Corman protégés (Martin Scorsese, Joe Dante, Jonathan Demme *et al.*) who went on to make big-budget movies. This critical espousal of certain exploitation directors does not generally take exploitation cinema itself seriously. Rather, exploitation is seen as a stepping stone to mainstream production.

An important aspect of 1960s and 1970s low-budget exploitation produc-tion was indeed to provide a training ground, a pathway to mainstream cinema for young, inexperienced directors. But it is misleading to view the films as simply practice exercises on the way to making 'proper' cinema. Exploitation films can be seen as a genre in their own right. The fact that they were often low-budget remakes of more up-market productions has led many critics to measure them against those productions, and to find them lacking in comparison. But much of the appeal of exploitation films to the drive-in cinema and student audiences for whom they were primarily intended derived from the knowing way in which they played on audience expectations of narrative and genre, parodying mainstream conventions. Low-budget exploitation scandalises some of the most hallowed canons of film criticism – the assumption that the critic or academic knows better than 'unsophisticated' audiences how to judge a good or bad film, for instance, or that a 'good' film is judged in terms of taste, aesthetic coherence, serious themes, and so forth. Instead of inferior products that fail to conform to the classic ideal, these films can be seen as offering alternatives to the dominant representational system, opening up the possibility of saying something different.

A further problem lies in the term 'exploitation' itself, which implies a process of 'ripping off'. It also implies an economic imperative – very low budgets; tight production schedules; low-paid, inexperienced, non-union personnel; minimal production values; sensational selling campaigns; and widespread saturation bookings aimed at specific markets (predominantly the youth/drive-in cinema audience generally uninterested in critical reviews), all in the interests of making a quick profit. One of the reasons that exploitation films are deemed unworthy of serious critical attention is their blatant commercialism – they do not aspire to be art; indeed, they seem to revel in their own trashiness and aura of immediate disposability. In exploiting, or capitalising on the success of more up-market, mainstream productions, they parody rather than emulate them.

Being so tightly tied to market forces has inevitable consequences for form: the elements that give big-budget films their coherence (stars, psychological realism, narrative development, expensive production values) are often absent. In the late 1970s, however, independent companies such as Roger Corman's New World Productions took advantage of co-production deals to make films that fell between art cinema and exploitation. *I Never Promised You a Rose Garden* (1977), for example, produced by Corman, scripted by Gavin Lambert, with a budget of $1 million, was a solid commercial success. This budget, though still low by major studio stan-dards, was much higher than early New World productions such as Jack Hill's *The Big Doll House* (1971), which cost roughly $150,000, recouping something like $3 million in rentals. In the mid-1970s, budgets rose to $250,000–$500,000, allowing bigger name stars and better production values, as in films such as *Big Bad Mama*, *Cockfighter* and *Jackson County Jail*, which were more 'quality' productions.[5]

Instead of up-market production values, then, exploitation films offer schematic, minimal narratives, comic-book stereotypes, 'bad' acting, and brief film cycles that disappear as soon as their audience appeal is exhausted: the student nurse cycle, initiated by the success of Stephanie Rothman's *Student Nurses* (1970), and more or less ending with Allan Holleb's *Candy Stripe Nurses* (1974), is a prime example. The films' conditions of production have consequences for content too: in order to attract/exploit their target audiences, exploitation films contain a high degree of sensationalised sex and/or violence, apparently playing on the more retrograde, sadistic/voyeuristic fantasies of young male viewers.

Given the apparent limitations of the form, and the lack of human values in the content, it seems paradoxical that many of New Hollywood's most interesting (that is, cinematically and politically aware) and highly rated young directors not only started out as exploitation film-makers, but made films whose cult status has resulted in them entering a different distribution and exhibition context in art-house theatres, college campus cinemas and film festivals – a 'sophisticated' context far removed from their original audiences. This paradox is only partly explained by the fact that low-budget exploitation offers young film-makers their first opportunity to direct. A company such as New World, knowing how difficult it is for aspiring film-makers to break into the industry, takes film-school graduates and pays them minimum wages in exchange for giving them their first break. This 'contract' throws up one of the first contradictions in the exploitation ethic – the exploitation is to some extent mutual. There is also a challenge for film-makers in the necessity of shooting fast and cheaply, in displaying ingenuity and in injecting ideas that do not entirely go along with hardcore exploitation principles. In other words, the director can also exploit the exploitation material in his or her own interests, and have fun at the expense of the genre. This kind of playful approach characterises films such as Stephanie Rothman's *The Velvet Vampire* (aka *The Waking Hour*, 1971), a send-up of the horror film, and Joe Dante/Allan Arkush's *Hollywood Boulevard* (1976), which parodies exploitation film-making itself.

A second contradiction is generated by the exploitation film's schematic form and its appeal to audiences who are assumed to care little about style. This allows for a degree of experimentation. Thus, within a fairly routine exploiter such as *Humanoids from the Deep* (aka *Monster*, 1980) – an ecological horror story that had mutant sea beasts attacking the young women in a fishing village – director Barbara Peeters included, along with the requisite scenes of of nudity and sexual violence, a sequence reminiscent of Hitchcock's

The Birds (1963) and John Carpenter's *Halloween* (1978) in which a woman is trapped with her child as her house is besieged by the monsters. Playing with point-of-view shots that are sometimes attached to the monsters, but sometimes clearly are not, she gave the camera a life of its own so that it became the aggressor itself – and, by implication, so did the viewer. The sequence conforms to exploitation woman-and-child in jeopardy rules, but it also questions them, partly by drawing attention to them. In a similar way, Jonathan Kaplan (who went on to direct the 1988 mainstream rape drama *The Accused*, starring Jodie Foster), faced with the requirements of the student nurse cycle as outlined to him by Roger Corman ('... exploitation of male sexual fantasy, a comedic sub-plot, action and violence, and a slightly-to-the-left-of-centre sub-plot ... frontal nudity from the waist up, total nudity from behind, no pubic hair, get the title in the film somewhere and go to work ... '[6]) made *Night Call Nurses* (1972) into a film that, by using a back-tracking camera at key moments, rejected the voyeurism implicit in the conventions.

This seems a good point at which to return to the relationship of feminism to exploitation films. In a 1981 interview, Stephanie Rothman remarked:

> *Student Nurses* was a big success. The male buddy films were out. There was a correct hue and cry about the fact that there were no more roles by women for women ... There was a wide market out there for films about women and a very responsive audience, not just men.[7]

This is an interesting comment in the light of assumptions about exploitation genres' targeting of predominantly young, male audiences. The exploitation film's subject matter, its presumed appeal to retrograde male fantasies, may not appear to be congenial material for women film-makers. Nevertheless, women directors, including a declared feminist such as Stephanie Rothman, a University of Southern California (USC) film school graduate, have worked successfully in exploitation. Indeed, Rothman's films not only acquired cult status on the art-cinema circuits in the USA during the 1970s, they were also widely shown at women's film festivals. It is interesting that more than twenty years later this is still the case, despite the fact that she, unlike many of her male colleagues, has not made the transition to mainstream directing. That Rothman herself is aware of the sensitive nature of exploitation films for feminism is revealed in several interviews.[8] Nevertheless, as she and others have pointed out, within the necessary economic constraints, the low-budget exploitation director, particularly at New World under Roger Corman as producer, had considerable artistic freedom. It was also the case that, because of Corman's liberal-left leanings, directors and writers were encouraged to address contemporary political issues, cashing in on what had currently caught the public imagination.

After graduating from USC in the early 1960s, Rothman obtained a Directors Guild of America directing fellowship (the first ever awarded to a woman) and moved straight into second-unit work for Roger Corman at American International Pictures and New World Productions. Her first solo venture as director was the beach-party teen-pic *It's a Bikini World* (1966), but her reputation as a stylish, politically aware film-maker rests on the five films she directed subsequently – two for New World and three for her and Charles Swartz's own company, Dimension Pictures. Rothman's first film for New World, *Student Nurses* (1970), coming at a time when there was a growing demand for more interesting women's roles, no doubt partly influenced by 1970s feminism, was a commercial success that inaugurated the short lived student nurse cycle referred to on p 57

Student Nurses involved a friendship between four young nurses from different backgrounds whose sexual, professional and political adventures made up the episodic narrative. The 'nurse' format enabled social issues such as abortion, drugs and the ethics of the nurse's commitment to a political cause to be raised. At the same time, Rothman took every opportunity to parody the basic principles of exploitation – in particular, its reliance on displaying the female body. Viewing it today, *Student Nurses* is a remarkable achievement. It is striking not only for its high production values, but also for its sophisticated discourse on 1970s sexual politics – neither of which would necessarily be expected from an exploitation film. Also unexpected are the drug-induced fantasy sequences, which are more in line with European art cinema than the rough and ready codes of exploitation. Rothman's inclusion of a relatively graphic abortion sequence, cut against scenes of one of the other nurses having casual sex, still has a powerful impact. One of the main themes of *Student Nurses* is the relationship of the individual to the group collective, a preoccupation common to many of Rothman's films.

Her next production *The Velvet Vampire* was less commercially successful, but has remained a cult art-house hit. An offbeat female vampire film set in southern California, it satirised contemporary sexual mores while reversing many of the expectations of vampire mythology. Comic reversals could be said to be the keynote of Rothman's exploitation films, combined with a playful approach to stereotypes and clichés that enabled her to turn the tables on the more voyeuristic and sadistic pleasures offered by the genre. This combination of satire and serious social comment is particularly marked in *Terminal Island* (aka *Knuckle-Men*, 1973), a women-in-prison action movie containing a high level of violence. Clearly uneasy about the violence, Rothman none the less refused to shirk it; instead she used the conventions to

Figure 4.1   Working girls: publicity material for *Student Nurses* (1970). Courtesy BFI Stills, Posters and Designs.

make a film about the transition from a brutal patriarchal regime to a more cooperative, egalitarian social system, led by women.

The action movie has traditionally been one of the most macho of genres. However, within New World exploitation in particular, the action film had often been given a feminist inflection through sexual role reversal in which strong, assertive women were put in roles usually reserved for men, often with a modern backdrop of an Asian or South American country in which a 'revolution' was taking place. These positive-heroine figures were physically active, capable of violence, taking their destiny in their own hands, and often using machine guns. The positive heroine would parody male violence, often 'raping', sometimes devouring her male victims. As already noted, many of these films were made in response to public demand for more women characters, and Jack Hill's *The Big Doll House* (1971), or Joe Viola's *The Hot Box* (1972), celebrated a popular version of 'Women's Lib'.[9] In spite of the potential here for more active roles for women, these sexual role-reversal films generally cast super-aggressive women as mirror-images of men, without questioning those images too much.

Rothman was aware of the problem of dealing with violence, and set out to make *Terminal Island* more than just a violent film, while at the same time arguing that women should be allowed to be as aggressive as men in certain circumstances. The result was a movie in which violence was used to defeat a cruelly authoritarian system and to set up an alternative founded on mutual dependence and respect. Where it differs from other exploitation action films is perhaps in the way it projects a vision of a cooperative system in which violence would be unnecessary, rather than simply celebrating the aggressive female figure. *Terminal Island* begins with the stereotype of the aggressive 'positive' woman; in the progress of the narrative, the protagonists fight as a group, in which all contributions are equally significant, to establish a utopian society, initiated by the women, and the narrative closes with the stereotype of woman as mother presiding over their utopia.

Like Rothman's other films, *Terminal Island* includes numerous feminist jokes, many of which depend on role reversal, or on women turning the tables against male aggressors. The 'bee stinging' sequence, which is a reversal of the conventional strip-tease (and, incidentally, part of a rape-revenge sub-plot), is a fine example, and there are others, for instance the overt jibes at the expense of genres such as the western and the biker movie, or the chessboard perched precariously (and strategically) on Bobby's lap. With its revenge theme, *Terminal Island* is closely linked to the low-budget 1970s rape-revenge movies that Carol Clover discusses in *Men, Women and Chainsaws*, which feature the Final Girl survivors who wreak revenge on male aggressors by maiming and castrating them. What is interesting, though, is that *Terminal Island* ends on a relatively optimistic note: the survivors are in the form of a group who begin to set up an alternative society, whereas in low-budget rape-revenge, the notion of 'society' is more or less redundant. *Terminal Island* can also be seen as an important forerunner of films such as

Kathryn Bigelow's *Blue Steel* (1990), which is also a critique of masculine power, violence and gun fetishism. However, Bigelow's postfeminist film is rather more pessimistic than Rothman's: rookie cop Megan (played by Jamie Lee Curtis) finally shoots down the rapist/serial killer, but seems to destroy herself in the process.

Despite her success in exploitation film-making, and her obvious talent as a writer/director (she co-scripted *The Velvet Vampire*, *Group Marriage* and *Terminal Island* and wrote *The Working Girls*), and despite setting up her own production company, Dimension Pictures, with Charles Swartz, Rothman has not directed a film since *The Working Girls* (1974), when Dimension Pictures was dissolved, and since then has concentrated on writing scripts. She has not taken the route to mainstream production travelled by many of her male contemporaries.[10] This raises the interesting question of whether exploitation film-making does in fact operate as a successful 'training ground' for women, as it does for male directors. During the mid-1980s, a second wave of women directors who worked in low-budget exploitation emerged, but this genera-tion seemed more aware of the dangers of being categorised as exploitation directors. Amy Jones, for example, who directed *Love Letters* in 1983, was keen to shed the reputation she had acquired for *The Slumber Party Massacre*, a low-budget 'slasher' project scripted by Rita Mae Brown, which was a commercial success, though not a critical one. As Jones explained:

> One of the reasons I wanted to do *Love Letters* was that I felt *Slumber Party* was not going to do anything for me as a director; because unless you get reviews and make a picture with more quality you don't get much attention.[11]

While *Love Letters*, produced by Roger Corman, had some exploitation elements – for example, sex, nudity (mostly female), reworking an already successful genre (the women's picture), and a low budget (around $1 million) – it was nearer the art-movie end of the market. It had a serious approach to its subject, a coherent narrative, psychologically developed characters, well-known actors (Jamie Lee Curtis, James Keach, Amy Madigan, Bud Cort), and its low-budget origins were well disguised. Another successful exploitation director, Penelope Spheeris, in an interview in *The Face,* disclaimed the exploitation provenance of *Suburbia* (1983) and *The Boys Next Door* (1984):

> Just because they're about rough-neck teenagers doesn't mean that my films are 'exploitation'. So were *The Outsiders* and *Rumblefish*. Exploitation films have nothing to say about the human condition and I always take responsibility for my films' moral statements.[12]

Clearly this disclaimer does not stand up in the face of the films, which, in spite of being exhibited on the art-cinema and festival circuits in the UK, were produced by New World as exploitation pics directed at the youth market (*Suburbia* cost $560,000, while *The Boys Next Door* had a relatively high budget of $1.6 million). Aesthetically, too, they had all the hallmarks of exploitation – minimal, episodic narratives, characters who had iconic significance rather than psychological depth, actors who spoke their lines as though rehearsing them, and substantial doses of sex and violence. In spite of her success as an exploitation director, Spheeris, like Jones, was anxious at that stage in her career to shed the exploitation label and discussed her next project, *Boy Child*, in terms of movies such as Truffaut's *L'Enfant sauvage*, Cocteau's *La Belle et la bête*, David Lynch's *The Elephant Man* and Hugh Hudson's *Greystoke: The Legend of Tarzan*, characterising it as an art-movie rather than exploitation.

Jones and Spheeris were clearly aware of the critical bias against taking low-budget exploitation films seriously, and saw their future as directors depending on a move towards a more acceptable art cinema. It is interesting that the outcome of this strategy has been uneven in both cases, with neither of these directors succeeding so far in establishing long-term mainstream careers in cinema. Spheeris' mainstream comedy hit *Wayne's World* (1992), despite its considerable merits, was nevertheless a far cry from the *Boy Child* project, with its art-house aspirations. On the other hand, the move by the major American studios in the early 1980s to penetrate the exploitation market, in particular the youth audience, has enabled Amy Heckerling to carve out a successful directing career. Her teen-pic *Fast Times at Ridgemont High* (1982) was produced by Universal, and her gangster parody *Johnny Dangerously* (1984) by Twentieth Century Fox. Following their success she went on to make such major comedy hits as *Look Who's Talking* (1989) and *Look Who's Talking Too* (1990).

However, when it came to big-studio remakes of projects that had their roots in low-budget exploitation, such as the rape drama *The Accused* or the serial killer/slasher film *The Silence of the Lambs*, both feminist-influenced, they went to Jonathan Kaplan and Jonathan Demme respectively, both of whom had cut their teeth on low-budget exploitation film-making with Roger Corman. Without being uncharitable – both *The Accused* and *The Silence of the Lambs* are of considerable interest to feminists – one cannot help but wonder why these projects were not offered to equally well-qualified women directors.

There seem to be no simple answers to the question of why it has proved so difficult for women directors working in low-budget exploitation to cross over into the mainstream. It could be, as I suggested at the beginning of this article, that too much emphasis is placed on the director at the expense of

63

other film-makers. Historically, directors have not always been in a position of power within the industry, and a different map of women's contribution may well emerge if patterns of employment across the full range of production at different periods are considered. What I have tried to do here is to sketch the historical significance of 1970s exploitation film-making for feminism, and to establish the central importance of the work of Stephanie Rothman and others to feminist debate about the possibilities and limitations offered to women by exploitation films. Low-budget exploitation has provided significant entry points for some women film-makers into the industry, and produced some fascinating feminist films, which remain relevant. Their influence can be discerned in low-budget independent material produced by younger feminists today,[13] as well as in mainstream blockbusters. Nevertheless, they remain renegade outsiders, relegated to the margins of conventional histories.

Notes

1　Pam Cook, '"Exploitation" films and feminism', *Screen* 17(2) (summer 1976), pp. 122–7.
2　See, for example, Alison McMahon's book *Alice Guy Blaché: Lost Visionary of the Cinema* (New York: Continuum, 2002), which challenges the widely accepted notion that D.W. Griffith can be seen as the 'father' of cinema.
3　An interview with Stephanie Rothman in Carla Despineux and Verena Mund (eds), *Girls, Gangs, Guns*, (Marburg: Schüren, 2002) pp. 55–75 [in German] is revelatory in this respect.
4　Pam Cook, '"Exploitation" films and feminism', *Screen* 17(20) (summer 1976), p. 124.
5　See Jim Hillier and Aaron Lipstadt (eds), *BFI Dossier No. 7: Roger Corman's New World* (London: BFI Publishing, 1981).
6　Quoted in Hillier and Lipstadt, *Roger Corman's New World*, p. 63.
7　Interviewed by Tony Williams, *Journal of Popular Film and Television* 9(2) (summer 1981), pp. 84–90.
8　See especially the interview with Tony Williams, *Journal of Popular Film and Television*.
9　Apparently Roger Corman asked Stephanie Rothman to direct *The Big Doll House*, but she refused. Jack Hill was appointed director, while Rothman did Second Unit.
10　The reasons for this are complex, as explained by Rothman herself in the interview in Despineux and Mund (eds), *Girls, Gangs, Guns*.
11　'Amy Jones and *Love Letters*', interview with Amy Jones by Robert S. Birchard, *American Cinematographer* 65 (January 1984), pp. 42–5.
12　Interview with Penelope Spheeris by Elissa Van Poznak in *The Face* (August 1985).
13　See, for example, Jennifer Reeder's *White Trash Girl* cycle, which arguably takes exploitation aesthetics to their limits.

Memory in popular British cinema

INTRODUCTION

The early 1980s witnessed a sharp increase in interest in melodrama and the women's picture, both critically neglected genres in comparison to the amount of discussion afforded to the western and the gangster film. The interest was partly a response to the cultural pessimism afflicting much 1970s film theory, which had constructed cinema as a closed system of representation, tying spectators in to capitalist and patriarchal ideologies. Melodrama's potential for social critique, and its role in siphoning off painful emotions resulting from historical and political change, suggested that the situation was rather more complex. There were also signs of unease with the negative view of cinema as an industry producing films made by men entirely for male consumption, since this failed to account for the significance of women audiences and the pleasures enjoyed by them. While the idea that women experienced cinema second-hand, through the dominant male perspective, inhibiting the expression of their own desires, may have been useful in articulating a dissatisfaction with the perceived marginalisation of women, it led to an impasse. As a way forward, theory began to look to those genres that foregrounded women's desires and interests, and were in many cases directly addressed to female audiences. At the same time, the critique of text-based theory and demand for a more historical approach gave rise to the proliferation of audience and reception studies, which looked to the contextual material circulating around film texts for evidence about their meanings. It was argued that the film could no longer be perceived as the locus of immanent meaning; instead, it was the site of conflicting discourses, spanning various media from newspaper reviews to the Internet, which constructed its meaning differently at different moments.

A further development in this move to historicise film studies was a burgeoning concern with national cinemas and their relationship to Hollywood. American cinema's domination of world markets, its apparently global

67

appeal to audiences, and the difficulties experienced by other national cinemas in breaking in to the US market, left smaller national industries struggling for survival. Historically, British cinema had been perceived as a victim of American cultural imperialism and economic power, lacking both the resources and the technical and artistic ingenuity of Hollywood and the critically respected European art cinemas. To combat this negative picture, British cinema historians turned their attention to key periods in which British films held their own at the home box-office against competition from American output. The 1940s were identified as a golden age in which British films were more popular than before or since, and critical work on this decade flourished. However, the films under scrutiny were by and large those sanctioned by criteria of quality, restraint and realism traditionally held to be desirable characteristics for British cinema. Further research uncovered a hidden history of popular British films, hugely successful with the predominantly female 1940s audiences. The flamboyant, stylish Gainsborough melodramas produced in this period became the focus for debate about the way British cinema was perceived, and the way its history had previously been constructed.

The work on Gainsborough melodrama produced fresh ideas not just about British cinema, but also about feminist-influenced thinking about melodrama, since the films provided a historically specific example of the genre. Much feminist writing on Hollywood melodramas and women's pictures had emphasised their conservative elements. The Gainsborough melodramas provided evidence of the genre's capacity to provide fantasies of female empowerment as a key feature in their appeal to women, opening the door to a more positive perspective on the pleasures offered by cinema to female audiences. The article 'Melodrama and the Women's Picture' (1983) engaged with the melodrama debates, locating the Gainsborough films in the context of discussion that had focused principally on Hollywood examples, and arguing for a historical approach that would recognise the connections and differences between British and American cinema. While focusing on the British social and industrial context in which the Gainsborough films were produced, it also attempted to move beyond their national provenance to their links with the wider, international film culture. Other research on Gainsborough made similar connections with European artistic traditions brought to British cinema by continental expatriate film-makers who worked for the studio, mainly in the area of visual design. Further study on the 1920s and 1930s revealed that Gainsborough had been actively involved in attempts to set up a pan-European cartel capable of breaking America's stranglehold on world markets. A more complex picture of national cinema began to emerge, one that positioned British cinema on the world stage as an international player with global aspirations.

Work on Gainsborough, and on the 1940s melodramas in particular, was influential in changing perceptions of British cinema history, which had largely been approached in terms of realism. There had been comparatively little writing by historians on the output of British studios – with the exception of Ealing, whose films had come to represent a particular brand of Englishness in the public imagination, and had inspired influential research by scholars. In contrast to Gainsborough, Ealing was perceived as projecting a cosy, parochial view of British national identity, through a predominantly realist aesthetic. In retrospect, this opposition was simplistic, and depended on too narrow a view of the output of both companies. But the contrast had the effect of drawing attention to the diversity of British cinema, and broadening the scope of debate to include the vast quantity of successful, popular films produced by Britain. Perhaps for the first time, discussion focused not just on institutional and social analysis of those films, but on their visual style.

The Gainsborough melodramas were a relatively short cycle, and the widely held view is that with their demise in 1950 their extravagant aesthetics and irreverent spirit went underground, to re-emerge later in the decade with the arrival of Hammer horror. This is an interesting situation, since just at the time that major Hollywood studios began producing the lavish Technicolor weepies by the likes of Vincente Minnelli and Douglas Sirk that had inspired the melodrama debates, British companies apparently stopped producing melodramas. Nevertheless, a different strain of the genre – the social problem melodrama, usually made in black and white – was widely produced and formed a staple of 1950s British cinema. *Mandy* (1952), directed by Alexander Mackendrick for Ealing, provides a striking example of this shift. While the Gainsborough melodramas had dealt with current social issues, they had favoured escapist fantasy scenarios as a means of exploring sexuality and desire. The social realist melodramas took a more exterior approach, placing characters in recognisable contemporary locations and situations. However, they did not sacrifice melodramatic feeling: *Mandy* is a classic weepie, generating powerful emotion from the predicaments faced by its protagonists. It focuses on female desires and aspirations, set in the context of a postwar Britain in the process of reconstruction, and it works through a typical melodramatic theme – the softening of rigid patriarchal attitudes to accommodate the needs of women. The discussion of *Mandy* in Chapter 6, like the account of Gainsborough melodrama in Chapter 5, situates the film in the context of its production circumstances and sociohistorical background, in order to demonstrate its reformist attitude to the changes faced by postwar Britain. However, it fails to consider its melodramatic visual aesthetic, and the innovative use of sound to encourage empathy with the young deaf mute Mandy, which might have produced a more complex analysis of the place of the film within Ealing's output, and in British cinema at the time.

'*Mandy*: daughter of transition' (1985) discusses the film in terms of the way it mediates and reflects on a historical transition from tradition to modernity in 1950s Britain. The final piece, 'Memory in British cinema: brief encounters' (2001) detects a similar resistance to the shift to modernity depicted in two films made at the end of the Second World War: David Lean and Noël Coward's *Brief Encounter* (1946), and Michael Powell and Emeric Pressburger's Scottish romance, *I Know Where I'm Going!* (1945). The comparison between the two films, both of which deploy memory and nostalgia to reach audiences, with very different results, opens up a general discussion about memory in cinema, and about cinema as memory. Both *Brief Encounter* and *I Know Where I'm Going!* can be seen as nostalgic memory films, and both, like the Gainsborough melodramas and *Mandy*, privilege the perspective of their female protagonists. This testifies to the historical importance of female audiences in British cinema, and to their influence on film-makers and the kinds of films that are made. Even if those films can be seen to circumscribe the power of women, they nevertheless acknowledge that power.

The studies of Gainsborough melodramas also drew attention to the ways in which they challenged prevailing notions of Britishness, partly as a result of their bias towards continental European locations and visual styles, and partly, perhaps, due to the number of European expatriates involved in their production. While the presence of European émigrés in British cinema had been well documented, their cultural impact was not widely recognised. Historically, European film-makers have worked across the board in the British industry, often gaining considerable power and influence, transforming working practices and contributing innovatory techniques. Nevertheless, British cinema scholars have hardly begun to assess the full extent of their influence. 'Memory in British cinema' approaches this task by tracing the memories and aspirations of the émigré film-makers who worked on *I Know Where I'm Going!* through the film's narrative and allusive visual style. The debt to European aesthetics, and to German Expressionism in particular, is revealed to be far more extensive than previously recognised, with the result that the film, though apparently very 'British' in its subject-matter and provenance, proves to be a cultural hybrid. Thus ideas about memory are used to bring to the fore the transnational nature of national cinema, and its links with other cultures as well as its own. In a way, this takes us back to melodrama once more, since it has been identified as an international form, continually transformed by different contexts and periods. 'Memory in British cinema' suggests that the notion of memory can provide the means to understanding and analysing the processes of historical transformation, and to formulate new ways of thinking about national cinema.

Further reading

Barr, Charles (ed.), *All Our Yesterdays: Ninety Years of British Cinema* (London: BFI Publishing, 1985).

———— , *Ealing Studios* (London: Studio Vista/Cameron Books, 1994).

Batsleer, Janet, 'Pulp in the pink', *Spare Rib* 109 (August 1981).

Brunsdon, Charlotte, 'A subject for the seventies', *Screen* 23(3/4), (September/October 1982).

Christie, Ian, *Arrows of Desire* (London: Waterstone, 1985).

Cook, Pam, *Fashioning the Nation: Costume and Identity in British Cinema* (London: BFI Publishing, 1996).

———— (ed.), *Gainsborough Pictures* (London and Washington: Cassell, 1997).

———— , *I Know Where I'm Going!* (London: BFI Film Classics, 2002).

Creed, Barbara, 'The position of women in Hollywood melodramas', *Australian Journal of Screen Theory* 4 (1977), pp. 27–31.

Dyer, Richard, *Brief Encounter* (London: BFI Film Classics, 1993).

Ellis, John, 'Art culture and quality: terms for a British cinema in the forties and seventies', *Screen* 19(3) (autumn 1978), pp. 9–49.

Elsaesser, Thomas, 'Tales of sound and fury: observations on the family melodrama', *Monogram* 4 (1972), pp. 2–15.

Geraghty, Christine, *British Cinema in the Fifties: Gender, Genre and the New Look* (London: Routledge, 2000).

Gledhill, Christine (ed.), *Home Is Where the Heart Is. Studies in Melodrama and the Women's Film* (London: BFI Publishing, 1987).

Halliday, Jon, *Sirk On Sirk* (London: Secker and Warburg/British Film Institute, 1971).

Harper, Sue, *Picturing the Past: The Rise and Fall of the British Costume Film* (London: BFI Publishing, 1994).

Haskell, Molly, *From Reverence to Rape* (Harmondsworth and New York: Penguin, 1979).

Higson, Andrew (ed.), *Dissolving Views: Key Articles on British Cinema* (London and Washington: Cassell, 1996).

Landy, Marcia, *British Genres: Cinema and Society 1930–1960* (Princeton: Princeton University Press, 1991).

Lant, Antonia, *Blackout: Reinventing Women for Wartime British Cinema* (Princeton: Princeton University Press, 1991).

Mulvey, Laura, 'Fear eats the soul', *Spare Rib* 30 (December, 1974).

———— , 'Notes on Sirk and melodrama', *Movie* 25 (winter 1977/78), pp. 53–6

———— and Halliday, Jon (eds), *Douglas Sirk* (Edinburgh: Edinburgh Film Festival, 1972).

Pollock, Griselda, Nowell-Smith, Geoffrey and Heath, Stephen, 'Dossier on melodrama', *Screen* 18(2) (summer 1977).

71

Screen 12(2) (summer 1971): special issue on Douglas Sirk.

Street, Sarah, *Transatlantic Crossings: British Feature Films in America* (London and New York: Continuum, 2002).

Further viewing

Brief Encounter (David Lean, UK, 1946)
I Know Where I'm Going! (Michael Powell and Emeric Pressburger, UK, 1945)
Madonna of the Seven Moons (Arthur Crabtree, UK, 1944)
Mandy (Alexander Mackendrick, UK, 1952)
Memento (Christopher Nolan, USA, 2000)

Chapter 5

MELODRAMA AND THE
WOMEN'S PICTURE

Melodrama has been more hotly debated than any other genre in cinema. Its potential to move the audience deeply while laying bare the impossible, painful contradictions of social and personal relationships appeals strongly to radical film critics, and recent feminist interest has focused on the way in which it deals with aspects of women's experience marginalised by other genres. Feminist criticism has shifted the terms of the debate and enlivened it. In particular, it has brought forward the women's picture, a sub category of melodrama and one of the most despised and neglected genres, as an important object of critical investigation. The women's picture is differentiated from the rest of cinema by virtue of its construction of a 'female point of view' that motivates and dominates the narrative, and its specific address to a female audience.

At the beginning of the melodrama debates in the early 1970s, attention focused on the most sophisticated, 'accomplished' examples in Hollywood cinema of the 1940s and 1950s, authored by great directors such as Douglas Sirk, Vincente Minnelli and Fritz Lang. Hollywood's women's pictures, the 'weepies', were either subsumed within this category, or – in the case of those that were unauthored, blatantly generic and identified by their female stars rather than by directors – were mentioned in an aside, or not at all. Subsequently, the relationship between melodrama and the women's picture has been assumed rather than argued, although feminist criticism has begun to draw some distinguishing boundaries. The Gainsborough melodramas provide an opportunity to look at these critical debates in terms of a particular historical manifestation of the women's picture, and to suggest some directions in which future discussion might move.

Cinema melodrama: roots and definitions

It is notoriously difficult to define melodrama. Everyone has their own idea of where its roots lie, and attempts to trace its history often take on the complexity characteristic of melodramatic plots themselves. In 1972 Thomas Elsaesser made one of the earliest and most influential attempts to trace a line through its multiple traditions in literature and drama to the high point of Hollywood melodrama of the 1950s. He separates out 'the melodramatic' as an expressive code which uses drama and music to heighten and intensify emotional effects, and which can be found in widely different cultural forms. He identifies its origins and generic development in the medieval morality plays, oral narratives and folk songs, through eighteenth-century romantic drama and sentimental novels to the nineteenth-century historical epics of Charles Dickens and Victor Hugo, pointing to a radical ambiguity at the heart of melodrama: its moral emphasis (stories of innocence persecuted and virtue rewarded) was countered by the ironic use of music and voice to comment critically on the moral tale. Moreover, the focus on individuals as the site of sexualised class conflict allowed it to present social struggle and change explicitly, and, depending on historical and social context, criticise the *status quo*. The complex narratives of melodrama, deriving from its focus on social transition, the twists and turns of 'outrageous fortune', provided another level on which the simplistic moral content was complexified, and often undermined or contradicted. Extending this to Hollywood cinema melodrama of the 1940s and 1950s, Elsaesser describes the use of 'cinematic counterpoint' in the most 'sophisticated' melodramas to work against the current of ideology: the most gifted directors used all the potential of *mise-en-scène* (colour, lighting, wide-screen) and narrative structure (compression, displacement, ellipsis) to create a closed, hysterical world bursting apart at the seams in which the protagonists, unable to act upon their social environment, suffered severe psychological and emotional symptoms (paranoia, masochism, hysteria) which were displaced onto the expressive codes of the films themselves. For Elsaesser, the power and importance of melodrama lies in its ability to produce a criticism of the oppressive domestic property relations of the middle-class bourgeois family, and it is this argument that set the terms of the debate: under certain historical conditions, and depending on the presence of a gifted director who can use the ironic potential of *mise-en-scène* and narrative, melodrama can be mobilised in the interests of social criticism.

Elsaesser's argument was taken up and explored by a number of critics; its auteurist bias meant that it was developed in a certain direction, interest focusing on a small number of 'sophisticated' melodramas that could be defended as 'progressive', rather than on a historical appraisal of the genre in cinema as a whole. The historical approach emerged subsequently, after feminist critics intervened to shift the terms of the debate towards the general question of the representation of women in Hollywood cinema.

Feminist approaches to melodrama

Laura Mulvey's 1977–8 discussion of Douglas Sirk's melodramas, while retaining an auteurist approach, shifts the emphasis away from the search for the 'progressive text' towards the function performed by melodrama in working through the contradictions of women's position in society. Reconstituted as an object of feminist study, melodrama is useful in helping us to understand how women are positioned under patriarchy so that we can formulate strategies for change.

Mulvey finds the roots of melodrama in Greek drama, and distinguishes two traditions: the tragic melodrama, in which male Oedipal problems dominate the scenario, and melodrama 'proper', which is dominated by the female protagonist's point of view as a source of identification. In the former, the feminine domestic sphere acts as a critical corrective to the overvaluation of virility by the male social order, whereas in the latter the male perspective is displaced by the point of view of a female protagonist whose desires structure and order the narrative. This distinction opens the way to discussion of the women's picture as a separate strand of melodrama, and Mulvey takes up Elsaesser's description of the ironic function of the expressive visual code: in women's melodrama, she argues, the protagonists are unaware of the forces that shape their destiny; the visual code provides the audience on the one hand with an indication of the characters' emotional state, and on the other with privileged knowledge of their situation, offering the spectator a position of moral superiority from which to judge the characters. Using *All That Heaven Allows* (1955) as an example, Mulvey describes how, in the women's melodrama, the woman transgresses socially accepted class and sex barriers, only to find her transgression turned against her by society: family and friends punish her, and her final happiness is marred by a bitter twist of fate. The woman who acts on her desires, challenging conformity, suffers, and it is this conservative moral emphasis in the women's picture that feminist critics object to. Mulvey hints that the women's picture is potentially more contradictory than this. The positing of a female point of view at the centre produces a problem, an excess which the Hollywood narrative cannot contain and which troubles its resolution. These 'troubled narratives' mark the woman's desire to escape her fate as pure fantasy, ultimately unrealisable. In Mulvey's example, *All That Heaven Allows*, the heroine's desire to return to a lost pastoral ideal is both marked as a dream in the overblown romanticism of the *mise-en-scène*, and rendered unobtainable by a final cruel twist of fate. In

1982, Charlotte Brunsdon explored this question of the self-consciously fictive element in the romantic happy endings of women's melodrama in relation to 1970s Hollywood women's pictures, arguing that their lack of plausibility works both to recognise and accentuate the impossibility of the fulfilment of women's romantic fantasies. I would argue that the marked ambiguities inherent in the narrative structure and ironic *mise-en-scène* of the women's picture are the cinematic equivalent of the discourses of fantasy and romance in women's romantic fiction, which, as Janet Batsleer pointed out in 1981, relies on an overt and excessive use of cliché, superlatives and purple prose to create a utopian dream world. The women's picture is similarly marked as 'fiction', or daydream, locating women's desires in the imaginary, where they have always traditionally been placed.

For Barbara Creed, writing in 1977, the woman's melodrama is a moral tale. She emphasises that the trajectory of the films is along an 'axis of female transgression, desire, sexuality, temporary happiness, opposition, separation, atonement, capitulation. It is one of mutually contradictory states: possession and loss, desire and frustration, presence and absence, power and impotence, fulfilment and lack'. For Creed, whatever the contradictions worked through, the narrative emphasis is on replacing women within patriarchal ideology, within the confines of marriage and the family, where they are ultimately unable to act on male society to change it.

The feminist emphasis on the conservative bias of melodrama stems from a wider critique of classic narrative cinema. Feminist film criticism has constructed this cinema as the site of the working through of male Oedipal problems, and the retrenchment of male/female power relations in favour of male domination. The resolution of the drama may not be unproblematic: in melodrama in particular the feminine is frequently valued as a corrective to masculine values. But the feminine corrective is defined in traditional terms: 'feminine' virtues of caring, compassion and sensitivity are set against 'masculine' aggression, violence and destruction. The feminine corrective is mobilised to redress the moral balance; it can modify, mediate, but it can never act to destroy, or to radically change society. (The powerful, destructive heroines of melodrama rarely survive; if they do, they lose whatever they most wanted.) Moreover, it is a femininity defined exclusively as maternal.

In my view, feminist scepticism about melodrama is totally justified. But there is a pessimism about many of the arguments that tends to close down discussion by emphasising the ways in which melodrama forecloses on female desire. It is important, I think, not to lose sight of the basic contradiction Mulvey points to: in order to appeal to a female spectator, melodrama must first posit the possibility of female desire, and a female point of view, thus posing problems for itself that it can scarcely contain. Furthermore, if, as

Elsaesser suggests, melodrama characteristically comes to the fore at times of social and economic upheaval, which inevitably produce repercussions in the film industry too, then melodrama emerges from, and must negotiate, a matrix of contradictory determining factors: economic, social, historical, ideological and industrial. At different moments different elements predominate, allowing for a wide variety of different emphases on the basic problematic.

In *From Reverence to Rape*, Molly Haskell attempted to define the many different varieties of women's picture, and the different patterns of female experience they articulate. She identifies three kinds of heroine: the extraordinary, upper middle-class woman who aspires to an independent existence; the ordinary middle-class woman who is a victim of her society; and the ordinary working-class woman who aspires to be mistress of her fate, but whose aspirations are defeated by the primacy of passion, love and emotion. One or more of these heroines are set in the context of four thematic categories, which can co-exist or overlap: Sacrifice (the woman must give up whatever is most important to her for the sake of moral order); Affliction (the woman is struck down by illness or misfortune as atonement for transgression – her own or another's); Choice (the woman is faced with a choice between two suitors, representing two different ways of life); and Competition (women compete for the attention or love of the hero, often discovering in confrontation that they prefer one another to him). Haskell also points to the 'middle-classness' of the women's picture; the way in which middle-class values and aspirations are set up as ideals, or are used as the standard by which actions are to be judged.

Feminist film criticism has been enormously productive in opening up the women's picture and in indicating the strategies it uses to position women. One question insists: why does the women's picture exist? There is no such thing as 'the men's picture', specifically addressed to men; there is only 'cinema', and 'the women's picture', a sub-group or category specially for women, excluding men; a separate, private space designed for more than half the population, relegating them to the margins of cinema proper. The existence of the women's picture both recognises the importance of women and marginalises them. By constructing this different space for women (Haskell's 'wet, wasted afternoons') it performs a vital function in society's ordering of sexual difference.

In trying to understand what is at stake in the construction of a sub-genre called the women's picture, it is important to look at the ways in which it differs from other 'male' genres, and also how it is related to the genre of melodrama itself, since this relationship is not always self-evident. Laura Mulvey has argued that cinema melodrama deals with the private world of sexual relationships and the family, and represents the 'other side' of the stoical heroism of genres such as the western, which marginalise women.

Within this general distinction, Mulvey distinguishes further between tragic melodrama, in which the male point of view predominates, and women's melodrama, in which events are seen from the female protagonists' point of view. I should like to take Mulvey's distinction as a starting point, elaborating on some of her observations in the interests of a more general approach to the women's picture. I will also draw on some of the other arguments about melodrama and women's pictures outlined above, and my remarks are, at this stage, speculative.

Tragic melodrama and the women's picture

Mulvey's distinction is useful on several levels: by focusing on the different construction of 'masculine' and 'feminine' points of view, it shifts emphasis away from the representation of women in melodrama to a more complex notion of the ways in which the genre orders and contains sexual difference; it draws attention to the problematic status of the woman's point of view placed at the centre of the Hollywood narrative; and it enables us to look at the women's picture as a separate but related strand of melodrama, to begin to understand why it has suffered from wholesale critical neglect, while maintaining mass popular appeal.

The distinction between masculine and feminine points of view is not always easy to maintain, particularly in melodrama where there is often a softening of sexual difference, and a merging of masculinity and femininity. Also, the construction of point of view in cinema is a complex process that is not simply reducible to identification with characters. Here, in talking about the construction of a female point of view, I am referring to the ways in which, in the women's picture, the female protagonist's perspective is presented through a combination of first-person (subjective) and third-person (objective) strategies roughly equivalent to those used in novels. In practice, the distinction between tragic melodrama and women's melodrama is not clear-cut; to imply that a masculine point of view predominates in tragic melodrama is not to suggest that it does not also offer feminine points of view, and vice versa in the women's melodrama, or that real spectators simply identify with one or the other according to their sex. But if, as feminist film theory has argued, classic narrative cinema is marked by the predominance of a masculine perspective to which the feminine is subordinated, then it is important to ask what the consequences are of the apparent reversal of this state of affairs in the women's picture. Women's melodrama shares many of the basic characteristics of tragic melodrama, but it also reverses some of them.

OEDIPAL CRISIS

It has been argued that male Oedipal problems are the mainspring of the action in tragic melodrama. The hero's incestuous desire to challenge the power of the father and take his place drives the narrative forward along a linear trajectory, though ironic twists of fate can complicate the narrative. The tragic hero is brought low, redeeming himself through a new-found humility. He becomes aware of his guilt, and the reasons for his suffering (for example, *Tarnished Angels*, *Written on the Wind*).

In the women's melodrama the heroine's Oedipal desire to take the place of the mother predominates, but in contrast to the tragic hero her position as subject of desire is presented as a problem of lack of knowledge and under-standing of the forces which control her destiny (*All That Heaven Allows*). She frequently finds herself in a world she does not fully understand, and which she must investigate (the 1940s Hollywood women's pictures, *Rebecca*, *Suspicion*, *Secret Beyond the Door*). Her perspective is often distinguished as paranoid, and the status of her perceptions (are her intuitions right or wrong?) is always in question. Her access to knowledge is blocked, and her desires are presented through narrative and *mise-en-scène* explicitly as fantasy. The construction of the woman's point-of-view privileges intuition, emotion, accident, questioning the validity of female desire in that very construction. The narrative structure is often circular rather than linear, circles within circles, delaying final resolution (as in *All That Heaven Allows*, where the heroine is returned, ironically, to the position of mother in the very act of trying to escape it).

SOCIETY

In tragic melodrama, society is kept at a distance, subsumed into Fate or Destiny. The hero is alienated from society, unable to act to change it, trapped in a closed world of domestic property relations where power rests in kinship structures and patterns of inheritance. This world is oppressive and inward-looking, leading to violent emotional excess (*Home From the Hill*, *Two Weeks in Another Town*, *Written on the Wind*).

The women's melodrama reverses this situation. The heroine's transgression resides in her desire to act against socially accepted definitions of femi-ninity, bringing her face to face with society. Work or a career is set against maternity and the family, and the heroine often gives up both for the sake of love, the 'grand passion' (for example, John Stahl's 1930s women's pictures *Back Street* and *When Tomorrow Comes*). The heroine suffers for her transgres-sion, sometimes with death, but her humiliations are small-scale and domestic compared with the tragic hero's epic downfall.

79

THE VISUAL CODE

In tragic melodrama, the expressive visual codes of *mise-en-scène* are used to heighten the intense emotional suffering of the protagonists, and so can act as an ironic visual commentary on the simplistic moralism of the plot, or can undercut middle-class values by showing that they lead to repression and violence. In women's melodrama, the visual code can also be used to express the feelings of the heroine, and to offer her point of view as a focus for identification. Household objects, furnishings, clothes are all important as indications not only of her social status, but also of her state of mind. But as Mulvey points out, codes of lighting and colour cannot be perceived by the characters, and are used to provide privileged information about them to the spectator. As outlined above, the women's melodrama uses the visual code to mark the woman's world as fantasy, and to show that the woman's point of view is limited in comparison with the spectator's. So female desire is problematised, located outside knowledge in the realms of the imagination.

From these preliminary remarks I should like to offer some general speculations about the women's picture, which would clearly need to be tested against specific historical examples. The construction of a genre specifically addressed to women, demanding a central female protagonist who is the active subject of desire rather than the object of male desire, presents a problem for the classic narrative that it can only contain by in turn problematising the woman's point of view, by representing it as paranoia or hysteria, or by overtly fictionalising it. The woman's ability to see is frequently questioned; she may be literally blind (*Magnificent Obsession*) or blinded by desire (*Spellbound*), or lost in a world of shadows and uncertainty (*Rebecca*, *Suspicion*). Her desire is often presented as a symptom, resulting in mental and physical illness (Joan Crawford in *Possessed*, Bette Davis in *Dark Victory*) so that her body becomes an enigma, a riddle to be read for its symptoms rather than an object of erotic contemplation. This hysterical body is inaccessible to the male protagonist, often a doctor or psychiatrist who fails to understand it adequately, to explain it, or to cure it (for example *Three Comrades*). Thus it threatens to slip out of male control, and the only solution is frequently the heroine's death. The male body, by contrast, is presented as an object of erotic contemplation for the heroine, who actively desires the romantic hero, but the problematisation of female desire in the women's picture means that her choice of the romantic hero as love object is usually masochistic, against her own best interests, and she suffers for her desire.

The women's picture as commodity

'The women's picture' does not only evoke a specific and exclusive mode of address; it also suggests an object of exchange, designed to be consumed by a particular group. Its existence is an indication of the film industry's recognition of the importance of women as an audience, and in a wider economic context, of women as consumers of commodity products. One element in the women's picture's address to a female audience is to women as consumers, whether mothers, housewives or working women, although the emphasis on consumption depends on the period. Charles Eckert has analysed the way in which the Hollywood studios of the 1930s set up a system of 'tie-ins' with other consumer industries, arguing that films became show-cases for product display. Stories were set in 'fashion salons, department stores, beauty parlours, upper and middle class homes with modern kitchens and bathrooms, large living rooms and so forth'.[1] Female stars reached an unprecedented zenith during this period, endorsing consumer goods such as cosmetics, fashion, jewellery, kitchen and other household equipment, while Hollywood produced a steady output of women's pictures dealing with contemporary women's experience from the heroine's perspective, featuring female stars whose faces and bodies appeared everywhere in advertisements for consumer products. Eckert's analysis is useful for demonstrating that audience address does not simply reside in the textual strategies of films themselves; but the strength of his closing remarks on the women's picture lies in his recognition that in order to capture its target female audience, the film industry had to mobilise desire in that audience. Eckert's account leaves off precisely at the point where feminists begin: the specific ways in which women's pictures activate feminine desire. As he suggests, a combination of his historical approach and detailed analysis of particular films could throw light on the powerful appeal of the women's picture to female audiences at different historical moments.

History and the women's picture

On one level, then, the women's picture emerges from a historical economic imperative: the attempt to capture and exploit a female audience in the interests of consumerism, which vary according to the given moment. In this sense, it is explicitly tied to history: it must deal with the images of women in circulation in society (even if set in another period) in order to gain recognition from its audience. It has to stimulate desire, then channel it through identification into the required paths. It negotiates this contradiction between female desire and its containment with difficulty, often producing an excess that threatens to deviate from the intended route. Eckert's analysis cannot account for this excess: it implies a complex but rather neat process. Feminists, on the other hand, look for excess as a sign of the system threatening to break down.

Both Eckert and Haskell suggest that the Hollywood women's picture emerged in the 1930s, when the American economy grew wise to the potential of cinema as a vehicle for product display, and to women's purchasing power, coinciding with changes in the film industry that led to an influx of women scriptwriters and stars. It continued into the 1940s, when various kinds of women's pictures proliferated in Hollywood,[2] and were shown on British cinema screens, a period that is of particular interest to the Gainsborough melodramas produced at this time.

I have argued that any attempt to theorise the women's picture must be sensitive to historical change. No genre evades history: although basic patterns and concerns may remain constant, their particular configurations shift, emphases change, certain elements are excluded, and so on. A brief look at the Hollywood women's pictures of different periods reveals enormous differences between, for instance, John Stahl's 1930s films, the Joan Crawford/Bette Davis/Barbara Stanwyck 1940s 'weepies', and Douglas Sirk's 1950s Universal melodramas, to mention but a few.

The Gainsborough 1940s melodramas, while retaining some of the characteristics of Hollywood's melodramas, are different again, differences that can be traced to their circumstances of production in wartime and postwar Britain and its film industry. Although the links between history, production conditions and films are not straightforward, I would argue that any discussion of the Gainsborough women's pictures in terms of the way they construct femininity in order to appeal to a female audience should recognise the historical specificity of this female audience as British and wartime, or immediately postwar.

As feminist historians have indicated,[3] the period of the war and the years immediately following was contradictory and confusing in its attitude towards women. Women's labour was important (albeit temporarily) to the war effort, and married women were encouraged to work by the provision of childcare facilities. At the same time, there was a prevailing anxiety about the falling birth rate and the disintegration of the family under pressure of wartime sexual mores, leading to planned population control and the growth of contraceptive education that could potentially free women's sexuality from reproduction. During the war, short-term sexual relationships, adultery and illegitimate births flourished: sex, passion and the drama of emotional life were brought to the fore, breaking up family unity.[4] After the war, although the temporary concessions to working mothers were withdrawn, and married women were once more predominantly thought of as mothers rather than workers, there was still a need for female labour in certain areas. It was not entirely a question of pulling women back into the family, rather of placing them differently in relation to postwar social democratic ideals, to which a healthy family life and the 'good mother' were indeed vital. I haven't space to develop this history here, but I want to emphasise the unstable nature of this transitional period, characterised by a prevailing climate of opinion that gave rise to a number of different, often contradictory, representations of femininity. Moreover, although the actual economic and sexual emancipation of women the war years encouraged was more or less submerged by the postwar emphasis on motherhood and family, I would argue that the idea of the emancipated 'free' woman, monogamous, but active, dedicated to self-help and capable of fighting for what she wanted, was important to postwar social democratic ideals of a better world for everyone.

In their attempt to capture the female audience, then, the Gainsborough women's pictures had to negotiate this complex network of shifting influences, to dramatise the contemporary sexual and emotional conflicts of women's lives. The films work through these conflicts, bringing contradictions to the surface. They present their heroines' lives as in transition, undergoing radical changes as the result of choices wisely or unwisely made. Women are presented as active, able to affect the progress of history, but the choices they make must be the right ones if a healthy British society is to be built. A number of ideals of social health are set up (for example, in *They Were Sisters*), among them the ideal family (no more than four children), the ideal mother (active) and father (tolerant), the ideal house (large enough to contain an array of attractive consumer goods and a maid), and the ideal relationship (heterosexual monogamy). Each film gives a different emphasis to these ideals, depending on its specific context. For example, middle-class ideals of wealth and consumption can be posed as less important than stable family values (*They Were Sisters*), or, in the context of postwar economic hardship and restraint, openly criticised (*Root of All Evil*). And though the films do, on one level, most particularly in their narrative resolutions, confirm prevailing social ideals of women as faithful wives and mothers, the contradictions inherent in those ideals, and the emphasis of the women's pictures on fantasy and romance, work to seriously undermine their value as social propaganda.

The Gainsborough women's pictures' address to a British female audience is also coloured by conditions prevailing in the British film industry at that time. Briefly, for my argument: after the war the industry made a number of attempts to expand, seeing its major task as providing effective competition

Figure 5.1   Haunted by the past: Margaret Lockwood in *A Place of One's Own* (1945). Courtesy Gainsborough and the Kobal Collection.

for Hollywood cinema, both at home and abroad. In 1978, John Ellis described the aim of British cinema in the 1940s as that of producing a national 'quality' product, which would both educate the British public and promote British culture abroad. Popular medium-budget melodramas such as

The Wicked Lady were blatantly escapist and hardly fitted prevailing critical notions of 'quality' (aesthetic coherence, psychological realism, humanist values). They went far beyond the bounds of 'good taste' in their emphasis on sex, sadism, violence and brutality. But they succeeded in differentiating themselves from, and competing effectively with, Hollywood, maintaining good production values on small budgets, and drawing large female audiences.[5] But while these films were clearly dedicated to criteria of mass entertainment and profit, particularly under Maurice Ostrer's control, it is possible to argue that the film-makers were also to a certain extent caught up in prevailing ideals of British cultural merit, even though the films were seen by critics to fall far short of those ideals. They were often adapted from respected British novels (Margery Lawrence's *Madonna of the Seven Moons*, L.A.G. Strong's *The Brothers*), and the music was conducted and played by eminent musicians (Muir Matheson and the London Symphony or the Royal Philharmonic). *Madonna of the Seven Moons* was publicised as part of the industry's move to produce a new kind of British picture, showing British ideas and ideals to the public at home and abroad, combining entertainment with fine techniques and originality in story design. In 1947 Sydney Box defended *The Brothers* in the columns of *The Evening News* (Friday, 16 May) against charges of gratuitous sadism in terms of its serious *literary* merits, and announced a forthcoming series of productions 'based on the work of this country's best writers'.

These claims may seem extravagant in the face of the films themselves but, I would argue, an understanding of the Gainsborough women's pictures in terms of a double impetus to provide entertainment without losing 'artistic quality', to exploit controversial subject matter without sacrificing British ideals, is necessary to an understanding of the way in which they construct femininity very specifically in terms of class and nationalist ideals. The 'feminine point of view' constructed by these films is explicitly British and middle class, tied to a specific historical period, and this partly accounts for their popularity, the success of their attempt to compete with Hollywood.

I would argue, then, that the Gainsborough melodramas of this period emerge from a complex network of determining factors: industrial imperatives to compete with Hollywood while maintaining British cultural standards; the desire to maintain postwar audiences of wartime capacity by addressing a female audience, and dramatising women's contemporary experience; an increasing understanding of the propaganda function of fiction films, and the consequent attempt to negotiate a number of conflicting images of women circulating in society.

Gainsborough women's pictures in the 1940s

As a result of their specific location in British history, the Gainsborough films, for the most part, appear very different from Hollywood melodrama, although it can be argued that they reveal similar patterns and preoccupations. Gainsborough melodramas have no great auteurs, for instance, and though *mise-en-scène* can sometimes be seen to be important, it has nothing like the force of 1940s Hollywood. At the same time, they do have their own cinematic vocabulary, a repertory of female stars, and, in the case of the 'contemporary' women's pictures, a concern with women's lives: their hairstyles, fashions, houses and furniture. They were also overwhelmingly British, set in British locations, projecting a British middle-class way of life. I believe the films would benefit from a close reading in terms of their relationship to British social history though, as I have argued, this relationship is contradictory. However, I only have space here to look briefly at the way some of the women's pictures that deal with contemporary women's issues attempt to negotiate those contradictions.

Schematically, it is possible to trace a shift in the women's picture's address to its audience between the wartime and postwar films. *Love Story* (1944), like many women's pictures, ostensibly deals with the tragedy of its central heroine, a London concert pianist played by Margaret Lockwood, who tries to join the WRAF, only to find that she is fatally ill. Previously dedicated to her work, she decides to spend her remaining time becoming involved in life, taking more risks. On holiday in Cornwall, where she stands out in the closed, moralistic world of the community because of her glamour, youth and open-minded attitudes (Lockwood's appearance, her clothes, underwrite her 'independence of spirit' and are important in giving positive value to her social transgression) she falls passionately in love with a local Lothario (Stewart Granger) whose own tragedy is his impending blindness, which prevents him from going back to war. He is also loved by a faithful woman friend (Patricia Roc), a successful theatre director, who, it becomes clear, sees his blindness as a way of keeping him dependent upon her, the only way she can get him to marry her.

The narrative is extremely convoluted, concentrating on the point of view of Margaret Lockwood, whose status as a 'good woman' is gradually established by the playing off of the desires of its two strong heroines against one another. Lockwood sacrifices her desire so that Granger can regain his sight and Roc can marry him, undertaking a gruelling concert tour for the benefit of British soldiers, which brings her close to death. Her self-denial is rewarded by fame as a pianist, and she is released from her promise by Roc, who realises that a marriage based on friendship rather than desire would be hopeless. Lockwood and Granger agree to marry, grasping the happiness of the moment rather than looking for permanence.

Love Story is striking for the way in which it dramatises sexual and emotional conflicts without resolving the contradictions it throws up. Female desire is first mobilised, then channelled by the presentation of two paths: sacrifice or self-interest. Ironically, it is only through sacrifice that Lockwood achieves her desires, but that sacrifice is negated in the film's resolution, which affirms the value of short-term passion rather than long-term fidelity. The film manages to present at one and the same time an ideal of femininity based on sacrifice and denial, a validation of women's desires outside home and family, and an endorsement of monogamy based on ephemeral passion.

Madonna of the Seven Moons (1944), while dealing with a similar problem of the mobilisation and channelling of female sexual desire, and mounting a critique of marriage based on love without passion, shifts the emphasis of its resolution towards the need for a new kind of independent woman, resourceful and courageous, capable of forming egalitarian relationships with men. This 'new woman' is seen to be important to the founding of a new social order based on honesty and democracy, allowing for the woman's freedom of action, unlike the 'old' order based on a religious suppression of women's sexuality. This aspect of the film is interesting in the light of British attitudes to women's freedom of choice in family planning towards the end of the war.[6]

Set in Italy, the film tells the story of a young convent girl who is raped by a peasant, then married off against her wishes to a wealthy merchant, whereupon she leads an apparently saintly life, protected from the outside world by her patient and loving husband. The smooth surface of her existence is, however, troubled by her strange hysterical symptoms, inexplicable to both husband and to family doctor, and a crisis is precipitated by the arrival of their daughter, fresh from her education in England (representing the 'new democratic order'), who tries to bring her mother round to her own modern ideas (involving much play with fashionable clothes). The mother's 'other self' takes over, and she runs away to live as a peasant with her jewel-thief lover. The sexual freedom and passionate fulfilment offered by this 'other world' is powerfully presented, and acts as a criticism of her married life on one level. However, it is also presented as a transgression, in class and sex terms, and as a symptom of repression, of the failure of a certain social order to cope with female sexuality. It is this repressive order which must be changed. The film sets up the daughter as the new, independent, resourceful heroine, who can bring about this change by becoming the investigator who will solve her mother's secret where her father and the doctor have failed.

Madonna of the Seven Moons addresses itself to a British female spectator who is active, and capable of contributing to changing society. Crucially, hetero-sexual monogamy, albeit more egalitarian, is at the centre of this new order, which is projected in middle-class terms. Maddalena/Rosanna is a victim of the old order: she dies with the two signs of her impossible existence on her body, the red rose (passion) and the cross (saintly love). Unity, rather than contradiction, is the hallmark of the new order. But it is one of the contradic-tions characteristic of the women's picture that while Maddalena/Rosanna is clearly a sacrificial victim, her symptoms, her retreat into illness, also perform a positive function. Her symptoms represent one way in which her body manages to elude the control of her husband and family doctor by becoming a text to be read for its symptoms, rather than an object of erotic contempla-tion. Moreover, the male protagonists' inability to interpret, explain or cure those symptoms indicates the limits of male control of the female body. In *Madonna of the Seven Moons* the incomprehension of the male characters in the face of the mother's symptoms makes space for the daughter, the new woman, to act.

The question of the limits of male control can provide the mainspring of the narrative in melodrama, as it does in *The Upturned Glass* (1947). James Mason plays a paranoid doctor who is initially unaware of his psychosis. He plans the perfect murder as just revenge for the death of the woman he loves. The film is tragic melodrama rather than a women's picture, because it pres-ents events through the eyes of its male hero (using his voice-over and occa-sional subjective shots to do so), who gradually comes to realise his guilt, and the limits of his power to act in society. Mason is a brilliant doctor with a strong sense of social responsibility who becomes the victim of his compul-sions, so that his ability to distinguish between right and wrong, to understand the limits of his power, is severely impaired. The hero's tragic flaw necessi-tates his death if a healthy social order is to be maintained. Mason comes to understand his guilt after a confrontation with another doctor, who is detached, objective, cynically aware of the limits of his ability to achieve good in society. He kills himself when he realises that his actions were the result of overweening pride, or tragic 'hubris'.

They Were Sisters (1945) is a women's picture that deals with the problem of the constitution of the ideal family, posing its problem in terms of making the right choice of love object. It opens with a montage of images from fashion magazines, clearly setting up its address to a female audience. The emphasis on fashion in women's pictures functions to establish women as both subjects and objects of desire. Women adopt the accoutrements of femininity in order to attract men in the stories: fashion is an integral element of desire. But it can also function as a focus of identification for women in the audience[7] and as a means of offering the audience information about the characters. Often in the women's picture, to be 'well dressed' suggests order, stability and balance, whereas excess, or lack of taste, in clothes indicates transgression, or inability to negotiate social codes (for example, King Vidor's *Stella Dallas*).

Of the three sisters, one (Phyllis Calvert, the stable, 'good' woman) dresses with restrained good taste; another (Anne Crawford, the selfish woman) goes for a rather calculated elegance; while the third (Dulcie Gray, the masochistic victim) is hopelessly badly dressed. Calvert chooses her husband well: a middle-class professional man, tolerant and willing to allow her considerable freedom, as befits her independent spirit; she has a happy, but childless marriage. Her two sisters choose unwisely: Crawford marries without loving her wealthy husband, a weak man who cannot control her and whom she despises; Dulcie Gray, blinded by desire, chooses a husband from a lower social class (James Mason), who turns out to be a sadistic brute of whom she's in constant fear. Both these unsatisfactory marriages produce unhappy, neglected children, and it is up to Calvert to act to redress the moral balance. She is mobilised as the agent of the narrative, acting to save her weaker sister from destruction by Mason. Although she fails, and her sister commits suicide, Calvert exposes Mason in court and so defeats him, finally ending up with all her sisters' children and the family she always wanted. In a final, idyllic scene that is almost conscious of its utopian, fictional quality, the ideal middle-class mother and father assert euphorically 'God's in his heaven and all's right with the world', and 'There are millions of families like us ...'.

Complicated, unbelievable narratives with blatantly fictional resolutions are one of the hallmarks of the women's picture, and one of the reasons, perhaps, that critics condemn them as trivial and escapist. *Root of All Evil* (1947) takes this fictional aspect of women's desires as one of its main problems. The story opens with a discussion between the heroine (Phyllis Calvert) and her fiancé about what she hopes for from love and marriage, set in idyllic rural surroundings. Before long, she is brutally disenchanted, and her loss of her romantic illusions about love motivate her to renounce romance in favour of revenge and power. She is enormously successful as a businesswoman, though family and friends criticise her hardness, and becomes a partner in an oil business with a man she falls in love with. She buys and furnishes a luxury house for them both, only to discover he is already married. Betrayed again by love, she takes over his share of the business as revenge, but the refinery burns down, and only when she has lost everything does she discover her true love: a farmer she's known since childhood.

Once again the women's picture negotiates an impossible contradiction between the mobilisation and validation of female desire, and the need to channel it in the required direction. In this case, romantic illusions about love and marriage are set up, questioned and relocated in order to mount a criticism of materialism, speculation and consumerism. But in the process, and even in its resolution, the film seems to ironise its own moral trajectory.

Through these very schematic readings, I've tried to indicate some of the ways in which, as I see it, the Gainsborough women's pictures, while retaining some of the characteristics of Hollywood's women's pictures, are necessarily transformed by the historical context of 1940s Britain and its film industry. I think my discussion of the difference between tragic melodrama and women's melodrama might be extended to an examination of the differences between, say, *The Upturned Glass* and *Root of All Evil* in terms of the way each deals with the downfall of its central protagonist, in order to throw light on the way each film constructs sexual difference. But I think it is important to stress the tentative nature of my attempt to theorise the women's picture, and the fact that I do not see it as having a direct or necessary application to the very different context of Gainsborough melodrama. It is intended rather as a filter through which to view the Gainsborough films, and I hold the differences between those films and Hollywood melodrama to be as important as any similarities. Throughout this discussion I have tried to make space for historical difference and contradiction as a vital part of theory, and would like to suggest that this approach might prove fruitful for future discussion of the women's picture and its construction of femininity.

Notes

1 Charles Eckert, 'The Carole Lombard in Macy's window', *Quarterly Review of Film Studies* 3(1) (winter 1978), pp. 1–21; p. 20.
2 Charles Higham and Joel Greenberg, *Hollywood in the 40s* (New York: Barnes, 1968).
3 Denise Riley, 'The free mothers: pro-natalism and working mothers in industry at the end of the last war in Britain', *History Workshop Journal* 11 (spring 1981) pp. 59–119; Elizabeth Wilson, *Only Halfway to Paradise* (London and New York: Tavistock, 1980).
4 Raynes Minns, *Bombers and Mash* (London: Virago, 1980).
5 Robert Murphy, 'Gainsborough pictures: a popular commercial studio', Polytechnic of Central London MA Thesis, 1981.
6 See Riley, 'The free mothers'.
7 See Eckert, 'The Carole Lombard in Macy's window'.

Chapter 6

MANDY
Daughter of transition

Mandy, a film about a deaf child's struggle to enter 'normal' society, was shot at Ealing in 1951 and released in July 1952. It is commonly identified as a film 'authored' by Alexander Mackendrick, an Ealing director who worked against the grain of the studio's preference for safe subject matter and a realist aesthetic. It is, equally, a key film of the early 1950s, appearing at an important moment for Britain, Ealing, and British cinema. Also released in 1951 – the year of the Festival of Britain, which celebrated the achievements of the outgoing Labour government – were *The Lavender Hill Mob* and *The Man in the White Suit*, described by Charles Barr as the last of the 'buoyant' Ealing comedies.[1] The year 1951 was a turning point for the film industry in general: the 'X' certificate was introduced in an attempt to stem the decline in cinema audiences by moving into sensational and previously forbidden areas of sex and violence, under pressure on the one hand from the influx of 'continental' sex films and European art cinema, and on the other from competition for audiences from television.

It is simplistic to pin down a change in social climate to a single year, but it does seem that 1951 can be seen as a pivotal year for British society, marking a shift from a period of postwar austerity, presided over by a Labour government dedicated to welfare capitalism, to the consumer boom of the 1950s managed by a new tough breed of Conservatives. The shift can also be characterised in terms of changing national values, community spirit giving way to individualism and an increasing emphasis on the private domain of home and family. Culturally, the British dedication to high art values of 'quality', 'taste' and 'realism' was to be assaulted by the influx of American consumer goods and popular culture, scandalising intellectuals from both left and right.

None of these shifts was particularly sudden: the seeds of Americanisation, and of greater laxity in moral values, for instance, were obviously already there during the war and postwar years; and when the Conservatives came to power in 1951, they did so by a narrow margin, suggesting that there was no major swing to them, and that the postwar Labour government's commitment to gradualism and reformism may have helped pave the way to Conservative victory and an ideology of 'classlessness' and consensus. However, it would also be a mistake to characterise the shift as entirely smooth. This transitional period was marked by a proliferation of competing ideologies, testifying to a national uncertainty about traditional values and their effectiveness in the postwar Britain of new technologies, egalitarian social democracy, and sexual emancipation. The social democratic rhetoric of radicalism, of a social revolution achieved painlessly, masked a suspicion of new ideas and a cautious attachment to traditional structures. The Festival of Britain itself perhaps exemplifies these contradictions – on the one hand celebrating the benefits of the Welfare State and nationalisation, and calling up the New Commonwealth as an ideal family of nations; on the other, promoting a particular style of living, a superficial 'Scandinavian' modernism that could easily be imposed upon traditional structures of home and family.[2]

Ealing had flourished during those years when the values of community and cooperation, which were to come under pressure in the 1950s, were mobilised in the interests of national unity. In a way, it came to represent those values itself, becoming something of a national institution. When faced with the decision either to exploit changing values, as Hammer did subsequently, or to accommodate them, Ealing took the latter road, producing a series of staid, normative comedies and dramas, which have come to be seen as representative of the studio's 1950s output. In this linear version of events *Mandy*, which appeared in 1952, fits neither into Ealing's buoyant period, nor into the 1950s consensus films. Thus it stands out as an isolated work, a powerful masterpiece that paradoxically marks the beginning of the studio's decline. But it seems less exceptional if considered as, precisely, a transitional film, an attempt by Ealing to negotiate a shifting terrain at a time when its future was uncertain; an attempt, perhaps, to take on board changing values, to explore and even exploit them, and finally to project an Ealing version of Britain in transition that would show the future as developing gradually from the past. In this sense, *Mandy* could be seen as exemplary, not only of Mackendrick's authorial concerns, but also of the relationship between social, cultural and economic factors at the particular historical moment of its production.

Mandy was promoted by Ealing as having its inspiration in a social problem – the institutionalised care of deaf and dumb children – and as using a real institution – the progressive Royal Residential School for the Deaf in Manchester – as a model. At the same time, the film was described by the studio as a powerful and moving human drama based on a novel that had been serialised for BBC radio's 'Woman's Hour'. Here are the first indications of an attempt to straddle contradictions. The appeal to a notion of documentary social realism both recalls a respected tradition of British 'quality' cinema and capitalises on an emerging genre of 'social problem' pictures. The social realist mode also connotes the realm of the public. This appeal to 'quality' confers respectability on the melodramatic/women's-picture aspect of the film – its blatant appeal to the private, personal realm of the emotions in order to capture an audience and manipulate its responses. (This was a direction often taken by mainstream British cinema in the 1950s – see the combination of melodrama and social realism in *Yield to the Night*, 1956, and *Woman in a Dressing Gown*, 1957, for example.) The tension between public and private, the shifting boundaries between them, is a major theme in *Mandy*, intersecting with the tension between past and future and worked through in terms of different institutional spaces (home/garden vs. school/playground/park).

Ultimately, these tensions are resolved by finding a new balance between the conflicting terms, and a space that lies somewhere between the basic oppositions, representing a compromise. Certain characters represent the poles of the oppositions: Mandy's grandparents stand for the old, traditional, monogamous middle-class family; Mandy herself, Kit (her mother), and Searle (headmaster of the school for the deaf) stand for the new, democratic, egalitarian ideal; Harry (Mandy's father) vacillates between the two, caught in his own resistance to change. This resistance is echoed in Ackland, representative of the institutional old guard on the school's governing body, in conflict with the progressives, Jane Ellis and Searle. The drama of shifting attitudes and ideas is worked through in Kit and Harry's relationship, torn apart by the conflict: the melodramatic mode evokes the power relations at stake in the private space of the family, the private pain of transition, while the social realist mode is used to depict power relations in the institutional hierarchy. Importantly, the public and private overlap – in the close relationship that forms between Kit and Searle, for instance, and in the scheming one between Ackland and Harry. These areas of overlap provide another locus for the playing out of the drama of shifting boundaries: Kit and Searle must sacrifice their relationship, Harry must disentangle himself from Ackland so that a new balance between old and new, public and private, can be found, and new boundaries drawn. The value of progressive ideas has been proved, but only in so far as they put pressure on established, traditional structures to change – a truly reformist, gradualist philosophy.

The point of this account of *Mandy*'s thematic and narrative structure is not to reduce it to an impoverished schema, nor to prove that the film is reactionary, or reformist rather than radical. I want to argue that the film is contradictory, that in negotiating sets of competing and conflicting ideologies it produces a vision of Britain that is at once forward-looking and backward-looking – looking forward, that is, to a new egalitarian society in which boundaries of class and sex are broken down, and looking backward to traditional structures in order to preserve them. *Mandy* projects a picture of a nation on the brink of change, from which it ultimately draws back, sadly unable to rise to the challenge. Ealing itself was in the same position.

To explore this contradiction further, I'd like to look at the film more specifically in terms of the way it mediates postwar ideologies of femininity and the family, particularly those of mother and child. The war years had encouraged economic and sexual emancipation for women, a situation not entirely reversed in the postwar reconstruction period, when labour shortages meant that women, including wives and mothers, were required for certain forms of work. However, in the postwar period women's main role in society was seen as lying within the family, a trend that continued into the 1950s as the economic boom made housewives increasingly important as purchasers and consumers. Nevertheless, the active social role envisaged for women during the war years continued in the postwar vision of a democratic and egalitarian society. Women had their own clearly defined contribution to make to the building of this new society, primarily as housewives and mothers. But if femininity was defined mainly in terms of hearth and home, which many feminists would now see as essentially oppressive and limited, it was also seen as having a positive effect on the overbearing, aggressive aspects of masculinity, softening it, making it more tolerant and flexible. There was a merging of masculinity and femininity in which each could benefit from taking on certain qualities of the other. This egalitarianism extended to the family too, which was no longer envisaged as authoritarian and patriarchal, but as a partnership of equals, albeit with clearly defined, different roles.

The emphasis on the family had repercussions for women; their employment, indeed all activities outside the home, had to be fitted round their primary role as housewives and mothers. During this period new meanings were attached to motherhood.[3] The war years had given rise to anxieties about the lives of mothers and children, about the depleted population, the declining birth rate, and the detrimental effects of evacuation and institutional care on young children separated from their mothers. Studies during and after the war began to address the importance of the emotional and psychological well-being of the child, stressing the mother–child relationship and relegating fathers to shadowy, background figures. Paradoxically, the stress on the presence of the mother both confined the mother to the home and gave a new status and power to motherhood itself. Simultaneously, female sexuality was increasingly defined as active. The Kinsey Reports of 1948 and 1953, given wide publicity in Britain as well as in the United States, suggested that

Figure 6.1 Painful transitions: Phyllis Calvert and Mandy Miller in *Mandy* (1952). Courtesy Ealing Studios and the Kobal Collection.

women's sexual needs were more diverse and demanding than had generally been thought, and, moreover, that they did not fit neatly into the assumptions underlying the heterosexual couple relationship. As if to counterbalance the threatening implications of such evidence, traditional notions of the family as a

95

site for reproduction were rejigged to accommodate these disturbing new ideas. On the one hand the family became a central organising principle in the new British society, and on the other it was posed as the place where conflicting ideologies of parenthood, childcare and sexuality would be battled out and finally contained.

Against the background of these shifting definitions of femininity and the family, Ealing films in general subscribed to traditional ideologies.[4] Criteria of realism, quality and taste dominated the studio's output, producing a repression of certain questions, particularly those of female sexuality – though the films of 'maverick' directors Robert Hamer and Alexander Mackendrick have been identified as focusing on such issues in interesting ways. Thus *Mandy* can be seen as exceptional in dealing quite directly with problems of sexual desire and restraint in the 'new family' of postwar and 1950s Britain. Nevertheless, like Mackendrick's preceding film, *The Man in the White Suit* (1951), it remains pessimistic about the possibilities for radical change, in spite of, even perhaps because of, its apparently positive 'happy ending'.

In its construction of femininity, *Mandy* draws on postwar images of the New Woman – equal to, but different from, men. It centres, as we have seen, on the relationship between Kit and Harry, Mandy's mother and father. Phyllis Calvert's performance as Kit recalls the parts she played as an active and desiring mother in Gainsborough women's pictures of the 1940s (*Madonna of the Seven Moons*, *They Were Sisters*), where the woman's desire was validated, as long as it did not transgress the social and moral order. Nevertheless, the focus on feminine desire in these films produced contradictions: the inevitable repression of desire consequent upon sacrifice of self-interest to a higher moral order frequently produced tragic scenarios in which loss remained more palpably significant than the victory of the social order. In *Mandy*, Kit's desire manifests itself primarily in relation to her struggle on behalf of her child, though she and her husband Harry have a passionate and, for Ealing, highly charged sexual relationship. The problem posed, and finally worked through in the film, is how far the acting out of each of the major characters' desires is for the good of the child, and therefore for the future health of society. It is significant that Mandy is a girl, for what is also at issue is the role of women in the New Britain – indeed, the film opens with Kit's voice-over asking explicitly what Mandy's future prospects might be. Mandy's entry into society is blocked by her father's self-interested pride and authoritarian attitudes.

Harry's patriarchal attitudes must change if Mandy is to play an active role in society, and it is primarily Kit's acting out of her own desire that brings about such a change. In the process, the traditional bourgeois family is split. Kit and Mandy are reconstituted as a single-parent family, finding in Searle a surrogate father-figure who has many of the attributes of a mother. Kit temporarily takes over control of the family, becoming more 'masculine', while Harry must become, like Searle, more 'feminine'. The boundaries of sexual difference are significantly shifted; hence the apparent optimism of the happy ending.

It becomes clear, however, that this shift is heavily circumscribed. The incipient love affair between Kit and Searle is curtailed, the alternatives to the monogamous, heterosexual family unit – the 'extended' family, the single-parent family, the state institution as family in the form of the residential school – are all found to be inadequate, or rather, are seen as intermediate stages in the progress towards the 'new', reconstituted heterosexual mono-gamous family; no longer quite so patriarchal, the power relations altered to take account of the 'equal but different' status of the mother, allowing Mandy to run out from the private, enclosed space of the family to join the rest of society. Restraint and curtailment are marked in the closing moments of the film. As Mandy runs to join the other children, Harry holds Kit back from following her: a tiny gesture, but significant enough to be repeated, and undermining the 'happy ending' with a question – with the father now back in control, the mother held in place, just how egalitarian is the new social order?

It is not reading too much into this small gesture, I think, to see in it a pessimism about the nature of reformism that makes *Mandy*, finally, less a celebration of the New Britain than a critique of the gradualist philosophy underlying its vision of change.

Notes

1 Charles Barr, *Ealing Studios* (London: Cameron and Tayleur/David and Charles, 1977).
2 Elizabeth Wilson, *Only Halfway to Paradise* (London: Tavistock, 1980).
3 Maggie Millman, *What is a Family?*, booklet accompanying the Channel 4 series *Flashback*, 'What is a Family? Images from the 20th century', first transmitted in February 1984 (London: Eyre and Spottiswoode, 1984).
4 John Ellis, 'Made in Ealing', *Screen* 16(1) (spring 1975), pp. 78–127.

Chapter 7

MEMORY IN BRITISH CINEMA
Brief encounters

Memory is a central preoccupation of cinema, and a crucial part of the development of cinematic language. The flashback, for example, one of the most basic and familiar devices for articulating memory in film, plays a fundamental role in establishing character, and in narrative exposition. Indeed, narrative continuity itself, and our ability to understand or read a film, depends on memory, as Christopher Nolan's *Memento* (2000) demonstrated so brilliantly. This was a thriller featuring a hero suffering from amnesia, whose confused perspective the audience was invited to share as he tried to make sense of events and objects around him. The *Memento* website carried a tag line, 'Some things are better forgotten', suggesting that the ability to remember is a mixed blessing, and that it is inextricably tied to forgetting. The idea that we might prefer to forget the past, or that memory is not necessarily a reliable way of accessing the truth of the past, is something that I shall return to. In a wider cultural sense, memory is often connected to trauma, and perceived as a way of coming to terms with terrible events, or a devastating loss of some kind. Recollection therefore has therapeutic value, and can be seen as a form of exorcism, in which the past is laid to rest in order that the person remembering can move on. As a social ritual, memory is crucial to the process of mourning that accompanies progress towards modernity. Paradoxically, memory is essential to forgetting or overcoming the past.

Given the scope and complexity of the role of memory in helping us to understand the world as well as the stories we construct to make sense of our place within it, it is hardly surprising to discover that the significance of memory in cinema is multifaceted. From the role of archives in preserving cinema's past and the compilation of archive material in films and television programmes, to the utilisation of oral testimony in cinema history, the deployment of memories of other films and film-makers in advertising campaigns, and in press reviews and other forms of reception – not to mention those aesthetic strategies intended to attract certain audiences by awakening nostalgia through music, costume, landscape and so forth – memory seems to pervade every aspect of cinema. Here, I shall limit myself to discussion of some of the basic strategies deployed by films in articulating memory, exploring what they have to tell us about memory itself.

There are valid reasons for beginning this way round – that is, with the texts rather than with theories of memory. Film texts do not necessarily simply use memory in a functional manner, they also embody memories – those of the film-makers themselves, for example. Sometimes this is a conscious process, as when directors such as Hitchcock or Scorsese include self-referential quotations to previous films. The audience is invited to engage in a game of recognition, which adds to the viewers' pleasure, and gives them kudos: they are asked, 'Do you remember this?' And if they do, they gain a few brownie points. Sometimes, the game of recognition is used emotively to evoke a sense of loss: the audience is asked, 'Do you remember what it was like then?' And viewers are invited to mourn, or to celebrate the passing of an era, which the film-makers set out to reconstruct.

Sometimes the film-makers' memories can be used to cross boundaries of nation, gender and class, as I hope to show in my analysis of *I Know Where I'm Going!* (1945). What is important is that these are shared memories – they have an intimate, personal dimension, but they also enable connections to be made between film-makers and audiences – or not, if the game of recognition does not succeed. I shall look at this in more detail when I come to discuss *Brief Encounter* (1946). Whether such strategies are used consciously or unconsciously, the films themselves are not just instruments in the process of recollection, they actively participate in that process, and in many cases reflect or comment upon it. They can therefore be treated as intellectual discourse, as presenting and exploring sets of ideas and assumptions. There are films, such as Chris Marker's *La Jetée* (1962), that deliberately set out to be intellectual ruminations on the subject of memory and cinema, but I would argue that such rumination or discourse can be found not only in the modernist avant-garde, or in independent cinema, but also in more mainstream popular films.

My interest in memory in cinema began when I was working on the British studio Gainsborough Pictures, and on the process of cultural exchange between British and continental European film-makers during the 1920s and 1930s. At that point, I was primarily concerned with the implications for national identity of the impact of non-British personnel on British cinema. Although the presence of continental Europeans in the British film industry had been relatively well documented by historians, their cultural and aesthetic impact had not been adequately recognised. As well as their creative skills and technical expertise, the European émigrés brought with them cultural memories which had artistic value, and which were sought and prized by British film-makers as a form of cultural capital. It is hardly surprising, then, that traces of the legacy of European aesthetics, such as German Expressionism or Surrealism, should be detected in some British cinema – but it seemed to me that the impact of the continental Europeans went much deeper than this, and that British cinema owed more to them than was first apparent. My research into Powell and Pressburger's *I Know Where I'm Going!*, which was produced by an international team (the Archers) comprising British and continental European personnel, and which clearly owed much to this mixed cultural heritage, proved revelatory in this respect.[1]

However, I shall start by looking at a film that on the surface appears to be a very different project, in that it celebrates a more local, domestic notion of Englishness: *Brief Encounter*, co-written by Noël Coward and directed by David Lean, which was completed in 1945 and released in 1946.[2] Since both films were made at the end of the Second World War, at a period when Britain was looking forward to postwar reconstruction, at the same time as trying to come to terms with the past, it is useful to compare their treatment of modernity and progress. They have other things in common too – both were made under the auspices of British film magnate J. Arthur Rank at a time when the Rank Organisation was making a determined assault on the American market by producing relatively expensive prestige pictures. Both, therefore, can be placed in the category of 'quality' British cinema, though they were intended to reach popular audiences too. Both share the iconography of trains used metaphorically to suggest a headlong, unstoppable drive forward into the future, while also creating a sense of multiple, conflicting directions that results in stasis rather than movement.

Both films feature characters on the brink of momentous social and personal change, both express uncertainty and hesitation about moving forward into a brave new world, and both use memory to articulate that anxiety. The context in which they were made is significant here. Towards the end of the Second World War, as the full horror of the atrocities in continental Europe began to come to light, the issue of memory, and of coming to terms with trauma, took on greater importance. But also, as Britain itself struggled with continuing austerity conditions, the domestic economy was in an uncertain condition, and the move to a bright, prosperous future seemed a very long way off. Both *Brief Encounter* and *I Know Where I'm Going!* look to the past to find a vision for the future.

As I have indicated, *Brief Encounter* was made in 1945, but the story was set a few years earlier, in the mid- to late 1930s. This was no doubt partly to do with the fact that the screenplay adapted Noël Coward's playlet *Still Life*, first performed in 1936. However, it would have been easy enough to update the story of frustrated adultery to the war period, and there is in fact a misapprehension in some quarters that the film is set in the 1940s. In *Forties Fashion*, a book about wartime Utility fashions, a still from *Brief Encounter* shows Laura's costume as a typical example of Utility design.[3] Indeed, in the course of the film Laura wears two versions of the military-style hat that was fashionable during the war, and a single-breasted, tailored tweed suit that is inspired by Utility. The Utility programme was introduced in Britain in 1941, so those elements of Utility design in the costume of *Brief Encounter* are clearly anachronistic. It is well documented that the film-makers went to great lengths to reconstruct the pre-war era, partly in order to create a sense of realism and verisimilitude, seen as crucial to quality British cinema, but also to induce nostalgia in postwar audiences still in the grip of wartime austerity measures.[4] In fact, in the context of austerity conditions, the film-makers were forced to fake many props, such as chocolate and fruit, which were still in short supply. Indicators of prewar habits and fashions can be found everywhere in *Brief Encounter*, almost to the point of excess. The windows and curtains of Fred and Laura's comfortable suburban house remain wide open at night, emphasising the lack of wartime blackout conditions; Laura and other female characters wear cosmetics and furs, both subject to restrictions during the war; sugar appears to be readily available, as do cakes, which would require the use of butter and eggs, all rare commodities. In a memorable scene, Fred and Laura enjoy after-dinner coffee made in a Cona coffee machine, given unusual prominence in the shot. In the light of such attention to detail, it seems unlikely that the anachronistic references to wartime were a matter of oversight.

There is no doubt that *Brief Encounter*'s film-makers aspired to realism and authenticity, and that they visualised that aspiration in an accumulation of archival detail, to paraphrase a criticism that has been directed at the English heritage films.[5] However, the element of anachronism is also much in evidence, though it is rarely taken into account. Anachronism is the key to *Brief Encounter*, and it seems to cause incomprehension, embarrassment and hysteria in some viewers. Although the film did reasonably well at the box-office, it was not an outstanding popular hit when it was first released, and some audiences in 1946 were reported to have been in fits of giggles at the outmoded English stereotypes and outdated sexual mores. Part of this is due to the fact that the film's nostalgic vision of the past is very class-specific – it depicts the imminent collapse of a middle-class way of life, which may not have appealed to all sectors of its contemporary audiences. However, this very anachronism has become a vital factor in the appeal of the film to gay audiences, who delight in the artificiality and campness that seems to have alienated some contemporary popular audiences.

What seems to be going on in *Brief Encounter* is a deliberate collapsing of boundaries between past and present. The story is told in extended flashback, through the reminiscence of the central character, Laura Jesson, played by Celia Johnson, a middle-class, happily married woman with children who falls in love with Alec, a dashing young doctor played by Trevor Howard. Laura tells the story in voice-over, and it is her perception of events, her memories that are foregrounded. It has often been pointed out that Laura's account of events is marked in the film as unreliable, not only because we see two slightly different versions of the scene in the railway cafeteria when Alec leaves her for the last time, but also because her voice-over tells us several times that she forgets incidents and details. She is also revealed more than once to be an accomplished liar. One can look at this is a number of ways: it has been argued[6] that, since Laura's status as narrator is undermined, she is deprived of authority. Others have claimed that Laura's feelings, her suicidal state, dominate her narration, and that her version is completely credible as an account of her emotional perspective. Celia Johnson's performance projects Laura as a straightforward and honest person who is deeply unhappy at having to deceive those she loves, which seems to contradict the apparent ease with which she thinks up lies to tell her husband. I would suggest that there is no need to come down on either side of this argument, since the film is saying that memory is a matter of retelling and reordering events, *which may be real or imagined*, from the perspective of the present. It is not a question of accurately retrieving the past, and, in fact, this is seen as an impossibility, since forgetting is part of remembering. Memory is perceived as more like a screen on which we project a fantasy of the past, inspired by present desires. It is only if we expect memory to accurately recall past events that Laura's veracity or unreliability becomes an issue.

The fusion of present and past in memory in *Brief Encounter* is expressed through a particularly interesting and complex use of flashback. Flashback is a common way of articulating memory in classic cinema, and its most usual form is a close-up on a character's face or eyes, suggesting that we are entering their head or thoughts, followed by a scene that represents their recollection of something that happened to them in the past. This is presented as a subjective, introspective moment in which the audience is invited to share the inner thoughts and feelings of the character, and to understand their motivation. A well-known example is the scene in *Casablanca* (1942) when Humphrey Bogart as Rick asks the pianist, Sam (Dooley Wilson), to play the special piece of music that triggers his memory of his love affair in Paris with Ingrid Bergman, who he believes betrayed him. As Sam plays the piano, the camera moves in on Rick's face and a fade leads into the flashback. We know that the memory is in Rick's head, and we take it as an accurate representation of his personal experience – this may encourage empathy and identification with Rick, so that we share his ambivalent response to the Ingrid Bergman character. Eventually, of course, we learn that his memory was not so much inaccurate as incomplete – he did not know the full reasons for her behaviour, and when he discovers the reason he is able to overcome the trauma and move on.

This aspect of empathy and identification through sharing a character's innermost thoughts is central to the way memory is used in classic cinema. The flashback offers access to a character's perception of events, and through identification it validates that perception. Because of the emphasis on subjectivity, there is usually an element of doubt – did this really happen in this way? – and in *Casablanca* this doubt is central to the narrative resolution. In *Brief Encounter* the element of doubt – is this Laura's fantasy? – is more emphatically articulated, and, in fact, at the end of the film Laura's husband Fred refers to her flashback as a dream – not a very happy one. The element of narrative resolution is weaker than in *Casablanca* – although Laura returns to her husband and family, the question of her state of mind, the hysteria induced by frustrated desire, is not settled.

Laura's flashback shares some elements with Rick's in *Casablanca* – the trigger for her reminiscence is a piece of music heard over the radio, Rachmaninov's Piano Concerto No. 2, and the camera moves in on her face as she begins to narrate her memory. However, the boundaries between reality and fantasy are more blurred in *Brief Encounter*. The scene begins in the present as Laura tries to convince Fred that her 'fainting spell' (in fact, a suicide attempt) is nothing to worry about. We know that she is lying to him, albeit with the best of intentions, and before the flashback begins we have already shared her inner thoughts and feelings through her voice-over. The use of music in the scene is interesting – the Rachmaninov Piano Concerto is played all the way through the film on the soundtrack, but when Laura plays it on the radio, this is the first and only time that it is used diegetically, as part of the narrative. This seems to imply the lack of a boundary between fiction and reality. As the flashback begins, a very slow dissolve shows Laura sitting in her armchair watching herself in the station cafeteria, as though watching a screen. It has been argued that this may be intended to suggest a cinema screen, which once again implies a fusion of fiction and reality. There is also a collapsing of time and place here, as Laura 'now' dissolves into Laura 'then' – however, Laura in the cafeteria is wearing 1940s Utility clothing, which actually places her as more 'now' (that is, in the time of the film) than Laura sitting in her 1930s living room. This is a complex representation of time: the film is set in the past, in a middle England apparently blissfully unaware of the imminent war. But the

103

Figure 7.1   At the crossroads: Celia Johnson and Trevor Howard in *Brief Encounter* (1946). Courtesy BFI Stills, Posters and Designs.

present depicted in *Brief Encounter* is a deliberate melding of past and present – and, indeed, the future of the characters.

Brief Encounter uses memory to mourn the passing of innocence, associated with a middle-class notion of Englishness that was itself anachronistic. At the same time, it employs the cinematic devices of memory in a self-conscious, ironic manner, as though the film-makers were implying that this innocence is all a façade, so that it is possible to see *Brief Encounter* as an ironic commentary on the very Englishness it seems to celebrate. I want to explore the ideas on time, place and memory that it plays with in relation to *I Know Where I'm Going!*, where they are treated rather differently. I have suggested that films can embody the shared memories of film-makers and audiences, and that *Brief Encounter* attempted to reach audiences by consciously employing memories of 1930s and 1940s Britain – though it appears they may not have been shared by everyone at the time. *I Know Where I'm Going!* also employs memory in order to reach audiences, and can be seen as offering a discourse on the processes of memory itself. It can also be seen as embodying the shared memories of a group of European expatriates working in 1940s Britain – and, indeed, the reminiscences of those involved in the production have played a significant part in critical discussion of the film.[7]

I Know Where I'm Going! (1946), completed in 1944 and released in 1945, was made during a hiatus in the Archers' career. The spectacular extravaganza *A Matter of Life and Death*, commissioned by the Ministry of Information with the intention of improving postwar Anglo-American relations, had to be postponed because of the unavailability of Technicolor. To fill the gap, Powell and Pressburger conceived a simple moral tale in black and white, a romance set in the Scottish Highlands with an anti-materialist message apparently well suited to postwar austerity conditions. Despite its simplicity, however, the film, produced under the umbrella of J. Arthur Rank's Denham Studios, is technologically ambitious. It uses an extensive amount of visual special effects and relies heavily on the expertise of the German expatriate cinematographer Erwin Hillier, whose work on earlier Archers productions such as *The Silver Fleet* (1943) and *A Canterbury Tale* (1944) had been singled out for lavish praise by critics, who often found Powell and Pressburger's films otherwise difficult to understand. The special effects, especially the rear projection, are a key element in the film's deployment of memory.

I Know Where I'm Going! is a love story that follows the journey of a modern, materialistic young Englishwoman from Manchester to the Scottish island of Kiloran, where she is to marry her wealthy boss, the head of Consolidated Chemical Industries. On the way, she meets and falls in love with the impoverished Laird of Kiloran, her journey is interrupted and her priorities reassessed. Apart from the opening sequences in Manchester, the film is set in Scotland and one of its central themes is the current impoverished condition of Scotland and its desperate need of modernisation. The closing titles dedicate the film to 'true Scotsmen everywhere', and the Rank publicity for the US release targeted the Scottish diaspora in America as a primary audience.[8] Nostalgia and longing for homeland play a key role in this respect. Nevertheless, I would argue that Scotland is not the only, and maybe not the primary, thematic concern of the film. Rather, Scotland provides a pretext for the exploration of a diasporean aesthetic that is only partly concerned with constructing a specific place or region, and is more concerned with creating an imaginary space that crosses national boundaries. This oscillation or tension between the search for authenticity of place and the creation of placelessness is central to diasporean aesthetics, which attempt to construct a fiction of 'home' that is acknowledged to be unrecoverable in reality.

The tension between longing and loss is present in *Brief Encounter* too, and seems to be a key element in nostalgia. In *I Know Where I'm Going!*, however, this fictional construction of home is consciously forged from myths and memories that derive from a mixture of cultural sources rather than drawing on a particular regional or national identity. It is not entirely clear what role this emphasis on cultural in-mixing may have played in the marketing of Scotland and Scottishness to US audiences, since the press book makes much of the production's aspirations to authenticity, focusing on the ceilidh sequence and including an endorsement from 'famous Scot' Harry Lauder. But it may perhaps be seen as a comment from the international, cosmopolitan team of the Archers on the 'Britishness' of British cinema at a time when the future of that cinema and how it should be conceived were being hotly debated. It is worth mentioning that *Brief Encounter* figured quite strongly in that debate as an example of the kind of quality cinema that Britain should be producing, and was highly praised by critics for its realism.

My argument about the deployment of cultural memory in *I Know Where I'm Going!* hinges on a comparison between that film and German director F.W. Murnau's 1927 classic *Sunrise*. Although there is no hard evidence in Pressburger's original script or in Powell's account of the making of *I Know Where I'm Going!* that *Sunrise* had a direct or acknowledged influence on the Archers' film, the latter shares a surprising number of formal and technological features with *Sunrise*, to the extent that Murnau's film provides a kind of ur-text that can be detected in *I Know Where I'm Going!*, turning it into a palimpsest. I should emphasise that *Sunrise* is not the only reference point for the Archers' film, which includes playful allusions to a number of other cinematic and cultural sources. The notion of a single point of origin is inappropriate in the context of the pastiche of styles that characterises *I Know Where I'm Going!*. However, I only have space here to follow up the *Sunrise* association. I would claim that *I Know Where I'm Going!* conjures up a memory of Murnau's masterpiece almost as a displacement for the spectacular the Archers themselves had intended to make: *A Matter of Life and Death*. This may partly be due to unconscious nostalgia on the part of the continental émigrés for the studio resources they had left behind in Europe, but it can also be seen as a statement of the aspirations of this group of film-makers working in Britain in the 1940s under austerity conditions and with comparatively outdated equipment.

The link between F.W. Murnau's *Sunrise* and *I Know Where I'm Going!* was made by William K. Everson in a Museum of Modern Art programme note (dated November 1980) on the Archers' film, reproduced by the National Film Theatre for a season entitled 'Location Magic'. Everson claims that *I Know Where I'm Going!* deserves the classic status accorded to *Sunrise*, 'and for the same reasons' – though he does not elaborate on the reasons. Intrigued by this connection, especially since *Sunrise* is one of my favourite films, I decided to follow it up to see whether or not it would stand up to scrutiny, with some surprising results. It may seem perverse to compare an apparently modest project such as *I Know Where I'm Going!* with the epic tale of desire and death that is *Sunrise*. Nevertheless, there are enough similarities between the two films to suggest an unconscious relationship, one that goes deeper than the level of visual style or artistic homage to what might be called a collective world view, or a shared way of looking at things.

Though eighteen years and many miles separate them, both films were part of a deliberate strategy to encourage prestige, quality productions that would enhance the power of the companies for which they were made. In both cases, the film-makers had privileged access to sophisticated studio facilities, and enjoyed the participation of highly skilled technicians and creative personnel – though the production circumstances of *I Know Where I'm Going!* were intended, in theory at least, to conserve resources and avoid the kind of profligacy associated with *Sunrise*. Both films convey a sense of adventure and excitement about the film-making process, celebrating cinema's utopian possibilities by putting on display a dazzling array of visual special effects. Both were also made at a time of industrial change and economic uncertainty – *Sunrise*, of course, was made on the cusp of a major technological and economic crisis, the transition to synchronised sound. In 1944, the makers of *I Know Where I'm Going!* were also facing an uncertain technological and economic future: austerity conditions had already postponed the move into Technicolor, while postwar relations between Britain and America – on which so much, including the survival of the British film industry, depended – were far from settled.

I shall briefly outline the production context for *Sunrise*. In the late 1920s, when his artistic reputation was at its height, the German director Murnau was invited to Hollywood by William Fox, who had invested in a series of prestige productions in an attempt to upgrade the status of the Fox Film Corporation in the industry. During this period the major Hollywood studios, in common with their British counterparts, courted continental film-makers, particularly those trained in Germany at Ufa, the largest and most powerful film company in Europe, controlling an impressive array of production, distribution and exhibition facilities. During its heyday in the early and mid-1920s, Ufa produced technically innovative and aesthetically ambitious films that were the envy of the world. Murnau and his collaborators, scriptwriter Carl Mayer and cinematographer Karl Freund, had a huge international success with *Der letzte Mann* (*The Last Laugh*, 1924), which must qualify as one of the most influential films ever made. In the late 1920s, Ufa ran into financial difficulties, and many of the film-makers associated with the company left Germany for Britain and Hollywood. Murnau was offered a lucrative contract by Fox to make *Sunrise*, with a high degree of artistic control and a generous budget, most of which was spent on constructing a massive city set on the Fox

107

studio lot. As it turned out, the film was not popular with US audiences or critics, and Fox's investment did not pay off.

The Archers also had strong links with Ufa. Pressburger started his scriptwriting career there in the 1930s, and is known to have particularly admired *The Last Laugh*. He subsequently formed a friendship with Carl Mayer, the scriptwriter on the latter film and *Sunrise*. *I Know Where I'm Going!*'s composer Allan Gray also worked for Ufa in the early 1930s, while production designer Alfred Junge joined the company in 1920, and cinematographer Erwin Hillier worked as a cameraman there between 1926 and 1928. If there can be said to have been an Ufa style, or ethos, it was probably to be found in the emphasis on visual elements such as décor, costume, cinematography and visual effects, and the attention paid to the overall design of a production, which meant that pictorial qualities were usually dominant. There was also a strong emphasis on collaborative methods of working between teams of creative personnel and a climate of technical experimentation and ingenuity – both also characteristic of the J. Arthur Rank ethos in the 1940s, when Rank invested in technologically innovative projects in a bid to put British cinema on the world map.

The resonances between the two films extend beyond their conditions of production. A notable feature of *Sunrise* is its hallucinatory quality, the impression it creates that audience and characters are caught somewhere between sleep and waking. *I Know Where I'm Going!*, too, generates a fantasy world, from the moment its heroine falls into a dream state on the train taking her to Scotland to meet her future husband, to the primeval nightmare of the Corryvreckan whirlpool that almost swallows her up. In both cases, the dream-like ambience was achieved largely through special photographic effects – in particular, through the use of remarkably subtle rear projection, but also through superimposition, and patterns of light and dark that are at once atmospheric and symbolic. Rear projection was used extensively in *I Know Where I'm Going!*, partly to solve some practical problems, such as Roger Livesey's unavailability for location shooting because of other acting commitments. The Archers got round this by employing a double, trained by Livesey, to stand in for him in all exterior scenes. The interiors were filmed with Livesey at Denham, and rear projection was used to produce composite images, which created the illusion that he actually was in Scotland. Erwin Hillier used deep focus and telescopic lenses to ensure that all elements of the image were in focus, and only on several viewings does the extent of the rear projection in *I Know Where I'm Going!*, which was used for some of Wendy Hiller's scenes in Scotland as well as the whirlpool sequence, become evident. Apart from its practical function, the rear projection can be seen as a mechanism for articulating memory, since a process shot precisely combines the past

Figure 7.2   Cross-cultural romance: Roger Livesey and Wendy Hiller in *I Know Where I'm Going!* (1945). Courtesy the Archers and the Kobal Collection.

(that is, location footage) with the present (that is, studio footage), superimposing one upon the other.

I Know Where I'm Going! echoes *Sunrise*'s dramatic diagonal compositions and tendency to have characters break the frame by erupting unexpectedly into it, which intensify the sense of urgency and underlying violence. Both films utilise the ironic 'double ending' technique that was also a feature of *The Last Laugh*, tacking on a happy ending as a makeshift resolution of the conflicts still bubbling away beneath the surface. But the most striking resemblance is in the shared narrative structure, based on journeys – between the city, representing modernity, and the countryside, representing tradition – and on deviations from a planned route brought about by the intervention of nature in the guise of a storm. In *I Know Where I'm Going!*, as in *Sunrise*, the elements perform a redemptive function, reminding the protagonists of basic human values.

There are several sequences in both films that illustrate the kind of rhyme between them that I have indicated. One obvious example of synchronicity occurs between the storm sequence in *Sunrise* and the whirlpool sequence in *I Know Where I'm Going!*. Both these scenes rely heavily on special effects, and represent a *pièce de résistance* in both cases. In the case of *Sunrise*, the young couple return to the countryside after a day in the city. At the behest of his mistress, a modern woman from the city, The Man tried to kill his wife on the outward journey, but realised the error of his ways, and they were reconciled. The irony is that during their boat trip back home, she is swept overboard in the storm and believed dead. In the Corryvreckan whirlpool sequence in *I Know Where I'm Going!*, the heroine Joan insisted, against all advice, on braving the storm to get over to the island where she is to marry her wealthy English boss, putting her own life, and that of the young boatman Kenny and the Laird, at risk. They all narrowly escape being swallowed up by the whirlpool. Both sequences utilised a large studio water tank, as well as location footage, models and rear projection, and both were technically accomplished, displaying high levels of craftsmanship and studio resources.

I have used *I Know Where I'm Going!* and *Brief Encounter* to demonstrate that memory works in many different, and not necessarily obvious, ways in cinema, which go beyond the common narrative use of flashbacks. Both films see memory as a creative process closely linked to fantasy, rather than as a matter of accurately reconstructing or retrieving the past, and both employ cinematic mechanisms such as sound and cinematography, as well as costume and props, to explore the complexities of the processes of memory. Indeed, both films suggest that the technologies of cinema could be seen as metaphors for memory itself, an idea that provides a fascinating starting point for further investigation and research.

Notes

1 See Pam Cook, *I Know Where I'm Going!* (London: BFI Film Classics, 2002).
2 See Richard Dyer, *Brief Encounter* (London: BFI Film Classics, 1993).
3 Colin McDowell, *Forties Fashion and the New Look* (London: Bloomsbury, 1997), p. 70.
4 See Antonia Lant's analysis of the film in *Blackout: Reinventing Women for Wartime British Cinema* (Princeton: Princeton University Press, 1991).
5 See, for example, Andrew Higson, 'Re-presenting the national past: nostalgia and pastiche in the heritage film', in Lester Friedman (ed.), *British Cinema and Thatcherism: Fires Were Started* (London: University College London Press, 1993), pp. 109–29.
6 By Richard Dyer in *Brief Encounter*.
7 See, for example, the documentary by Mark Cousins, *I Know Where I'm Going Revisited* (BBC Scotland, 1994).
8 See especially the US press campaign book, held in the British Film Institute library.

Stars, iconoclasm and identification

PART THREE

INTRODUCTION

Star study occupies a central place in the changing landscape of film studies, providing a focus for conflicting ideas about cinematic images and spectatorship. In the late 1970s, when film theory was heavily weighted towards textual analysis inspired by literary models, Richard Dyer's 1979 book *Stars* broke new ground by emphasising the links between stars as clusters of contradictory meanings and society. It also highlighted the identification of gay men with female stars such as Judy Garland and Bette Davis, drawing attention to the fact that, in the absence of positive representations of homosexuality, gay people in the audience had pilfered straight images to put to their own uses, whether in film-making or in critical responses that camped up those images. One of the most influential of Dyer's arguments was his notion that charisma, that indefinable something that makes the star image special, could work against the narrative drive to ideological closure by captivating the spectator's attention. Even if the story made sure that the strong female heroine got her comeuppance, her dazzling image lingered in the viewer's mind, overriding the knowledge of her punitive destiny. While others had put forward similar arguments about stars, Dyer's account was the first to bring sustained argument and scholarship to a subject generally neglected by mainstream film studies. It was at the forefront of a process of re-thinking issues of representation and sexual politics, and many subsequent studies acknowledged its impact on their own approach.

Dyer's arguments about charisma suggested that ideological meanings were not already embedded in images, they emerged from the contexts in which those images were produced and consumed. The promotional and other discourses circulating around stars and their films contributed to those meanings, but the situations in which they were received by different audiences were equally important, and could produce interpretations far removed from the film-makers' presumed intentions. Dyer's account of the responses of gay men to female star images implied that the processes of identification between viewer and star were less straightforward than had been claimed. He attempted to find a way out of the impasse created by psychoanalytically oriented studies that perceived the classic Hollywood system as ideologically closed, arguing that the contradictory nature of that system allowed for some freedom of interpretation and potential for opposition, albeit socially circumscribed. His bid to find non-psychoanalytical models for the relationship of spectators to screen reflected a general malaise with the tendency of psychoanalysis to produce conservative accounts of sexuality that shored up normative ideologies. Following Dyer, researchers moved on to consider the institutional and social contexts for stars, and began to develop audience reception studies as an alternative approach. These studies revealed that stars, and viewers' memories of them, played a significant role in people's lives. Moreover, identification with stars often formed part of struggles for identity and resistance. The rapturous response to the star image could provoke desires and aspirations that might be acted on outside the cinema, leading fans to mimic their heroes and heroines, whether in look and style, or in their actions. This suggested that such images, far from imprisoning spectators in false consciousness, could empower them.

Despite the growing resistance to psychoanalysis, not all star studies rejected psychoanalysis outright. Indeed, Dyer's work coincided with a general revision of the theories of voyeurism and fetishism that had been influential during the 1970s. The Freudian and Marxist concepts of fetishism had been employed to define ways in which idealised images in classic Hollywood encouraged illusory fantasies of empowerment in order to tie spectators in to capitalist and patriarchal ideologies. The implication of such arguments was that the Hollywood system of representation, and the pleasures it offered, should be deconstructed, through critical writing and through the new forms produced by the emerging independent avant-garde cinema. These arguments were perceived by many as puritanical – certainly they were inspired by iconoclasm, by a desire to overturn old, traditional images and stories and create new ones that would accurately represent the aspirations of political dissent. But they were also reaching towards a more diverse, heterogeneous film culture in which more voices could be heard. The outright rejection of the forms of popular cinema espoused by some radical critics and film-makers may have been both puritanical and elitist, but the activity of deconstructing familiar images to create new configurations is not that far removed from the processes of appropriation and transformation of star images engaged in by the fan. The end result, though, is different in each case; the independent film-maker aspires to change the system of representation, including its structures of production, distribution and exhibition, while the fan operates quite happily within that system.

The rethinking of fetishism led to the recognition that it is in fact a contradictory process rather than a fixed psychic structure. It was argued that fetishism depends on a suspension of disbelief: something that is known to be the case is disavowed in order to overcome the pain of that knowledge. Thus the fetishist vacillates between a state of knowledge, and the negation of knowledge – an unstable situation that both acknowledges reality and provides escape from it, rather like the audiences' experiences of cinema. Indeed, once divested of its negative associations, fetishism is a useful concept to describe the impulse, characteristic of the fan, to collect objects and memorabilia. These objects both bring the adored star or celebrity closer, and possess a magical quality that has the potential to transform lives. At the same time, there is no reason to suppose that the fan is not aware of the illusory nature of their attachment, while also indulging in a playful flight of fancy. This applies to cinema spectators too: rather than being entirely at the mercy of the illusion, they may experience a double reaction, in which they are aware that they have put aside reality, a knowledge that contributes to their pleasure. The extent of their pleasure may be measured by the success of the trip to the cinema in helping them forget reality by engaging in an imaginary experience – which may be one reason why audiences criticise films for not being convincing enough (that is, for not allowing them to suspend disbelief adequately).

The debates around audience responses to star images opened the way to different approaches to cultural analysis and to sexual politics. The strategy of making political interventions intended to lead to the overturning of prevailing systems of representation, and the existing structures of production and exhibition, gave way to a policy of working within the system, and to notions of resistance through appropriation. This shift can be detected in the articles included in this section. 'Stars and politics' (1982) steers a course through the current arguments, working its way towards a position that declines to espouse either the wholesale rejection of images perceived as contaminated by commodity fetishism, or the straightforward adoption of the 'charisma' model. The article anticipates reception study, suggesting that the relationship between stars and spectators could be transformed without destroying pleasure, by focusing on different, conflicting responses to the idealised star figure, including those of the fans along with critical and theoretical accounts. Needless to say, these are discourses that would normally not be brought together in the same analysis; however, if they were, some interesting and surprising convergences may well be revealed. Fans, journalists and academics may share more in their reactions to cinematic images than they are prepared to acknowledge.

'Stars and politics' engages with the issue of the politics of representation, which is also the concern of the interview with independent film-maker Sally

Potter, conducted on the completion of her first feature film in 1983. In *The Gold Diggers* (1984), Potter talks about her desire to create images of women that both acknowledged the power of existing screen heroines while trying to say something new. She is critical of star images that portray women as idealised figures whose beauty may intimidate women who do not conform to the ideal, and she discusses the psychic and financial investment made by spectators and film-makers in stars. However, rather than reject those images wholesale, she argues for a strategy of juggling stereotypes, of de-naturalising them and focusing on the performance of femininity. Potter describes the choice of Julie Christie – a star who represents a traditional ideal of blonde glamour – to portray Ruby, and black actress Colette Laffont to portray Celeste as a deliberate move to play stereotypes off against one another, in order to question traditional representations. At the same time, behind the stereotypes, each character is complex and contradictory, creating a sense of femininity as multidimensional. The stylised use of costume contributes to this by drawing attention to the many disguises adopted by the film's chameleon-like heroines, who perform a range of female identities.

In the interview, Potter defined *The Gold Diggers* as a 'musical describing a female quest'. It was also a costume drama, set during the Klondike Gold Rush, which reworked the narrative conventions of the western genre. Despite her assertion that the film was essentially a playful venture, and she had no intention of refusing pleasure, her background in avant-garde theatre clearly influenced the conception and realisation of the film, creating a kind of Brechtian distance which may not have appealed to audiences who enjoyed popular cinema. Nevertheless, *The Gold Diggers* was a critical success, praised for its stunning use of black-and-white photography and music. Despite this, it was ten years before Potter's spectacular, bigger-budget feature *Orlando* (1993) was produced, this time for her own company, Adventure Pictures. *Orlando*, a reworking of Virginia Woolf's novel, starred Tilda Swinton as the gender-bending, time-travelling protagonist. As with *The Gold Diggers*, Potter used the historical costume drama to explore the limits of cinematic representations of gender and sexuality, foregrounding elements of masquerade and performance. At the same time, she made the most of the visual spectacle, creating a dazzling display of images that drew attention to the sublime beauty of cinema itself as a foil for the androgyny of Swinton's performance. Once again, Potter broke with conventional ideas of beauty, and this time her efforts were greeted with box-office success as well as critical acclaim, bringing her a little closer, perhaps, to the Leicester Square opening she refers to in the interview.

Potter's refusal to place herself as a director in the ghetto of 'women's cinema', and her desire to be accepted as an artist on her own merits, is the subject of the article 'No fixed address: the women's picture from *Outrage* to *Blue Steel*' (1998), which calls for a complete rethinking of the place of women in cinema, whether as film-makers or as images. Taking a cue from Kathryn Bigelow's assertion that what is needed is a radical change in conceptions of women working in the Hollywood industry, and a breaking down of the generic categories to which they have traditionally been consigned, 'No fixed address' challenges the notion of a fixed, gender-specific address to audiences. It argues that film studies has overwhelmingly privileged the 'male spectator', while neglecting the historical contribution of women to cinema across the board, in a variety of roles as directors, stars, designers, scriptwriters, musicians, editors, producers and audiences. The article echoes Potter's call for women to claim their place in cinema, beyond the circumscribed limits of gender. It takes the work of Kathryn Bigelow, discussed more fully elsewhere in this volume, as a high-profile example of film-making that crosses generic boundaries and is difficult to assimilate in gender terms, deliberately using graphic sexual and violent material to confront issues of representation before much larger audiences. Bigelow's risk-taking strategy appears to be symptomatic of developments in women's film-making more generally: Jane Campion ventured into similarly difficult territory with *In the Cut* (2003), in which the heroine's life-threatening involvement in the dark, dangerous world of male sexual desire was depicted in disturbingly graphic detail. While acknowledging the significant achievement of such work, and the considerable difficulties faced by women film-makers, 'No fixed address' suggests that the time has come to acknowledge women's place at the centre, rather than at the margins, of cinema history, and to begin to think and write that history in terms of a more precise and historically specific concept of their contribution, beyond the focus on a handful of women directors.

Further reading

Bruzzi, Stella, *Undressing Cinema: Clothing and Identity in the Movies* (London and New York: Routledge, 1997).

Cook, Pam, and Dodd, Philip (eds), *Women and Film: A Sight and Sound Reader* (London: Scarlet Press, 1993).

Dyer, Richard, *Heavenly Bodies: Film Stars and Society* (New York: St Martin's Press, 1986).

Gledhill, Christine (ed.), *Stardom: Industry of Desire* (London and New York: Routledge, 1991).

Hillier, Jim, *The New Hollywood* (London: Studio Vista, 1993).

Mayne, Judith, *Cinema and Spectatorship* (London and New York: Routledge, 1993).

Stacey, Jackie, *Star Gazing: Hollywood Cinema and Female Spectatorship* (London and New York: Routledge, 1994).

——, 'Hollywood memories', in Annette Kuhn and Jackie Stacey (eds), *Screen Histories: A Screen Reader* (Oxford: Oxford University Press, 1998).

Williams, Linda, 'Learning to scream', *Sight and Sound* (NS) 4(12) (December 1994), pp. 14–17.

Further viewing

Blue Steel (Kathryn Bigelow, USA, 1990)
Christopher Strong (Dorothy Arzner, USA, 1933)
The Gold Diggers (Sally Potter, UK, 1983)
In the Cut (Jane Campion, USA, 2003)
Orlando (Sally Potter, UK/Russia/France/Italy/Netherlands, 1992)
Outrage (Ida Lupino, USA, 1950)
Strange Days (Kathryn Bigelow, USA, 1995)

Chapter 8

STARS AND POLITICS

In this chapter I am less interested in defining the institutional context of stars, or in looking at individual star images, than in the way they have figured historically in discussions around sexual politics and representation. As Richard Dyer has indicated, stars are important in the context of gay politics, and they have also been taken up by many feminists, who have argued for their value as potential role models for women. This argument rests on the idea that, through identification with those female stars who once represented 'strong' women able to resist their subordinate role in society, feminists can find a model for their own resistance today. I deal with some of these arguments here, and try to place them historically because it seems to me vital that if we want to mobilise any ideas in a political cause we should first understand their implications rather than simply assert their value. But I think I should also try to place my own position historically, since I am trying to negotiate a number of contradictory strands within film theory, and the difficulties and confusions that emerge are a symptom of an attempt to move beyond the present paralysis in film theory without jettisoning the hard-won gains theory has made. I am not cynical enough to believe that theory is only effective at certain moments, when it is fashionably current. At the same time theory, like everything else, is subject to historical change.

In the 1970s, feminist film theory produced a host of problems. This theory, drawing on semiology and psychoanalysis in particular, brought us to an impasse: it revealed that in patriarchal society the feminine was impossible to represent because sexual difference was defined entirely in relation to masculinity as the norm. What is more, all our pleasures were also thus defined, circumscribed by the endless repetitive playing out of male/female power relations in society – the subordination of femininity to masculinity. The only alternative seemed to be to reject pleasure offered on such terms, which amounted to a rather puritanical refusal of 'dominant' or mainstream pleasures in favour of their deconstruction. I shall try to play off this argument against others that can be used to question it, to show that it in no sense represents the final truth. However, I don't think it should be jettisoned as a worthless argument, though its conclusions can and have been criticised.

On a more personal note, which serves as a cross-cultural reference, I participated in a feminist film conference in Italy in 1981, where those of us representing Anglo-Saxon feminist film theory were strongly criticised by some as 'the puritans', and against our critique of patriarchal pleasures was placed a celebration of spectacle, of 'positive heroines', of glamour and playing on the dominant system. The Hollywood star system was seen as crucial to this position, which was concerned with recalling the past, a 'golden age' when women could be represented as 'strong' and in control of their lives, resisting patriarchy. I use this anecdote to indicate that our politics, feminist or otherwise, are culturally based, as, indeed, are our notions of 'pleasure'. I think it is important to recognise these differences, since 'pleasure' is often argued ahistorically, as an ideal or an end in itself.

Finally, I'd like to acknowledge the importance of Richard Dyer's book *Stars*,[1] since it provoked me to think through some of the ideas outlined above. The book is a scholarly and extensive analysis of stardom, which finishes with an almost guilty recognition of the pleasures that politics *removes*, leaving us, apparently, with nothing but analysis, understanding, knowledge. Politics also tends to leave us in a rather 'safe' position, set apart from the rest of the population who are still involved in those ideological traps that we have escaped. Perhaps we should begin to formulate a politics that enables us to risk the safety of given positions.

I'd like to make some observations about stars and the problems involved in appropriating them for a strategy of sexual politics. I hope my remarks will provide a way of looking at the film *Christopher Strong* (1933) that will illuminate those problems, and I'll try to show, by means of a detour through some feminist critical writing on the subject of stars and the representation of women, how the film can be used to bring into focus the more difficult and confusing aspects of the debate. I use different and conflicting arguments to interrogate one another, and I do not intend to arrive at a 'correct' conclusion: I think it's more useful to lay out the terms of the debate for further discussion.

Most feminist writing on stars has centred on the Hollywood 'star system', which is taken as the model for what stardom is all about, rather than as a particular historical manifestation of a general cultural phenomenon. Feminists agree that the Hollywood system depends for its continued existence on the spectacle of the female body, but they disagree on how a feminist politics should attempt to deal with this appropriation. For some, the star system at its height in 1920s and 1930s Hollywood represents a golden age in which the prevalence of female stars coincided with the emergence of strong heroines to invest the women represented in the movies with a power and influence that have never been equalled since. Molly Haskell argues that the influx of women scriptwriters into the film industry in the 1930s was an important determining factor, as was the emergence of the woman's film.[2] In spite of their powerlessness within the industry hierarchy (there were few women directors, no women producers), women were extremely important as an audience, and some female stars gained the power to influence economic and aesthetic decisions because of their status as bankable commodities. Haskell retains the idea that the Hollywood system is geared to male control, but, and in spite of the lack of historical analysis in her argument, she implies that at certain historical moments the industry, because of its need to capitalise on the female audience, has opened its doors to intervention by women almost in spite of itself. She accepts that these moments of intervention are short-lived, and that the system divests women of their temporary power through the narrative devices that give them their comeuppance. Nevertheless, she argues, it is those 'incandescent moments' when the great female stars were able to transcend their humiliating narrative destinies by virtue of their charismatic performances that we remember, and which can provide us with a model of feminine resistance for feminist struggles today.

Molly Haskell's argument is based on a defence of the golden age of classic Hollywood cinema, which produced a model of the heterosexual couple relationship that she sees as more egalitarian than anything cinema produces today, where relationships are reduced to narcissistic self-reflection, and the truly challenging heroine who asserted her equality with and difference from her male counterpart is no more. Examples quoted by Haskell are Lauren Bacall/Humphrey Bogart, and Carole Lombard/Clark Gable.

Other feminist critics, writing from a perspective influenced by theories of cultural politics emerging from France after 1968, have taken a more pessimistic view of the classic Hollywood system, arguing that its apparent 'openness' − that is, the way in which it seems to offer progressive images of women that depict them as strong, independent and a challenge to male domination − is predicated upon the expectation of closure. In other words, built into the classic system itself, the codes it employs, the relationships it sets up between spectators and the screen, is a way of viewing the figure of the woman as the powerless object of male domination. According to this argument, it is not that there is a pre-given ideal of female sexuality which the system works to recuperate, and which we can then appropriate for our own uses, as Haskell argues. Rather, the classic system produced definitions of female sexuality that are based on a promise of openness (a potential rupture in the male order) which is inseparable from the closure in favour of male domination, and it is in this *double* movement of aperture and closure that our pleasure as spectators is to be found. The emphasis, however, is on closure: the attempt by ideology to resolve its contradictions in its own favour, to present itself as coherent and natural.

The most convincing elaboration of this argument in relation to the Hollywood star system comes from Laura Mulvey.[3] She argues that the star system produces stars as ego-ideals, both similar to and different from us. Through a process of imaginary misrecognition we undergo a temporary loss of ego, which is the basis of our identification with stars, and which recalls for us the time before the ego was formed. However, this apparently open situation in which the spectator is 'free' to identify across the boundaries of sex, class, race and age is based on a system or regime of 'looking', which builds the way woman is to be looked at into the spectacle itself. According to this argument, classic narrative cinema plays upon the conventional social divisions that allocate a place for woman as passive, object of the (conventionally) 'male' gaze, and man as active bearer of the look. The psychic process of fetishism plays a crucial part in fixing the figure of the woman into its allocated place: in the Freudian definition of fetishism, the woman's body, lacking the penis, signifies the threat of castration, a problem that is resolved by an act of displacement in which the absent penis is replaced by another part of the body, or another object, as the focus of attention, taking on extra value as a phallic substitute. So the original problem of castration is contained by a process in which the woman's sexual difference, representing castration anxiety, is first recognised then denied.

In the context of the cinema and the discussion about stars, female stars in particular, this argument provides a convincing account of the pleasure offered to the spectator by the fetish figure of the female star: a perfect product offering reassurance and safety, the disavowal of castration anxiety. And one can see how, although castration anxiety is different for men and for women, the game of phallic replacement involved in fetishism can offer pleasure to both 'male' and 'female' spectators, since it is argued that the play of absence and presence, as resolved by the phallic substitution, offers the power of pseudo-domination to the spectator through the prolonged gaze at the fetish figure. In the Freudian castration scenario women are doubly powerless – they can aspire to, but never attain, the power of the phallus. Fetishism endows both the body of the woman with the insignia of power and the spectator with the powerful controlling gaze, enabling disavowal of the real social relations between men and women, although finally those relations are re-asserted, and sexual difference is imposed by the narrative resolution. Small wonder, then, that stars fascinate men and women and that we are reluctant to give them up.

For my purposes, the fetishism argument provides a very different approach to classic Hollywood cinema and the function of stars within it from that offered by Molly Haskell, a difference that has consequences for discussion of political strategy. The 'incandescent moments' described by Haskell in which the female star appears strong enough to transcend the subordinate place allocated to woman in society (a place reinforced by the classic narrative structure) become in the fetishism argument a built-in part of a system that controls female sexual difference, circumscribing it with the phallus as the primary signifier of power, thus precisely defining a subordinate place for women in society. Woman is endowed with the phallus in order that it can then be taken from her, confirming her status as powerless. But even if classic narrative cinema allowed her to keep it there would still, I think, be a problem: feminists should indeed be wary of giving progressive status to images offering an illusion of power founded in the phallocentric system that denies us our difference. Moreover, if, as Laura Mulvey suggests, classic Hollywood cinema is a mechanism for working through male fears engendered by a patriarchal society, what is the value of looking back to its heyday as a golden age of female emancipation? Surely one would have to ask first what the function was of that emancipation for such a system.

The main difference between the two approaches seems to be that the ecstatic, thrilling moments of transcendence that Haskell takes as a potential model for an ideal of female sexuality are, in the fetishism argument, part of a system that fixes the figure of woman as passive object of the 'male' gaze, outside the 'real' dimensions of time and space, which are controlled by the male characters. The fetishism argument therefore seems more pessimistic in its conclusions than the Haskell approach, defining a closed system of representation in which moments of excess, trouble or escape function as a prelude to ideological closure. However, it does attempt to define the ideological dimensions of the pleasure offered by stars in classic Hollywood cinema, and the vested interests at stake in holding on to it.

The problem raised is one of political intervention: if one accepts the fetishism argument, then it becomes impossible simply to appropriate the fetishistic image of woman as a model for feminists, as Haskell suggests; and even if one doesn't accept it, we should at least be cautious about taking as a feminist 'role model' an image of female sexuality that is predefined for us, however pleasurable.

The problem with the fetishism argument is that it lacks a historical perspective that would allow for differences within the system: differences of time and place, of genre, of director, studio and so on, or for that matter, differences in viewing situations that might transform the conditions required for the fetishistic process: the darkened secret room, the pleasure of uninterrupted viewing. Some feminist critics have argued that the definitions of female sexuality offered by Hollywood can be redefined from a feminist perspective. Patricia Erens defends her own re-reading of Shirley MacLaine's star persona in such terms.[4] MacLaine's image as the naive prostitute with a heart of gold, the eternal victim, is not forever tied to the system that produced it: its meaning can change in relation to shifts in point of view, and a contemporary feminist reading can create a positive image from one that was originally negative by shifting the emphasis away from the negative aspects – in this case, towards MacLaine's positive (for Erens) political activities in real life. While sympathetic to the argument for feminist re-readings of the work done by women in the Hollywood system, at all levels, including stars, I have reservations about setting up those women as ideal 'positive' figures for identification, since it involves removing them from the process of argument, struggle and contradiction on which I think politics depends. *The Doris Day Dossier*, which is based upon a similar project of re-reading and reassessment from the perspective of feminism, avoids the problem of idealisation by presenting three different feminist arguments around the Doris Day image, which sometimes conflict with one another.[5] The feminist perspective offered is not one of simple identification but of discussion and dissent, and the star image is presented as the focus for conflicting definitions of female sexuality rather than as a feminist role model. It is, in my view, extremely important to the intervention made by the Doris Day arguments that the discourse of fandom and its pleasures is kept in play along with other critical discourses.

Potentially, therefore, though not necessarily, a shift in point of view, a change of context can transform the fetishistic relationship between star and spectator without destroying the star figure, by reintroducing difference in the form of conflicting arguments around that figure. However, such a shift undoubtedly would destroy the fascination between star and spectator and therefore is unlikely to be attractive to any serious fetishist. The resistance to the feminist arguments around Doris Day bears witness to the extent to which those arguments threatened the security of the relationship between star and spectator.

It is possible to recast the fetishism argument in less pessimistic terms. I have already suggested that the process of fetishism depends as much upon the recognition of female sexual difference as on its denial: it's a contradictory process containing an instability that is open to intervention. An effective form of intervention into a system geared towards effacing difference is, I would argue, the exploitation of that difference, working on the instability of the system. This strategy can be effective at the level of production, in films that 'play' with star images, but more so, I would suggest, at the level of exhibition, where the viewing context can be changed. But it is also important to recognise, I think, when it comes to arguments about the 'subversive' value of stars, that Hollywood cinema is entirely capable of recognising and playing on the potential instability of its own system, that it invests just as much in difference as it does in closure. Terry Lovell has elaborated this argument in terms of Marx's theory of capitalist commodity production,[6] and has been taken up by Richard Dyer in his discussion of stars. To put it crudely: in order to perpetuate the situation in which commodities are used up and replaced, capital has to stimulate a demand for those commodities among consumers. To achieve this demand it has to recognise many conflicting interests in society, and frequently invest in commodities that work against its own best interests. Thus there can be friction or tension between commodities and the interests of capital, which allows those groups whose needs were initially exploited by capital to appropriate those commodities and use them against the dominant ideology. In the gap between the interests of subordinate groups and the interests of capital a power struggle takes place to decide how certain commodities should be used. The fetish figure of the female star can be seen as just such a commodity; capital invests in an image of woman that may, at certain historical moments, conflict with the place it allocates for women in society. Thus the image is potentially subversive of capital's interests and can be used against those interests.

The extent to which an 'image' or representation can be called a 'commodity' is not very clear, but the attraction of this argument is that it introduces the idea of power struggles in society over representations, rather than defining representation as a monolithic system controlled by capital; however, by locating subversion within 'commodities' themselves, such as the female star image, it assumes that such commodities are somehow free of capitalist ideology, and by the same token, the interests of subordinate groups are 'naturally' in conflict with those of capital. It also tends to ignore the extent to which capitalist commodity production plays on the contradictions within its own system to turn them to its own advantage, though not always successfully.

If the argument is applied to Hollywood cinema, one can find an abundance of examples of the way the system recognises its own contradictions through self-reflexiveness, self-parody, even self-criticism. Capitalist commodity production clearly recognises the value of 'subversion' to the perpetuation of its system. It seems problematic to me to designate certain representations (commodities) such as the female star figure as subversive in themselves, since the extent of subversion surely rests on how that figure functions within the fiction of the film in relation to the other images of femininity it offers, and to the images circulating in society. Moreover, the commodity production argument seems to me to reinforce the status of images as objects rather than as part of a process of producing meanings that change with history.

I'd like to offer some points for discussion in relation to *Christopher Strong*, bearing in mind some of the questions I've raised above, and using the film as the focus for a number of conflicting arguments. It was chosen specifically for this discussion of stars, rather than as an Arzner film, because of its place in the Hollywood industry of the 1930s, a period held up by Molly Haskell and others as a 'golden age' for female stars. It was made in 1933, when the Hollywood film industry was severely affected by the economic crisis. The years following the coming of sound and the effect of the Depression put stars in a weak position in relation to the studios: production had been drastically reduced and salaries were cut back. It was not unusual for studios to feature three or more stars in a film to boost its box-office appeal and keep individual star salaries low. Stars were expected to exercise economic restraint and show complete loyalty to the studio. In the light of these industrial determinants it is interesting that the film takes 'stardom' as its subject on one level, facing all of its characters with more problems of restraint and self-sacrifice, none more so than its central 'star', the young and exceptional aviatrix Cynthia Darrington, played by Katharine Hepburn. Hepburn was a theatre actress who brought with her a reputation for being difficult and uncooperative, an 'independent' woman; this was her second film and the studio's first attempt to make her a star. In the context of discussions about commodity production and fetishism, her 'newness', manifested in a rather stilted performance, could be seen as a disruptive element in the film, breaking the rapport between star and spectator. However, it is precisely her quality of extreme youth, and her exceptional courage, that sets her apart from the rest of society: her 'strangeness' has a value in the fiction that her performance supports rather than subverts.

The film was directed by a woman, Dorothy Arzner, and scripted by a woman, Zoe Akins; it is also a 'women's picture', in spite of its title, which means that it was directed at a female audience, had a storyline based on romantic fiction, featured a female star at its centre, and dealt with contemporary 'female' issues such as sex, love and marriage. It seems to conform, then, to Haskell's argument about the industry's openness to intervention by women at this time.

There were many different kinds of 'women's pictures' in Hollywood in the 1930s. It is interesting to speculate why they emerged and why a particular kind of female star, the exceptional heroine, was central to them. The economic crisis meant that certain bourgeois ideals were under threat: in particular the ideal family centred in a well-ordered, spacious home, attended by faithful servants, controlled by an authoritarian father and supported by a compliant mother dedicated to buying the consumer goods necessary to improving home and family. Such an ideal was no longer attainable; the women who identified with it would have to learn patience and self-sacrifice. At the same time the New Deal was in the air with recipes for coping with the economic crisis, and the strong independent heroine was an important part of New Deal ideology. The old society was seen as decadent and spent, in need of regeneration. The active energy of the 'new woman' was a necessary part of that regeneration, as long as it didn't threaten the basis of a healthy society, the monogamous family.

Christopher Strong has been celebrated by Gerald Peary and others as a proto-feminist film because of the way it endorses the courage and self-sacrifice of the active heroine, and the suffering of the wife and mother, while offering a critical perspective on the behaviour of the hero, Christopher Strong.[7] This account centres on the positive qualities of the central heroine, whose exceptional bravery is taken as a model for feminist identification. Katharine Hepburn's 'charismatic' performance, her glamour, seems on one level to support this reading of the film. However, it could also be argued that the way in which the narrative moves towards fictionalising her 'star quality' is underestimated.

A more recent account, in the form of textual analysis, shows how the active heroine performs the function of a catalyst in the fiction for the crisis in the monogamous family, which is finally reconstructed on a new, more liberal basis. Jacqueline Suter discusses the film in terms of the fetishisation of its heroine, Cynthia Darrington, demonstrating how her character (strong, independent, reckless) functions to work through a dilemma of patriarchy, so that in her final act of sacrifice, her suicide, she validates the patriarchal myth: monogamy is the only viable ethic, worthy enough to give one's life to preserve.[8]

The argument implies that the process of fetishisation is, in the case of this film, internalised in the fiction in such a way that it becomes a necessary part of the ideological movement of the film towards closure. The film's closing moments create Cynthia Darrington as a legend, a model of courage and self-sacrifice – indeed, a repression of difference, since she is pregnant with Christopher Strong's illegitimate child when she dies. She is transformed from an active speaker of resistance to the male order to the passive object permitting scrutiny and adoration without fear.

Suter's reading tends to emphasise ideological closure, conforming to a more pessimistic notion of fetishism. A third possible reading, and one that I would prefer, would be in terms of the contradictions at work in the film that render its ideological closure problematic. Rather than locating those contradictions entirely in the star figure, however, I see them as arising from a number of factors: the historical place of the film in the industry; the contradictory nature of the image of woman in New Deal ideology; the critical

127

potential of the 'women's picture'; the unusual conjunction of a woman director and scriptwriter; the film's attempt to negotiate the uneasy relationship between its female star and her place in its ideological project (in other words the power of the visual codes connoting 'stardom' to overcome narrative closure); and so on. But I want to emphasise the importance of keeping all these readings, and other potential readings, in play, since I think it is history and politics that will decide for each of us which we prefer.

In the context of discussion about stars and identification, on one level the film seems to be *about* the search for ideals of masculinity and femininity. One of the questions that circulates around the star-figure of the active heroine is her suitability as a role model for young girls. The film offers a number of competing definitions of femininity that reflect upon and transform one another: the role of the wife and mother played by Billie Burke is important in this respect. The figure of the active heroine fictionalised in the film as an ideal takes on meaning by virtue of its relationship to the other definitions of femininity (such as Billie Burke's 'ordinariness') offered by the film and in society at that time, and cannot, I would argue, be discussed outside that relationship and its particular historical context, as many arguments about identification and stars tend to discuss the subject.

Notes

1 Richard Dyer, *Stars* (London: BFI Publishing, 1979).
2 Molly Haskell, *From Reverence to Rape* (New York: Holt, Rinehart & Winston, 1974).
3 Laura Mulvey, 'Visual Pleasure and Narrative Cinema', *Screen* 16(3) (autumn 1975), pp. 6–18.
4 Patricia Erens, *The Films of Shirley MacLaine* (London: Thomas Yoseloff, 1978).
5 Jane Clarke, Mandy Merck and Diana Simmonds, *BFI Dossier No. 4: Move Over Misconceptions: Doris Day Reappraised* (London: British Film Institute, 1981).
6 Terry Lovell, *Pictures of Reality* (London: BFI Publishing, 1980).
7 Karyn Kay and Gerald Peary, *Women and the Cinema: A Critical Anthology* (New York: Dutton, 1977).
8 Jacqueline Suter, 'Feminine Discourse in Christopher Strong', *Camera Obscura*, 3–4 (1979), pp. 135–50.

Chapter 9

THE GOLD DIGGERS

One of the most exciting programmes of the 1983 London Film Festival was the combination of Helen Grace's *Serious Undertakings* with Sally Potter's feature *The Gold Diggers*. Sally Potter began making 8mm films in 1968, but she trained as a dancer, performing and choreographing for the Strider Dance Company while making films such as *Hors d'oeuvres* (8mm), *Play* (16mm) and *The Building* (an expanded cinema event). In 1974 she founded the Limited Dance Company with Jackie Lansley and toured in Britain and the USA. Subsequently she worked both on solo performance shows and in collaborations, including with the musical group FIG (the Feminist Improvising Group). In 1979, her short film *Thriller*, a feminist comedy, was released, and in 1980 she formed the Marx Bros group with Lindsay Cooper and Georgie Born. She then went on to choreograph two solo dances for Maedee Dupres and to lecture on feminism and cinema. *The Gold Diggers* was her first feature.

Sally Potter I see this film as a musical describing a female quest. Making it has demanded asking the same questions during the working process as the film endeavours to ask: about the connections between gold, money and women; about the illusion of female powerlessness; about the actual search for gold and the inner search for gold; about imagery in the unconscious and its relationship to the power of cinema; looking at childhood and memory and seeing the history of cinema itself as our collective memory of how we see ourselves and how we as women are seen. Working with two female central roles meant continuously asking how can I build/find characters and images of women that will serve our intelligence and mirror the complexities of our struggles. The feature film format sets up its own expectations in terms of what it must offer, which made a useful discipline to work with and learn from and also to push against where it seemed necessary to create a tension with the genre.

So much for intentions. In practice, the ideas were developed through a mass of technical details and decisions: the choice of lens, of light, of movement, gesture, location, timing, cut. There was a brief rehearsal period where I choreographed some sections, started to work on the two central characters and to build up a coherent screen presence for performers from diverse backgrounds and ranges of experience. Julie's presence resonates not only with her own work history, but also with the iconic power of the face in cinema; through her part we worked to suggest aspects of the history of the cinematic heroine: silent movie stars with their language of exaggerated gesture; the Hollywood belle descending the archetypal ballroom staircase; the film noir mystery woman, an enigma even to herself. I had worked with Colette before in *Thriller* and with her developed the part of the female investigator, the observer within the frame. The male parts were developed more as caricature – of bureaucratic anxiety, academic stasis (the expert and his assistant) and of anonymous pursuers and street terrorisers. I wanted to call the male bluff and disperse some of the fear and seriousness that usually surrounds those images, to clear the ground. The landscape itself was a performer – Icelandic light changing moment by moment and offering contradictory aspects of itself. In the shoot and in the editing process I attempted to create 'layers' in each scene – of genre references and internal cross-reference (the dancer who 'freezes', the frozen landscape, etc.), the frame as the inner projection (Ruby's memory) – and to work with the conventions of the musical (the dream sequence, the backstage scenes, the songs, etc.). Ultimately, my own desire was, and is, to give pleasure; to heal the 'pleasure time blues' of the opening song.

Pam Cook The central enigma of the film is the attempt to draw connections between gold, money and women. What drew you to these connections in the first place?

SP Do you remember the times a few years ago when there was a gold rush in London? Suddenly there was this amazing fascination with gold and everyone was bringing their gold to Hatton Garden and selling it. We were writing the script around then. But also, gold has been used as the subject matter of so many films; everybody thinks they know something about gold and what it means in relation to money. Many people still think of it as the universal equivalent, including some governments it would appear, even when they're not still on the gold standard. It's a kind of superstition. Gold as an image is rich on so many levels, not only on the level of economics and its symbolic function, as in the golden mean and the golden section, but also it's a chemical richness. It seemed like a kernel around which ideas could swivel and from which images could depart. So that was why gold. Why women? It seems impossible as a woman film-maker to get away from the topic of woman. The issue became how to make an image of woman in a feature film that related to the history of screen heroines and yet was a departure from it. Then gradually, almost organically, arose the idea of the circulation of money and the circulation of women. The film was a way of exploring what the connections were..

PC Did you find, as you worked through your ideas in the film, that you came closer to making those connections, or were you simply establishing them as questions? The connections are very enigmatically presented in the film.

SP A film doesn't set out to be an academic treatise. What it achieves, if anything, is a poetic clarity about the issues. But let me try and separate some of the strands: economics, beauty and the star. The basic Marxist concepts of surplus value and exchange value have an elusive quality. There seems to be something about the nature of money itself and its movement that crystallises that elusiveness because it is in fact a symbolic system, a system of representation. So when you're trying to represent a system of representation, you're dealing with this tantalising, just out of your grasp, phenomenon.

In the making of the film I used to go back, over and over again, to a remarkable phrase of Foucault about the metaphysics of money ... The relationship between contemplation of the cosmos and knowledge of the glittering metals.

> The marks of similitude, because they are a guide to knowledge, are addressed to the perfection of heaven; the signs of exchange, because they satisfy desire, are sustained by the dark, dangerous and accursed glitter of metal. An equivocal glitter, for it reproduces in the depths of the earth that other glitter that sings at the far end of the night: it resides there like an inverted promise of happiness and, because metal resembles the stars, the knowledge of all these perilous treasures is at the same time knowledge of the world. And thus reflection upon wealth has its pivot in the broadest speculation upon the cosmos, just as, inversely, profound knowledge of the order of the world must lead to the secret of metals and the possession of wealth.[1]

It has been interesting talking to some economists about gold, for even to them it has this elusive quality. About beauty: some of the things the expert says about the golden section I would think of as true, but the context in

131

which he says them makes them questionable. In the same way that fascists took over some ideas of proportion and called them the noble proportions of mankind, so even fundamental and harmonious principles of form, like the golden section, can be used to dubious ends. Physical beauty can become a tyranny if it's used to create anxiety in women who do not conform to the ideal. The star is often a manifestation of an ideal type and the part of Ruby, designed for Julie Christie, plays with these ideas. The star phenomenon is an actual form of investment and in real financial terms is a kind of circulation of the face. We asked ourselves what is the connection between capitalist investment in the circulation of the face and the necessary iconic power that the face will then take on through repetition, with, let's say, a religious icon that has no financial investment in it but has enormous metaphysical, spiritual and psychological investment in it.

The level on which these things are dealt with in the film is on the level of puns, given that punning is deep play with language, isn't it? So it's a cinematic pun, which means deep play with the language of film – a sort of semiotic shuffle.

PC Hollywood has often used the woman's body symbolically as a means of displaying gold – the blonde as an ideal of femininity for instance, or the female star in her glittering costume.

SP Yes. It's a means of displaying male wealth and ownership of the woman, too. The first image of Ruby is in the ballroom, being circulated between the men – passed from one partner to the next – that was a deliberate first image. The first time Celeste is seen without Ruby is in a computer room in a bank, asking questions about what her role is in relation to the money she's helping to circulate. At one point she says 'money flows through my body'. So that's where they're both positioned – Ruby herself is being circulated and displayed, and Celeste is helping to circulate money. From these relatively powerless positions their investigations lead them to make connections between money, power and energy and its symbolic relationship to the earth's resources. That's the voice that Celeste takes up in her song about imperialism towards the end of the film.

PC Is there a possibility for action for the two heroines coming out of that new position and understanding? Is that part of the project of the film, to change the situation?

SP Yes. Firstly by occupying the same space cinematically that has been designated for them historically, but subverting it from the inside, as in the repeated ballroom sequence where the prevailing order is disrupted, and falls into disarray. But Celeste's final words in the film are 'I know that even as I look and even as I see I am changing what is there'. Our first step towards change is the act of seeing.

PC Ruby's amusement in the ballroom is a kind of turning back on the codes which brings them all down. Can we talk about the formal structure of the film, which is also extremely complex? You've said that you see it as an adventure story or quest, a kind of epic form – but its narrative is not linear, as one might expect. Can you talk a bit about the way you saw it working on conventional genres and fictional forms as they've been used in cinema?

SP The film has a spiral structure, within which there are many genre refer ences, creating a tension with the expectations that the feature film format produces. The subject matter of the film is partly that – a reflection on the history of its forms. In a narrative linear structure which goes from A to Z there's not a great deal of room to go back and change things that were wrong in the first place. A spiral gives the room for constant re-evaluation – you can display the issues first and then go back and change them. So it's a sort of grounded revolution. The spiral is a very strong, sturdy structure, it's familiar in many natural forms and has a history, architecturally and spiritually and, of course, biochemically. And it is a life structure too.

PC What do you mean by that?

SP Well, in one's life one is continuously going through cycles in the process of change.

PC Female sexuality is supposed to be very closed in on itself and unable to take a distance from itself or the rest of the world. I think your film actually demands a position of distance and one of the threads running through it is the female voyeur, which is linked with the female investigator. Voyeurism demands a distance and it's often been theorised that voyeurism is masculine and that femininity cannot occupy voyeuristic space. Did you actually make the effort to include distance?

SP I think detachment is a virtue. The stereotype of the woman as incapable of detachment comes from the idea that women are closer to the emotions, closer to the dark side – being outside of language in the land of the uncon- scious. A certain kind of misogyny creeps into theoretical language on this

133

Figure 9.1   New horizons: *The Gold Diggers* (1984). Courtesy BFI Stills, Posters and Designs.

issue, just as it does in non-theoretical language. It's based on the misconception that because women are brought up to have certain emotions more accessible — it is part of the nurturing role to be able to feel and empathise and all that — that somehow they are, by definition, more emotional. If anything, it's the other way round — men are more conditioned by their feelings because they are less accessible to the conscious. The unconscious and the conscious have a bigger gap and are therefore more determining, because the more something is repressed, the more it actually determines behaviour. In that sense the supposed emotionality of women, the ability to express and discharge feeling, in fact can create a more detached world view. One can have the confidence that one's responses are a process of experience coming through to the conscious, take that on and say OK, this experience can be the basis of my detachment.

So I think the distance in the film is about that, rather than about voyeurism.

PC One of the themes of the film is that a robbery has been committed on woman, on femininity: the opening blues, for instance, and a discourse running through the film is that something has been taken from woman. So lack is inscribed in the film — how does that relate to what you just said?

134

SP Well, what I'm saying is that it's no good dwelling in the land of the victim. And that even though we have to acknowledge our oppression and all the things that have been taken away, including our pleasures, nevertheless there's a point of view which is extremely handy, which is to see the paradoxical advantages of our situation and to see our inner strength.

PC The film has a formal asceticism, some might say puritanism, reminiscent of avant garde minimalism.

SP Where is the puritanism?

PC In refusing the traditional pleasures that cinema offers through conventional representations of women, but also through conventional narratives, through all that we've come to accept and understand as natural in our normal cinema-going experience. When I go to the pictures in Leicester Square, or to my local, I enjoy the conventional pleasures that that experience offers, which is not just to do with what you see on the screen, it's to do with audience reaction and a darkened room. Now, there are ways in which your film, because of the black and whiteness of it, and partly because of its structure, refuses a lot of conventional pleasures of voyeurism and the multiple other pleasures that ordinary cinema offers us. It pares things down to a minimum.

SP For me there's a great passion in austerity and in the desire for a structure which is clean in the deep sense — for that kind of rigour. One of the things the film tries to do is to integrate certain aspects of passionate formalism with feminism.

And the truth is that when I was first confronted with minimalism in various forms, I found it deeply pleasurable. I also found certain aspects of what was called puritanical, pleasurable and I find much of what's called pleasurable, painful. Some of the big questions that the film ends up being about come out in the first song (*Seeing Red*) — where is the pleasure? What is the pleasure if it's based on female pain? If you're conscious of that and want to make something that is extremely pleasurable, but doesn't hook into — for want of a better way of expressing it — oppressive stereotypes, then the range at first sight is rather limited of where you can go and play. In that sense I'm a very moral person, but it can get confused with puritanism — though as a friend of mine says, puritans have more fun. But there's nothing wrong with ethics: it's a form of deep pleasure. There's everything right about wanting to dismantle oppressive stereotypes, there's everything right about fighting oppression, there's everything right about wanting to make pleasure that isn't causing somebody else pain. If that's called puritanism, then I think

135

puritanism is having a great time. But anyway, I think there are a lot of scenes in *The Gold Diggers* which do a lot of playing and are about cinematic pleasure – that's why I was a bit surprised when you said it was puritanical.

PC In the first viewing it could be seen as rather ascetic.

SP Monk-like. To me it did become a very meditative experience. It started out more heavily politicised and became very meditative in the cutting room.

PC There has been a move amongst a lot of feminists working in cinema, photography and painting not to represent the female body at all because of the traps that leads us into. Do you sympathise with that position?

SP Yes, I do, though I don't share it entirely. In my performance art in the past, I have been seen on an ice rink with no clothes on, holding a microphone, debating what it's like to be both the muse, the female nude, and speaking for the muse. In other words, I have put my own body on display, so I know from the inside what that dilemma is about. And I know I would find it hard to do that again. But I don't think it's impossible to represent the female body, it's just a bit difficult to get through the tangle of oppressive stereotypes. *The Gold Diggers* tries to take existing stereotypes and rejuggle them into a new alchemy, partly by looking at the performer, the woman behind the sign. The Julie Christie part, for instance, has to do with an accepted representation of femininity in the cinema, a certain kind of glamour and blondness and beauty; a certain ideal. In the process of the film she sheds that to an extent, it becomes evidently a form of disguise. What that does is open up a space somehow, a gap, which separates the accepted stereotype from the woman. That's perhaps the kind of space in which the female can appear without colluding with voyeuristic abuse.

PC One doesn't necessarily have to refuse the stereotypes or representations which exist. One can call them constantly into different spaces, produce different meanings. I see that as an important part of a certain kind of avant garde work – for instance, Marcel Duchamp's work taking ordinary, everyday objects and moving them to another social space where they mean something quite different.

You've used two central heroines and exciting forms like the adventure/epic. Nonetheless, the film doesn't offer the usual pleasures of identification.

SP The identificatory thread is not along the lines of the human being providing a model that one can live vicariously through and with, but rather

136

an identification with certain processes. There are arguments and ideas that run through the film that certainly, for me, provide an intellectual identification. The structure provides a possibility for identification with certain unconscious structures – dream logic, nightmares, or whatever. And there can be identification with both of the women through the theme of the split itself. Celeste and Ruby together make the 'celestial ruby' or 'philosophers' stone'; their unity is in the alchemical secret. Without the unity of the economic, analytical area (Celeste's journey) and the personal, subjective, dreamlike memory area (Ruby's journey), there can be no secret for transformation. So one can identify with that dialectical process, the friendship of opposites.

PC I think that the Ruby character is potentially more available for identification because she's more emotional. She cries, she's seeking her lost mother and her own past; she laughs, she goes through the gamut of emotions. The Celeste character is more logical and detached.

SP That is the division of labour between the characters, in a way. And as one is supposed to identify more with the emotional, then Ruby would be more invested with that sort of identification. Now, if women are stereotyped as being closer to the emotions, black women are doubly stereotyped as being closer to the earth, so it seemed important to have Celeste take a more detached position as a contradiction to that. Black actresses are often either reduced to sensual or subservient parts, or have to take up the banner of representing all black women, in an agit-prop way. It's a restrictive range.

PC It seems to me that the Celeste character has more positive overtones as the new-style heroine in your film than Ruby. I think there's a lot in the Ruby character that feminists would like to suppress in themselves and wish didn't exist, i.e. the contradictions we have to experience and which are very painful sometimes.

SP This is where looking at the performer behind the sign comes in. There's a great deal to be proud of in what has sometimes been dismissively analysed as collusion with the trappings of femininity. For the performers themselves, there's always that detachment, the knowledge that one is playing a part, and it takes a lot of skill. Ruby is a chameleon construction, full of contradictions created by the irreconcilable parts she must play.

PC Why did you choose to film the landscapes in Iceland?

137

SP Lindsay and I had been to Iceland in our music group (the Feminist Improvising Group). The landscape was so extreme, so bleak and relatively untouched, that it had all the connotations of virgin land and unexplored territory. In much female literature, landscape has been used as a metaphor for the territory of the mind and the unconscious, and of course in films there's often a quite comic connection, as at the moment of the kiss when thunder rumbles, lightning strikes and rain pours onto the barren land. Iceland seemed rich in metaphor of a kind appropriate to the film – the notion of the frozen self, the isolated self, with the hut as the body. Later, the frozen ice melts into water imagery, a more accessible consciousness that we can dive into. So the land is also a mutable element, a force. It's part of the alchemical subtext. And on the associative level, Iceland seemed to fit the popular image of the Klondike. Desperate men in thousands did tramp out in extraordinary conditions, trying to find gold. It's the epitome of the capitalist dream – you too can make it, if you try hard enough. At the same time, there's a sort of rape-of-the-earth feel about it.

PC So it functions on one level as an image for imperialist venture.

SP A bit, although the gold rush phenomenon is not really about imperialism. It was inconsequential what individuals managed to get out of the ground. Imperialism is a much more massively organised form of plunder. The individual quest for gold is much more about helplessness, really, and longing … longing to beat the system and get rich quick. It's also a longing at a deeper level, a more metaphysical level – it's Holy Grail material in the form of the quest for gold nuggets.

PC I was tempted to make an analogy myself between the frozen landscape as an image for colonial ventures and the body of woman similarly used, similarly appropriated, similarly colonised.

SP Yes, the Iceland landscape can stand for both of those things. But there is a difference between the tragedy of the working-class man and his quest and the other kind of tragedy – the capitalist or imperialist conquest of land and resources.

PC The film seems to turn the tables on men by reducing them all to stereotypes, using innocent signs to represent the good and stereotypes to represent the evil. The tragedy of the working-class male gold digger gets lost.

SP Firstly, I think there is no such thing as female sexism. The stereotyping of woman is a stereotyping of a relatively powerless position in the sexist structure, and so is a double injury. If you stereotype a powerful man, it doesn't have the same meaning at all. Now in a film, you make a choice of where you draw the line about who is the focus of the story and this film, indeed, does not focus on the working-class man.

PC It represents him as a thief, in a way. He's ripped out the gold; and he carries off the mother.

SP The image of the man coming in with the gold, to me functions less on a class level than it does as an image of male power. It's the promise of male 'gold' that separates the women from each other; in the first instance, the daughter from the mother. Sexism creates the separation. Ruby is searching for her trauma, isn't she, and what she discovers in the theatre scene is the origin of the division from herself, through the division from her mother.

Now I think that really the way the men are handled is much more in the genre of comedy. I don't think it's accusatory or destructive stereotyping, really, and I've been interested to see men's response because many don't feel under attack. They feel only a sense of relief. For example, the relationship between the expert and the expert's assistant, I think, makes pretty clear how men oppress each other within the power structure ... you know, the ricochet effect. There's a sub-plot there that indicates how men keep each other in their place, and eventually that scene turns round expressionistically to the emptiness of the place that 'maleness' of that kind occupies – the emptiness and confusion of the man.

Then the men in the streets who do the following and pursuing never find the women, they never catch up. They keep losing them, like the Ealing comedy, bungling type of character, a reference to the well-trodden path of the suited man in black-and-white British movies. They're as much occupying a space of threat as being the threat. People say, 'Why are they so anonymous, these pursuers?' Well, every woman knows that pursuers are often anonymous. When you walk down the street you are pursued by an anonymous man – that is an everyday fact of sexism. And then, in another sense, the men in the film form part of the inner landscape of women too – internalised sexism – which we all know is more powerful than the real thing. As women, we are in a slight majority all over the world and could rise up right now and put an end to sexism forever. There's nothing holding us back, apart from our internal chains and, of course, the external structures, but they're peanuts compared to the inner voices. I'm not trying to say that sexism doesn't exist in the real world – what I'm saying is the men in the film occupy that interior space. At the end of the film, when the women decide they've had enough and all become Scarlett O'Hara tripping over the battlefield of the ballroom, then the men are left to face each other. This, to me, is about the politics of the men's movement. The men have to get up and dance with each other and, watching themselves, are embarrassed. The kernel of the situation is that men have to face each other and learn to love each other. Men are alienated from each other as nurturers, carers and dancers with each other and their peculiar emotional dependency on women is a fundamental facet of sexism.

PC Can you talk a bit about music in the film?

SP I'm sure Lindsay would have lots of interesting things to say about the music. We wanted to establish a primary relationship between image and music and not have too heavy a reliance on verbal text. Many films have music but you're not supposed to notice it, it's just supposed to colour your emotional experience of the film, without you quite knowing why. We wanted to foreground it more than that. So it's partly a musical in that sense, and there are various structural devices that relate to the musical: the interlude structure, the dream sequence, and the use of backstage scenes, the rehearsal genre.

PC I'm interested in the way costume is used in the film. Celeste and Ruby both adopt a variety of costumes in contrast to the men.

SP Ruby is the belle of the ball in diamonds, the silent screen actress with a head of blond curls, the icon on the plinth and the investigator in a raincoat watching all those other facets of her chameleon self. Celeste's costume changes are more subtle. She is the observer within the frame throughout. So the costume changes are about the theme of disguise and also a comment on acting. The actress is not the same as her part, she is playing a part, and a large part of that job consists of changing the way you look – it takes a great deal of skill. It's part of the hidden labour of the actress. Similarly, this comes into our daily lives. Women often spend a great deal of time choosing and coding the part we will play for the day, through our dress, and are constantly aware of those roles. Whether feminist or not, it doesn't make any difference, there's still that act of choosing going on. And it often needs a great deal of humour to prevent it becoming a very heavy issue. There are endless feminist cartoons about having to dress a certain way to be acceptable to men and then being blamed for being provocative. It's a no-win situation as far as dress goes. There is a self-mocking cartoon of a woman in a boiler suit saying, 'I've rejected all the stereotypes and now I'm my real self'. What we're saying is that where oppression denies a free choice, there is no such thing as a real self.

PC Why did you choose to use two central heroines in the way that you did? Do you see them as different from heroines in conventional fiction?

SP I think there's room for lots of different kinds of heroines and we're on the crest of a wave as women produce more and ask what form of heroism is appropriate to us. Part of what happens is that the territory of heroism undergoes a shift, so that, for example, the adventures of the unconscious become just as much an arena for heroic action as what's conventionally thought of as heroic space. I'm not putting forward an argument that heroines have got to occupy a completely personal space   I'm very bored with heroism in the kitchen.

PC Is it just male heroic roles that are available to us?

SP Well, I think this is where our politics come into it. First of all, we've got to get out of the way this idea that anything we want to do is denied us. Nothing less than everything will do. If we want to ride in on white chargers and carry off our favourite film star, we can do that. If we want to be welders, we can do that. If we want to disrupt Freemasonry ceremonies in the City of London, we can do that. These are images from the film, but really there aren't any limits for us in the territory that has already been conquered by men. However, we may wish to redefine our territory and may wish also to redefine our heroism. So we come into the area of fiction as it is lived and fiction as fiction. Obviously, a film is occupying fictive space. Nevertheless, that fictive space has formed and shaped our uncon scious and how we see ourselves, and therefore determines and reflects the way we live.

PC But what about the real social conditions which prevent women from doing what they want – becoming welders, for example? You seem to be suggesting that everything is equally available to us if we want to do it.

SP I said that is the correct point of view to take. The basis of every action is a dream or vision.

PC We have to want.

SP We have to want, yes, and know it's possible, otherwise we limit ourselves before we begin. In a sense, that's the language of our desire which is the first territory to reclaim, and that's why our heroism takes a different form. I'm not saying it's all in our heads, girls, we can go out and be welders any time we want. No. Women in manual trades know it's a real struggle and are organising around it. But as *Rosie the Riveter* showed, at different times in history it's not a matter of women's skill or lack of it, it's what the economic climate demands. In wartime, women welders were suddenly in hot demand. After the war they had to go back into the home. So it's not that objective circumstances don't block us, but that we have to assume that the external difficulties don't reflect our internal capacities and potential.

PC To a certain extent, you must be concerned with creating new women's fictional forms and a new women's cinema. Are conditions of production important to that? Using an all-woman crew, for instance?

SP It would have been ironic to make a film with this subject matter and then accept a completely conventional male-dominated crew. So, along the lines of women can be welders, women can also be gaffers, riggers, camerapersons and carpenters and so on.

It seemed important to make a double statement in that respect. You can separate the product and the process of making it, but women's struggles have always been to draw attention to that split, and to try and heal it.

PC Do you see yourself as producing women's cinema and, if you do see yourself in that way, do you think there are problems in that concept? That actually a women's cinema can be placed in a rather marginal way as belonging to women, the possession of women?

SP Even if I didn't see myself as producing women's cinema, other people would see me that way. Anyway, I'd want to occupy the position with pride. But I think there's another facet: as an artist, film-maker, or whatever, one is on some level essentially androgynous. I mean my identifications historically are with Hitchcock, Godard, Tati and other great male mentors, and the exceptions too, like Dorothy Arzner. But in cinematic history most of the filming has been done by men. I think of myself as a director and want that sense of colleagueship, of history and tradition. It gets dangerous to say that because you're a woman you haven't got a cultural history. That's not true, that history is ours, too.

PC There is already a tradition of women's cinema in Hollywood, the women's pictures, which were quite often scripted by women. Dorothy

142

Arzner directed a great many women's pictures, and Ida Lupino, when she went into directing, also used that form. There is a sense in which a new, independent women's cinema could follow in that kind of tradition, which is both a historical recognition of the importance of women as an audience and also a way of saying, this belongs to you and that's where it is, over there, in a separate space from cinema itself.

SP It's true that there is a history of remarkable female cinema. I keep discovering more and more of it. But still, we're in a tiny minority on the production side, compared to the vast female audience. So it becomes doubly important that we reclaim universality for our own and don't accept the position of outsiders.

PC You have said before in an interview in *Framework* that you were interested in reaching what you described as a mass audience, the kind of audience that would go to a Leicester Square cinema and see a film.[2] Do you think the notion of a mass audience is actually a viable one any more?

SP I've had to revise my thoughts slightly. I think the concept of 'breaking through' was an internal device to try and escape the internalised forms of marginalisation. I still haven't lost hope about Leicester Square! It's obviously a fantasy in terms of this film but, in other words, it's a desire to occupy a big screen space.

PC The Hollywood women's pictures did reach a mass audience; British independent feminist cinema doesn't yet occupy that space. Some feminist cinema is emerging, like the new German cinema, for instance, which occupies the kind of big screen space you were talking about but, in fact, it's distributed on an art circuit over here, with a specific kind of minority audience. There have been certain changes in the production and consumption of cinema in Britain recently, partly to do with the input of television and funding from TV, and I would speculate that there's a new kind of British cinema emerging which is an art cinema, with its own channels of distribution and exhibition: the culture slot on Channel 4, or in the independent film theatres, which is where your film is most likely to be shown. It is a big screen space, if you like, but addressed to a minority intellectual audience. I wonder how you feel about that?

SP You're probably right about where *The Gold Diggers* will be shown. Different levels of production automatically lead to different levels of consumption, so they're partly predetermined – the Leicester Square

Odeon will only ever really be filled by the modes of production designed for it.

PC On the other hand, films that are shown there can be pulled into different slots. For instance, a film like *Julia* can be used in a number of different feminist discussion situations, whereas the art cinema is very rarely pulled into a popular space.

SP I can't quite remember, but what I think I was talking about in that interview in 1981, was that inside every independent film-maker lurks this little fantasy self that is a 'real' moviemaker. (Also, women in particular often feel that what they do is not 'real' because once they get into it they discover it isn't what it was made out to be by men.) But British cinema is gradually achieving a realistic appraisal of its own identity and more of an acceptance, both of its heterogeneity and of its eclectic roots. For example, in my own case, I went to the Film Coop when I was 18 and loved Joyce Wieland's *Sailboat* and other minimalists; but I also loved the Marx Brothers, Godard, Eisenstein and *The Third Man*. So, in a way, it's about a reconciliation between those kinds of cinematic spaces. I think what I reject is the idea that independent cinema is inherently superior to, or better than, mass cinema; it has slightly shifty class implications.

PC The art-cinema circuit has traditionally drawn its audience on the basis of offering those kinds of rather elitist pleasures and has depended on the idea that it's serious as opposed to the popular cinema, which is entertainment. The way the new independent cinema, as I've characterised it, is marketed, distributed and exhibited, means that it will never be in a position to break down those divisions between the serious film and the entertainment film, because it's a precondition of its mode of existence that it asserts itself against the entertainment film.

SP But entertainment isn't inherently reactionary. In fact, pleasure is a prerequisite for learning. It's true, though, that a lot of mass cinema is very deeply tied into market forces. It is made to a formula to try and gross a lot of dollars, though some slip through which are also doing something else. Independent film isn't so tied to market forces, even though it may be meeting other kinds of cultural investment, and so it's free to deal with unprofitable subject matter and to experiment with form.

PC Yes, it can, but can it reach the audience you were saying you would like for your film?

SP What I'm saying is that I want to communicate, and mass cinema offers a vast, imaginary space in which to do that. But the ultimate value of a film is not whether six million people have seen it, but whether it worked in terms of what it set out to do. If its function is to say something really important to 200 people, then it has reached its own zenith when that is achieved. Independent film has opened out all those different levels of production that are possible, useful and desirable. However, as women, we're generally 'allowed' to make the smaller kind of women's issue documentary film – it's more difficult to work at the larger end of the scale. So then, part of my job as a woman film-maker is to break out of the ghetto. However, I then find that the big screen space is occupied in such a way that my position, my vision and my desire, which is necessarily a revolutionary desire, is not quite going to fit in. So, then, another way of looking at the reality is this: maybe independent production meets thousands, rather than millions, but we're overly apologetic and self-critical when it's more important positively to acknowledge the ways in which independent film has changed things – and, at the same time, continue to make that demand for a big voice.

(London, February, 1984)

Notes

1 Michel Foucault, *The Order of Things* (London: Tavistock, 1970), p. 173.
2 Valentina Agostinis, Interview with Sally Potter, *Framework* 14 (spring 1981).

Chapter 10

NO FIXED ADDRESS

The women's picture from *Outrage* to *Blue Steel*

The women's picture has played a major role in the development of feminist film criticism since the early 1980s – partly in response to a certain tendency in some 1970s feminist film theory to prioritise 'the male spectator', and partly as a strategic move to reassess a critically devalued and neglected genre. This debate, which has centred on questions of female spectatorial pleasure and address, has produced some remarkable textual analyses and trenchant critiques of the ways in which classical Hollywood cinema both represents and positions women, opening up issues such as narrative structure, masochism and consumerism. Despite the revisionist impulse motivating much of this work, it has tended to locate itself within a more general critique, inherited from 1970s film theory, which perceives classical Hollywood as inherently bourgeois and patriarchal, and therefore inimical to feminist interests. My own article, 'Melodrama and the women's picture', written in 1983, while attempting to account for the genre's popular appeal, betrays a deep suspicion of the whole idea of the women's picture.

> One question insists: why does the women's picture exist? There is no such thing as 'the men's picture', specifically addressed to men; there is only 'cinema', and 'the women's picture', a subgroup or category specially for women, excluding men; a separate, private space designed for more than half the population, relegating them to the margins of cinema proper. The existence of the women's picture both recognises the importance of women, and marginalises them. By constructing this different space for women (Haskell's 'wet, wasted afternoons'), it performs a vital function in society's ordering of sexual difference.[1]

There is more than a hint of conspiracy theory in this formulation, which implies that the category of the women's picture exists in order to dupe female spectators into believing that they are important, while subtly marginalising and disempowering them. This is an intellectual position that echoes through much feminist writing on the Hollywood women's picture. More recent work in the area of audience response has suggested that through identification with stars and emulation of their image, female spectators may feel empowered and act out that feeling in their everyday lives.[2] Although I still consider that feminist discussion of the women's picture has been enormously productive, I no longer believe that popular texts necessarily operate in the way I suggest in the above quote, that is, to marginalise and disempower female spectators. However, nor do I think that a simple reversal of that position, which looks at the women's picture in terms of the way it offers pleasures of female empowerment, gets us much closer to understanding the complexities of audience engagement with popular films.

My concern here will be to trace, selectively, some of the shifts that have occurred in the way that the women's picture has been discussed by feminist writers, in order to ask some preliminary questions about genre and gendered address. At the same time, I shall explore the differences and continuities between a specific manifestation of the classical woman's film and some postclassical developments, with the aim of assessing what, if anything, has changed in Hollywood cinema since the 1950s with respect to women film-makers and audiences. First, a couple of caveats. Since the relationship of the woman's film to classical Hollywood cinema is often uneasy, to say the least, it is somewhat misleading to refer to 'the classical women's picture'.[3] Moreover, if the transition to what is known as 'postclassical' or 'new' Hollywood can be seen as spanning the period between the 1948 Paramount decrees and the completion of divorcement at the end of the 1950s, then the 'classical' status of films produced in the late 1940s, and the designation of 1950s Hollywood cinema as 'postclassical', are clearly both problematic.

While recognising the difficulties inherent in the terms 'classical' and 'postclassical', particularly when used to impose definitive formal or temporal boundaries, I employ them here to indicate a process of transformation of the Hollywood industry and its products rather than a strict demarcation between two distinct phases of production. The Hollywood film industry, like any other, is always in the process of transition; indeed, it has been argued that since the classical studio system has been reorganised rather than dismantled, new Hollywood and its products are not that different from the old.[4] Nevertheless, the changes following the Second World War – such as the reorganisation of the studio system, the relaxation of censorship, the expansion of low-budget independent production, the trend towards high-concept block-busters, and the growth of new production and exhibition sites such as drive-in cinemas, theme parks, television and video – seem to have initiated a profound shift in the way cinema is produced and consumed.[5] One of the characteristics that quite clearly differentiates postclassical from classical cinema is the move towards greater visibility of sex and violence, and it is this development that partly concerns me here.

The dissolution of boundaries – between different modes of production such as television, video and cinema, and between different generic forms – has also been identified as a distinctive postclassical characteristic.[6] The permeability of boundaries is central to my discussion of genre and gendered address. Approaches to classical generic categories have traditionally assumed a gender-specific address. Thus the woman's film is perceived in terms of a primary address to female spectators, an assumption supported by reference to textual strategies such as narrative and *mise-en-scène*, to extratextual discourses such as promotional material and fan magazines and to historical evidence of industry policy. Though it is sometimes accepted that women's pictures are also addressed to male spectators, these are perceived as secondary audiences and have received little or no critical attention. Most other genres – even those such as musicals and musical comedies that do not appear to be clearly gender specific – are discussed in terms of their address to the ubiquitous male spectator. The western, the gangster movie or the horror film, which appear to feature central male protagonists and secondary female characters, are perceived as 'masculine' genres.

I do not need to labour the point that, with the exception of feminist work on melodrama and the woman's film, film studies has overwhelmingly privileged male spectatorship, and has thereby contributed to the consensus that cinema is primarily addressed, and belongs, to men. Yet while teaching a course on John Ford and the western recently, I was struck by the similarity of many classical western narratives – with their emphasis on circularity, digression and delay – to the structure of classical women's pictures. The choices facing the western hero, between love and duty, family life and a wanderer's existence are not that different from those encountered by women's picture heroines. In several of Ford's classical westerns, the expressive use of music and *mise-en-scène* to heighten emotional affect can only be described as melodramatic – indeed, I would suggest that a comparative analysis of *My Darling Clementine* (1944) and *Written on the Wind* (1956) would produce interesting results in terms of generic cross-fertilisation. It's interesting that, in his study of *Stagecoach* (1939), Edward Buscombe examines the way that the film was marketed using Claire Trevor's costume and hairstyle, one of the strategies employed in promoting women's pictures.[7]

Of course, the idea that genres are mixed is not new, nor am I the first, by any means, to suggest that we cannot make easy assumptions about genre and gendered address. Broadly speaking, in discussion of such issues, a tension can be discerned between approaches that identify a single, gender-specific mode of address, and those that posit multiple address, whether in terms of gender duality, or spreading the net more widely to include groups defined by class, race and ethnicity, age, and sexual preference. In what follows, I shall navigate a path through some of this writing, following a particular course. Since it is the increased visibility of sexual violence in the postclassical period that has inspired a number of critiques, feminist and otherwise, I shall look at a certain tendency in the woman's film that concerns itself with sexual violence. This route will take me from the 1940s Gothic-influenced paranoid woman's film analysed by Mary Ann Doane, via its transformation in 1950s family melodrama, 1970s and 1980s low budget rape revenge and 1990s sci-fi blockbusters.

In her introductory chapter to *The Desire to Desire*, Doane outlines the ways in which psychoanalytic film theory's account of the cinematic apparatus has overwhelmingly privileged male subjectivity. One of her reasons for choosing the 1940s cycle of woman's films was to open up questions of female subjectivity in one of the few genres to put a feminine sensibility at the centre. In contrast to the voyeurism and fetishism associated with the male spectator, Doane sees femininity in cinema defined in terms of masochism, paranoia and hysteria. As she says:

> These scenarios of female subjectivity have generally not been instrumental in delineating the cinematic apparatus. Nevertheless, they are fully compatible with the scenarios of the woman's film as a genre, particularly when they concern themselves with masochism. For in films addressed to women, spectatorial pleasure is often indissociable from pain.[8]

She proceeds to examine a number of woman's films for the ways in which they narrativise masochistic and/or paranoid scenarios – such as *Rebecca* (1940), *Possessed* (1947) and *Secret Beyond the Door* (1948) – in which the heroines' assumption of active investigative and heterosexually desiring roles is turned around on them to reveal and confirm their destiny as victims.

Doane claims that it is through such scenarios of victimisation and suffering that the 1940s woman's films address a specifically female spectator. She is careful to assert on numerous occasions that audience address and spectator positioning are not at all the same thing:

> Women spectators oscillate or alternate between masculine and feminine positions ... and men are capable of this alternation as well. This is simply to emphasise once again that feminine and masculine positions are not fully coincident with actual men and women.[9]

She goes on to qualify this statement:

> Nevertheless, men and women enter the movie theatre as social subjects who have been compelled to align themselves in some way with respect to one of the reigning binary oppositions (that of sexual difference) which order the social field. Men will be more likely to occupy the positions delineated as masculine, women those specified as feminine.[10]

It is the slippage between the first and the second proposition that interests me. It would surely have been as easy, and as convincing, to reverse the second assertion: social subjects who have been compelled to align themselves with binary oppositions of sexual difference are quite likely to occupy other, opposing positions in the movie theatre. But what is significant is that there is no evidence to support either proposition. While the oscillations or multiple identifications offered by fictional texts may be defended, in theory, by recourse to psychoanalysis, there is no way, beyond the anecdotal, of knowing what happens when real spectators enter the cinema. I shall return to the question of audience address, response and evidence later. For the moment, I want to stay with the relationship between actual spectators and the films they go to see.

In her overview of recent developments in theories of spectatorship, Judith Mayne takes issue with the way many film theorists have oversimplified identification in the cinema, in that they assume both that identification takes place between spectators and characters, and that spectators identify with those characters that correspond most directly with their own identity. She sees this assumption as contravening the psychoanalytical theories on which much of this work was based, which questions the very idea of stable identities:

> There is something too literal about a notion of identification whereby I, as a woman or a US citizen or a middle-class academic, necessarily and supposedly unproblematically 'identify' with whatever I see on screen that most approximates my identity ... Identification understood as a position — and more properly as a series of shifting positions — assumes that cinematic identification is as fragile and unstable as identity itself.[11]

Mayne discerns a shift in notions of identification that has taken place with the emergence of reception studies, which takes spectators rather than the cinematic institution as the point of departure. This shift has opened up a gap between what is perceived as the homogenising impulse of the institution and the potentially multiple, conflicting responses to it, and a space between address and reception. Thus the implied spectator positions offered by popular Hollywood texts are not necessarily inhabited by real audience members, who may experience such films in ways that go against the ideological grain. Later in her discussion, Mayne develops one of the implications of the idea of the gap between texts and spectators:

> Film theory has been so bound by the heterosexual symmetry that supposedly governs Hollywood cinema that it has ignored the possibility, for instance, that one of the distinct pleasures of the cinema may well be a 'safe zone' in which homosexual as well as heterosexual desires can be fantasised and acted out. I am not speaking here of an innate capacity to 'read against the grain', but rather of the way in which desire and pleasure in the cinema may well function to problematise the categories of heterosexual versus homosexual.[12]

One could take this suggestion further by arguing that, contrary to the claims made by much film theory that 'the cinematic institution' works to endorse and sustain dominant ideology, popular cinema problematises all social categories – of class, race and ethnicity, national identity, gender, sexuality, age and so forth. The invitation to the cinema is based on the promise that spectators may experience the thrill of reinventing themselves rather than simply having their social identities or positions bolstered.

Despite the loosening of the bonds between spectators and cinematic texts in revisionist film theory, the implications of this 'gap' or 'safety zone' idea have not generally been embraced with enthusiasm, presumably because it opens up a hornet's nest of further problems. It challenges a number of film theory's underlying assumptions. For example, by positing that popular cinema is more ideologically open, and processes of identification more fluid than has previously been imagined, it suggests that opportunities for resistance are more available than the opposition between 'dominant cinema' and 'counter cinema' would allow. And, of course, the proposition accepted by so much feminist film theory – that Hollywood cinema works to exclude, marginalise and victimise women, whether as fictional characters, filmmakers or spectators – is radically questioned by the idea that all spectators may redefine themselves in relation to the dominant social categories, not only in the darkened space of the cinema, but outside it too.

My feeling is that these cracks appearing in the surface of film theory are the result of a change in perception of popular cinema and its ideological operations. The self-fulfilling prophecy whereby women are perceived as the dupes and victims of a patriarchal Hollywood machine is gradually giving way to a more historical sense of the relationship of women to cinema, one which could reveal their role as more significant and central than has so far been argued. But this is jumping the gun. To follow the trajectory of this shift, I shall return to my discussion of Mary Ann Doane's work on the 1940s woman's film. Doane's account is particularly useful because it limits itself to specific overlapping categories accessible to psychoanalytical interpretation, such as maternal melodramas, films with physically or psychologically afflicted female characters, and the Gothic paranoid cycle. All of these, she argues, dramatise female emotional over-investment, the despecularisation of the female body (that is, the woman often the object of a curious rather than an erotic male gaze) and the textual difficulties inherent in putting female subjectivity at the centre of the narrative.

I do not wish to reduce Doane's analysis, which is impressively detailed and elaborate in its mobilisation of psychoanalytic theory. However, in the space available here I can only pick up on a few of her points. In particular, I'd like to explore her notion, outlined above, that the woman's film addresses female spectators as masochistic victims. While I do not deny the masochistic pleasures offered by the woman's film, Doane's assumption that these pleasures are gender specific seems too limited. Moreover, her adherence to a negative notion of female masochism, defined in terms of passive suffering, ignores the extent to which many of the films she discusses have as their backstories dramas of male masochism. That is, titles such as *Rebecca, Secret Beyond the Door, Jane Eyre* (1943) and even, perhaps, *Now Voyager* (1942) feature damaged male characters who in the past have been punished and/or abused by dominant, powerful women who continue to exert a hold over them. In these films, then, the hero is not the only sexual aggressor, and he is also a victim. Thus, in the course of the women's picture narrative the heroine confronts not only her own victimisation, but that of the hero as well (and sometimes that of subsidiary characters). In the Gothic-influenced films in particular, female pathology is matched and often outdone by male psychosis in a kind of overlapping of male and female desire.

There are two significant points here: one is that these multiple masochistic scenarios bear a striking resemblance to those identified by Carol J. Clover in *Men, Women and Chainsaws*, discussed on p. 157, as being at work in the modern American horror film, where psychologically damaged and sexually impaired men turn their aggression against female characters. There are, however, two major differences – the 1940s heroines do not usually turn the tables on their aggressors in the same way as their 1970s counterparts (indeed, they often end up in an uneasy and haunted couple relationship with them), and the sexual violence is implied in the 1940s cycle rather than graphically depicted.

The other point is that the multiplication of masochistic scenarios in the 1940s woman's films implies a dual address to male and female spectators. This suggests that we should look again at the widely accepted notion that the woman's film is primarily addressed to female spectators. For example, a notable feature of the 1940s films discussed by Doane is their deferral of gratification. The possibilities of happiness and fulfilment offered by heterosexual romance and marriage are constantly postponed by the failure of both male and female characters to resolve their Oedipal problems. The much vaunted textual openness of the melodramatic narrative can partly be put down to this playing out of masochistic scenarios of postponement and deferral. Needless to say, this problematising of heterosexual romance and deferral of consummation is not confined to melodrama and the women's picture, and the pleasures offered by such narratives are presumably available to all spectators.

I have lingered on Doane's analysis because her psychoanalytic textual approach illuminates the problems inherent in the idea of a woman's film dependent on a gender-specific address. In the 1940s films in question, not only is the female masochistic scenario reciprocated by that of the male, but the scene set by the Gothic paranoid films in particular is one of total victimisation in which everyone suffers. Gender boundaries are blurred by the reciprocation of the characters' fantasies. A theatrical space – usually in the localised arena of a large house – is opened up where both men and women act out fantasies of victimisation in which the roles of victim and aggressor are often interchangeable. If male and female characters are more alike than different in these films, it might make more sense to talk, in textual terms at least, of an ungendered address. As I suggested earlier, the appeal of such movies may lie precisely in the way they offer the lure of the abandonment of socialised gender and other positions. Another significant feature of the Gothic paranoid cycle is that the stories are highly localised and rarely look outside the family for the causes of psychosexual disturbance. The family and home are defamiliarised, serving as external projections of psychic trauma and pain. In 1950s melodrama, this defamiliarisation process, together with the scenarios of sexual violence and psychological damage, does not disappear. Rather, the personal takes on an added dimension, shifting on to social and national levels. I shall discuss Ida Lupino's *Outrage* (1950) as a key transitional film in this respect. For the moment, I want to return to questions of address.

Barbara Klinger's work on the studio promotion of 1950s family melodramas such as *Written on the Wind* offers historical evidence of address to audiences defined in gender terms. In a chapter titled 'Selling melodrama' in her book on Douglas Sirk, *Melodrama and Meaning*, Klinger takes issue with the idea put forward by 1970s film theorists that the melodramas directed by Sirk, Minnelli and Ray articulated a subversive critique of 1950s repressive, consumerist America, particularly through their visual style. Instead, she argues, the visual excess characteristic of these 'sophisticated' melodramas participated in and was sustained by ideological discourses of sexuality and affluence prevalent at the time. I do not have space to do justice to Klinger's argument about the place of 1950s melodrama in relation to what she terms 'the adult film'. I want to focus on her attempt to establish – through a contextual approach that examines the promotion, reception and other discourses surrounding the movies themselves – multiple, often conflicting forms of address, and a dual gendered address to spectators. For Klinger, the liberalisation of discourses around sexuality in the postwar period privileged heterosexuality at the expense of others, such as homosexuality and African-American sexuality, that were demarcated as deviant. In addition, the increase in explicit representations of sexual display was, she argues, often focused on the nude or scantily clad female body. Magazines such as *Playboy*, launched in 1953, were devoted to a philosophy of extramarital male sexual freedom, while exposé journals such as *Confidential*, directed at women readers, luridly revealed the private lives of celebrities in articles devoted to such questions as Robert Wagner's problems in the bedroom.[13]

The promotion of adult melodramas during this period mobilised both discourses – that of female sexual display directed at presumably heterosexual men and that of sexual scandal directed at women. It is interesting that Klinger also identifies a discourse of sexual violence against women in the promotional campaigns, associated with a double language that exploited the films' adult, sensational content as well as their serious, realistic approach. At the same time, advertising foregrounded spectacular *mise-en-scène* devoted to displays of affluence in order to appeal to the upwardly mobile aspirations of audiences, thus introducing a class address. Since women were key figures in the shift to a postwar consumer economy, these discourses, according to Klinger, were primarily addressed to them. Thus sexual display was not only a source of erotic fascination, it was intimately linked to acquisitiveness. The images of sexual and material excess in 1950s melodramas were, in Klinger's account, embroiled in current strategies of capitalism and patriarchy, and there is reason to suppose that audiences would enter the cinema expecting to enjoy them in voyeuristic and consumerist terms.

Klinger's analysis of the promotional discourses employed by Universal suggests that both generic identity and audience address must be considered historically rather than via the attribution of transcendental, unchanging formal characteristics. It also implies that ideological meanings cannot be accounted for simply by authorial intention. However, Klinger is not concerned with displacing an authorial interpretation only to replace it with another, institutional one:

> Examples of social readings like those geared towards voyeurism and consumption are particularly important to consider in relation to assessments of the film/ideology relationship. They do not necessarily produce a unified text with a coherent ideology, but suggest that institutional and social forces can act to produce a heterogeneous text offering a variety of viewing pleasures grounded in various kinds of social ideologies – to its audience.
>
> From such a perspective, we cannot consider the family melodrama of the 1950s as necessarily subversive to the repressive regimes of the decade. Rather ... such films often helped realise the heightened sexual depictions and affluent ideologies that marked the culture.[14]

Convincing though Klinger's argument about multiple address in the studio's promotional material for *Written on the Wind* is, her assertion that 1950s audiences may have enjoyed the adult melodramas in the terms set up by the surrounding discourses without 'getting' the subversive critique of US society is on the level of speculation. Her contextual approach suggests that the potential shifts of identity offered by multiple modes of address are consonant with marketing strategies that tie spectators in to prevailing ideologies of consumerism, sexuality and class rather than loosen ideological and social bonds – but in the absence of historical evidence of audience response, the question of what actually happened to spectators in the cinema remains obscure. Nevertheless, her investigation does make it clear that although the 1950s melodramas, like the 1940s woman's films, were addressed to women, they were certainly not just addressed to women, nor were women the primary audience addressed in all cases.

Klinger's emphasis on the conflicting discourses in play during the 1950s, and her identification of multiple modes of address in and around the adult melodramas, usefully provides the context for *Outrage* (1950), directed and co-scripted by Ida Lupino – a film that occupies an interesting position in relation to the transformation of Hollywood industry at this time, and to the big-studio, sophisticated melodramas that have dominated discussion. It was independently produced for RKO by The Filmakers, a company formed by Ida Lupino and Collier Young in the wake of the dissolution of the contract system which tied stars to specific studios. Many other stars took the same route during this period. As producer–writer–director, and occasionally actress too, Lupino can be seen as an early example of the hyphenate phenomenon characteristic of modern Hollywood. *Outrage* is typical of the low-budget, black-and-white social-issue melodramas produced by The Filmakers company in the 1950s. Its story, which deals with the traumatic rape of a young woman by a psychologically damaged war veteran, quite clearly participates in liberal discourses prevalent at the time – for example, in the social message delivered by minister Bruce Ferguson to the court about the need for compassion towards all of society's victims. Many of the The Filmakers' films contained similar scenes of liberal pleading.

In the space it gives to the perspectives of different characters, *Outrage* is a particularly good example of multiple, conflicting textual address. Indeed, this multiplicity tends to obliterate the predicament of the rape victim, which has proved difficult for some present-day viewers expecting a recognisable feminist agenda. It is not my intention to rehabilitate *Outrage* as a feminist text. In fact, as I have argued elsewhere, I believe the film's resistance to present-day feminist analysis to be a strength, since it demands to be seen in historical context.[15] It is worth noting in this respect that at the time of their release in the UK, The Filmmakers' films were often praised by critics for their feminist take on social issues relevant to women. Lupino herself was a key factor in both promotion and reception.

In the context of my present discussion what interests me about *Outrage* is its symptomatic status. It occupies a position between different production contexts and between genres. It is a hybrid: part studio production (evident in the early city scenes, shot in noir style), part documentary (the exterior California sequences and the sections featuring the orange ranch); a mix of film noir, melodrama, social problem movie, teen pic and exploitation movie. Its emphasis on sexual violence and its relentless victimisation scenario, in which almost everyone is perceived as damaged in some way, recall the 1940s Gothic paranoid cycle, while its comparatively explicit depiction of the causes and consequences of rape looks forward to later adult melodramas. The narrative structure of flight and pursuit prefigures 1960s serial television narratives such as *The Fugitive* (1963–64), for which Lupino directed three episodes, while the postwar rehabilitation theme emulates bigger-budget postwar reconstruction movies such as *The Best Years of Our Lives* (1946), also independently produced for RKO. Thus, in looking backwards and forwards at the same time, *Outrage* appears to occupy a place on the boundary between classicism and postclassicism itself. Indeed, it seems to embody the fluctuating, unsettled nature of that boundary.

Outrage is also partly a rape-revenge story, though the revenge element is somewhat obscured by the narrative drive to pathologise the rape victim. As already remarked, its representation of sexual violence is relatively explicit when compared to the 1940s woman's films, and it belongs with the 1950s adult melodramas in this respect. But it can also be linked to low-budget exploitation movies, and to 1970s and 1980s rape-revenge, not least in the way it connects the personal trauma of sexual assault with wider moral and social issues. However, in the twenty or so years separating Lupino's rape movie from its 1970s sisters, quite a lot happened. Most obviously, in *Outrage* the rape discreetly takes place off-screen, while in 1970s rape-revenge the brutality of rape and sexual assault is represented in graphic detail, albeit mostly from the point of view of the victims rather than the perpetrators. Rape-revenge is usually associated with the modern American horror film rather than with melodrama, though we would do well to remember the Gothic roots of both – we are back in the realms of generic inbreeding.

Arguably, it is in postclassical horror and associated cycles such as slasher films and rape-revenge that sensationalised displays of sexual violence reach their apotheosis, a factor that has provoked critiques from a number of directions. Many of these antagonistic responses, feminist and otherwise, have focused on the *visibility* of sexual violence, claiming that such spectacularisation is both morally offensive and socially undesirable, in so far as it panders to sadistic, voyeuristic male fantasies. In her chapter on rape-revenge in *Men, Women and Chainsaws*, Carol J. Clover challenges this received wisdom, arguing that the focus of such films on the perspective of the female victim-turned-avenger may actually place viewers in a masochistic position – doubly so, in that they are invited to identify not only with the rape victim, but also with her male victims as she goes about killing, maiming and castrating those who have harmed her. Clover detects a shift – which she suggests may have something to do with the influence of 1970s feminism – from the male-centred rape films of the early 1970s such as *Straw Dogs* (1971) and *Frenzy* (1972), in which spectators are encouraged to collude with the rapist's sadism, to female-centred rape-revenge films such as *I Spit on Your Grave* (1977) and *Ms .45* (1980), where the female rape victim's perspective, and her quest for bloody revenge in kind, move to centre-stage:

> Ironically, it may be the feminist account of rape in the last two decades that has both authorised a film like *I Spit on Your Grave* and has shaped its politics. The redefinition of rape as an offence on a par with murder, together with the well-publicised testimonials on the part of terrified and angry victims, must be centrally

157

responsible for lodging rape as a crime deserving of the level of punishment on which revenge narratives are predicated.[16]

A similar argument is made by Linda Williams in *Hard Core* about changes in the depiction of rape in pornography in the early 1980s. Williams claims that due to a number of factors, including the heightened acceptance of the feminist critique of male sexual violence, enjoyment of rape scenarios became increasingly unacceptable in an industry trying to expand its viewership.[17] It is interesting in this respect that the mainstream blockbuster *Basic Instinct* (1992) – that least politically correct of films – contains a rape scene presented as 'bad sex', which, although its focus is on the psychologically disturbed Nick Curran character, also registers the pain and anger of the rape victim, albeit rather weakly. Clover seems to regard the rape-revenge cycle as an appropriation of, rather than an active engagement with, feminist politics. Despite the gender implications of her arguments about feminist influence and the female victim heroes and final girl survivors, and her problematisation of male spectatorial pleasure, she adheres to the commonly held opinion that viewers of low-budget horror are predominantly young men, and considers that the films are addressed to them, though she offers very little hard evidence in support of her claim. In her brief discussion of horror audiences at the beginning of her book, she glosses over the question of privatised video viewing and the lack of reliable statistics for the composition of horror film audiences in favour of the accepted notion of the younger male as 'majority viewer'.[18] Yet, as with the woman's film, the masochistic scenarios she identifies are surely not so gender specific in their address as her argument suggests. Nor should the greater visibility of young men as horror viewers lead us to assume that they are always the genre's primary audience.

Evidence that audiences for horror are not confined to men is offered by Linda Williams in an article about the exhibition context of *Psycho* (1960). The article includes frame stills from a cinema managers' training film that show a line of ticket holders waiting outside the DeMille Theatre in New York for a matinee screening. They are all women, mostly middle-aged. Other photographs taken with infrared cameras during a screening at the Plaza in London show audience members, men and women, reacting to what they see and hear. Williams interprets these images as performative responses to the unresolved gender disturbances at the heart of *Psycho*, suggesting that some gender destabilisation took place in the cinema audience as well as on screen. From the photographs it appears that some women were adopting contained, stoical ways of looking associated with masculinity, while some men reacted with anxious gestures closer to the histrionic performance of fear associated with femininity. Taken at the time of viewing, these photographs are perhaps the most convincing evidence so far of the potential fluidity of gender identification among the cinema audience, and of the cinema experience as offering a 'safe zone' for the enjoyment of such adventures in masquerade.

I find the notion of the performative nature of the viewing process explored by Williams intriguing. She links the gender performance in the film (Norman Bates' masquerade as his mother) with what takes place in the movie theatre, arguing that the exaggerated poses adopted by audience members suggest 'a pleasurable and self-conscious performance'.[19] Although Williams considers that such performative responses were initiated by *Psycho*, which she sees as inaugurating the 'thrill-producing visual "attractions" that would become fundamental to the New Hollywood',[20] some of the arguments that I have considered so far imply that this destabilisation of gender and other social categories in the cinema is more common than we are prepared to admit, and cannot be limited to a classical/postclassical division. Nor, I would suggest, can the performative response be limited to what takes place in the movie theatre itself, since people may adopt disguises outside the cinema too. I have discussed elsewhere a particular example of gender masquerade in the critical reception of Scorsese's *Cape Fear* (1991), in which some male writers reacted to the film's disturbing gender reversals by adopting the mantle of femininity.[21] This clearly has implications for studies of audience response that rely on the evidence of people recalling their experiences.

We should be wary of identifying a single film as a historical benchmark, and many of the elements identified by Williams as specific to the *Psycho* experience can be found earlier, in 1950s Hollywood cinema. Nevertheless, in some ways, *Psycho*, like *Outrage* ten years before, does seem to stand at a frontier of cinema history. In the shower sequence, Hitchcock created, through editing and sound, an illusion of graphic sexual violence. In fact, the audience had seen very little. Even so, a border had been crossed. Nudity and graphic sex and violence became more visible. This situation intensified with the move of low-budget exploitation into the mainstream as the major studios began to penetrate new markets in the 1970s and 1980s, and with the expanded availability of video. As I have already mentioned, the increased visibility of sex and violence in postclassical Hollywood cinema has been the subject of extensive feminist critique. The graphic representation of rape and sexual assault against women in exploitation genres has been vociferously contested by those concerned that such scenarios perpetuate misogynist attitudes and encourage men to perform real acts of sexual abuse. As we have seen, such critiques have had a powerful effect on what it is considered permissible to show.[22]

In the wake of such critiques, to an extent, the representation of rape and the viewing of such representations have become associated with the act of

159

rape itself. Those who enjoy watching sexual violence on screen, particularly in its 'low' manifestations, are highly suspect. If they are men, they are potential rapists, if they are women, they are potential rape victims. The revisionist work by feminist critics such as Clover on low-budget horror and Williams on pornography has demonstrated that the situation is more complex. The gender reversals characteristic of these 'low' genres allow for the empowerment of female victims and the disempowerment of male aggressors. Although we still cannot be absolutely sure what is taking place here, particularly with the proliferation of exhibition sites, the potential for multiple, shifting identifications seems to be there. It is important to note, of course, that this fluid situation is not necessarily in the interests of feminism. It is interesting, for example, that *Disclosure* (1994), in which a happily married businessman, played by Michael Douglas, is 'raped' by his female boss (Demi Moore), reverses the pattern of female victim/male aggressor in what can only be construed as a highly anxious response to the power of women in the workplace. However, it should also be pointed out that the film highlights with startling clarity the fact that its motivating fantasy of sexual submission and dominance is not gender specific.

This brings me back to genre and audience address – in the light of the above discussion, the assumption that genres employ a single gender address can no longer be taken for granted. Nor can the potentially fluid situation of multiple address and plural identifications at work in popular cinema be associated simply with postclassical Hollywood. By the same token, the idea that certain genres are, or ever have been, more 'suitable' for women as either viewers or as film-makers has come under pressure. This is Kathryn Bigelow, quoted in Jim Hillier's book *The New Hollywood*:

> Conventionally, hardware pictures, action oriented, have been male dominated, and more emotional material has been women's domain. That's breaking down. This notion that there's a women's aesthetic, a woman's eye, is really debilitating. It ghettoises women. The fact that so many women are working as directors now ... across the spectrum, from comedy to horror to action ... is incredibly positive ... You're asking the [Hollywood] community to reprogramme their thinking.[23]

Bigelow perhaps overestimates the numbers of women directors who have moved into contemporary Hollywood, and it is well known that those who have made that difficult transition rarely make the 'A' list. Without diminishing the real problems faced by women working in Hollywood, it is possible to argue that the focus on marginalisation and exclusion that has preoccupied

Figure 10.1   In a man's world: Jamie Lee Curtis in *Blue Steel* (1990). Courtesy Lightning Pictures/Joel Warren and the Kobal Collection.

feminist criticism since the 1970s needs to be rethought, and the historical contribution of women to cinema across the board recognised. This involves a shift in perception – away from counting the relatively small numbers of female directors towards a more historical and contextual analysis of different points of entry into the industry by women, in what is, after all, a collaborative medium. The influence of female audiences, and the considerable impact of feminism – or should I say feminisms – across the full range of production have scarcely begun to be addressed.

It is tempting to conclude, as Bigelow seems to suggest in the quotation on p. 160, that the postclassical period has seen an opening up of opportunities for women film-makers. Although there is an absence of statistical information, one nevertheless gets a sense of the presence of women in all aspects of the production process – as stars, producers, directors, technical and creative personnel – and in all genres. Bigelow herself is a high-profile example of a crossover phenomenon – a woman director who works with traditionally male action genres, who collaborates with male film-makers and whose work cannot easily be assimilated in gender terms. Her films *Near Dark* (1987) and *Blue Steel* (1990), both generic hybrids, confront head-on difficult questions of violence and sexuality, while the bigger-budget *Point Break* (1991) and *Strange*

Days (1995) both handle the technical problems of blockbuster action film-making with masterly style and verve.

Like Ida Lupino almost fifty years before, Bigelow is a writer and producer as well as director, and interesting comparisons could be drawn between their production contexts and their work, particularly between Lupino's rape film *Outrage* and Bigelow's cop movie *Blue Steel*, which includes a rape-revenge scenario. Such a comparison might suggest that the conjunction of post-1970s feminism and the entry of women film-makers at all levels of the industry with the greater visibility of graphic sex and violence, deplored by many, has had some beneficial effects for women, in that it has allowed feminism to move into a wider arena. Women film-makers can, it seems, now use sexually explicit and violent material to confront issues of representation before much larger audiences.

It also appears as though the concerns of the paranoid woman's film have moved from the localised, domestic arena they occupied in the 1940s on to the global stage in the 1980s and 1990s. It is interesting to note, for example, that in the *Alien* series of films, a paranoid woman saves the world, while in *Terminator 2: Judgment Day* (1993) a paranoid woman changes the course of history. Thus the question raised in my 1983 article, echoed in Kathryn Bigelow's comments on p. 160, about the ghettoising effect of a woman's film defined in terms of an exclusive address to female spectators, appears to have come full circle, and to have been answered, at least partially, by the increased gender fluidity and genre hybridity characteristic of the New Hollywood. However, I do not think we can make any assumptions about 'progress', in feminist terms at least, based on a classical/postclassical divide.

If it is true that there are greater numbers of women working in contemporary Hollywood, the nature of the impact of the presence of women as producers, directors and writers remains unclear. How, for feminist purposes, do we weigh up the value of Jonathan Demme's feminist-influenced *The Silence of the Lambs* (1990) against Kathryn Bigelow's *Strange Days*? Is it the case, perhaps, that female audiences have at times exerted greater control over Hollywood production than those working inside the industry? As I have already suggested, only a historical investigation of the contribution of women to all aspects of cinema can assess the significance or otherwise of that contribution at specific conjunctures.[24] I would anticipate that such an investigation will produce a more complex map of the role of women in Hollywood cinema than models defined by exclusion and marginalisation. After all, the conclusions we draw from historical enquiry and evidence depend to some extent on what we are looking for in the first place. The agendas and methodologies adopted by historians are just as much subject to social and cultural forces as the objects chosen for study.

Notes

1 Chapter 5 of this volume, p. 77.
2 See, for example, Jackie Stacey's study of the interaction of female audiences with star figures in *Star Gazing: Hollywood Cinema and Female Spectatorship* (London and New York: Routledge, 1994).
3 In *The Desire to Desire: The Woman's Film of the 1940s* (Basingstoke: Macmillan, 1987), Mary Ann Doane identifies an ironic approach to classical Hollywood narrative conventions as a characteristic of women's pictures.
4 See David Bordwell and Janet Staiger, 'Since 1960: the persistence of a mode of film practice', in D. Bordwell, J. Staiger and K. Thompson, *The Classical Hollywood Cinema: Film Style and Mode of Production to 1960* (New York: Columbia University Press, 1985).
5 An argument put forward by, for example, Jim Collins, 'Genericity in the nineties: eclectic irony and the new sincerity', in J. Collins, H. Radner and A. Preacher Collins (eds), *Film Theory Goes to the Movies* (New York: Routledge, 1993).
6 See Timothy Corrigan, *A Cinema Without Walls: Movies and Culture After Vietnam* (New York: Routledge, 1991).
7 Edward Buscombe, *Stagecoach* (London: BFI Publishing, 1993).
8 Doane, *The Desire to Desire*, p. 16.
9 Doane, *The Desire to Desire*, p. 8.
10 Doane, *The Desire to Desire*, p. 8.
11 Judith Mayne, *Cinema and Spectatorship* (New York and London: Routledge, 1993), p. 27.
12 Mayne, *Cinema and Spectatorship*, p. 97.
13 Barbara Klinger, *Melodrama and Meaning: History, Culture and the Films of Douglas Sirk* (Bloomington and Indianapolis: Indiana University Press, 1994), p. 54.
14 Klinger, *Melodrama and Meaning*, p. 68.
15 Pam Cook, 'Outrage', in A. Kuhn (ed.), *Queen of the 'B's: Ida Lupino Behind the Camera* (London: Flicks Books, 1995).
16 Carol J. Clover, *Men, Women and Chainsaws: Gender in the Modern Horror Film* (London: BFI Publishing, 1992), p. 153.
17 Linda Williams, *Hard Core: Power Pleasure and the 'Frenzy of the Visible'* (London: Pandora, 1991), p. 166.
18 Clover, *Men, Women and Chainsaws*, pp. 6–7.
19 Linda Williams, 'Learning to scream', *Sight and Sound* (NS) 4(12) (December 1994), p. 17.
20 Williams, 'Learning to scream', p. 17.
21 Pam Cook, '*Cape Fear* and femininity as destructive power', in P. Cook and P. Dodd (eds), *Women and Film: A Sight and Sound Reader* (London: Scarlet Press, 1993).
22 I am referring here to approaches to representation inspired by, for example, Catharine MacKinnon and Andrea Dworkin's radical feminist critique of pornography, cited by Linda Williams in *Hard Core*, pp. 17–18.
23 Jim Hillier, *The New Hollywood* (London: Studio Vista, 1993), p. 127.

24 This work has already begun – see, for example, Lizzie Francke, *Script Girls: Women Screenwriters in Hollywood* (London: BFI Publishing, 1994); Stacey, *Star Gazing*; and Miriam Hansen on Rudolph Valentino and female audiences in *Babel and Babylon: Spectatorship in American Silent Film* (Cambridge: Harvard University Press, 1991).

Martin Scorsese and postclassical nostalgia

INTRODUCTION

Martin Scorsese is a key figure in postclassical, or New, Hollywood. One of a new breed of 'movie brats' who emerged in the 1970s, he made intensely personal, aesthetically adventurous films which established him as one of the most significant and controversial directors of his generation. The movie brats included names such as Francis Ford Coppola, Paul Schrader, Michael Cimino and Brian De Palma, all like Scorsese influenced by European and world art cinema as well as classical Hollywood. Their films were peppered with references to cinema history, part homage to the work of the great auteurs they admired, and part iconoclastic attempt to rewrite the past, to produce new and exciting cinematic forms. In Scorsese's case, his work was consciously, though not necessarily directly, autobiographical, reflecting his obsessions and his Italian-American background, as well as his individual tastes. His dedication to personal film-making and refusal to compromise his ideas have gained him a reputation as one of the major auteurs of contemporary American cinema. He occupies an interesting, and sometimes uncomfortable, position both inside and outside Hollywood production, a situation which seems to mirror the way he views himself as a New York Italian-American – part of American culture, yet not assimilated within it. This fractured perspective results in a conflict between nostalgia for the idealistic aspirations of the American Dream, and despair at the unattainability of those ideals in the immigrant communities.

Scorsese's brand of personal, intellectual cinema emerged from a specific set of circumstances associated with Hollywood cinema following the reorganisation of the studio system after the Second World War, among them the growth of low-budget, independent production; the relaxation of censorship leading to controversial subject matter and graphic depictions of sex and violence; the influx of art movies and 'adult' films from continental Europe; the proliferation of new production and exhibition sites such as film festivals,

167

drive-in cinemas, television and video; and the rise of film schools giving birth to graduates proficient not only in film-making techniques but armed with knowledge of cinema history. As Hollywood struggled to gain new audiences, many of whom were increasingly cine-literate themselves, the stylish and sophisticated efforts of these film-school graduates played an important role in niche marketing to younger cinemagoers. Although schooled in classical Hollywood film-making, they took their inspiration from European and other cinemas, producing work that broke with classical principles of narrative coherence and closure, and harmony and unity of form, in favour of more allusive, elliptical and attenuated styles characterised by irony and ambiguity. There has been much debate about just how 'new' the New Hollywood was in relation to the old. Some have argued that the reorganisation of the old studio system left many of its modes of production and technologies relatively intact, with the result that the aesthetic principles of classical Hollywood were not radically transformed. For others, the changes in production, distribution and exhibition in the age of global electronic media have had profound effects on the way cinema is produced and consumed. In a way, the term 'postclassical' is best seen as encapsulating a state of transition rather than a clear boundary between old and new. It seems to imply a state of ambivalence: a nostalgic yearning for a lost innocence (manifested by the habit of quoting from 'classical' cinema) accompanied by an equal and opposite desire for freedom from classical constraints (evidenced by the use of non-classical forms, such as episodic, meandering narratives and a primary emphasis on the image).

It has been argued that the ambiguity characteristic of postclassical cinema is akin to the ironic stance of postmodernism, which is said to breed a cynical distance. In this respect, the allusions to classical cinema are seen to address a knowing audience who take pleasure in games of memory and recognition. Yet the games are often accompanied by a palpable sense of loss, producing an affective response that tends to be overlooked. The fusion of past and present in postclassical cinema, accompanied by the breakdown of classical linear narrative codes, creates a sense of the inevitability of the passage of time that is both celebrated and mourned. In Scorsese's case, the loss of the past is given a tragic dimension, as his flawed, alienated heroes, trapped by history, struggle to establish and maintain their identity. Scorsese's anxiety about the erosion of the past takes many forms: he makes sure that his own work is preserved in his personal archive, and one of his reasons for shooting his boxing film *Raging Bull* (1980) in black and white, besides as a tribute to Warner Bros films of the 1940s, was as a protest against the deterioration of colour values. But perhaps the most powerful and significant deployment of nostalgia is connected to his depiction of Italian-American male characters, focused on their disturbed psyche and deviant heterosexual masculinity. These anti-heroes are symptoms of the failure of the American Dream, which they act out in their lives. Their search for redemption is characterised by extreme violence, both physical and verbal, as they turn their anger, frustration and sense of betrayal against the world, frequently misdirecting it towards those they love, but cannot trust. Scorsese often uses traditional genres such as the gangster film, reworking them to produce modern versions in which the violence kept off-screen in classical Hollywood is portrayed in graphic detail, through a form of stylised, heightened realism that brings the audience very close to the action, encouraging them to share the pain and anguish of the characters. Rather than create an ironic distance, Scorsese sets out to forge emotional identification with tragic characters who are sociopaths, victims of a culture that has both seduced and rejected them. His use of cultural references may have an ironic dimension related to this sense of failure, but it is primarily a device for expressing emotion and achieving an affective response. Irony does not necessarily exclude such a response; indeed, there is no reason why irony and emotion should not co-exist.

The greater visibility of sex and violence in postclassical Hollywood has been a problem for many, who deplore what they perceive as gratuitous spectacle pandering to the lowest sadistic impulses of the audience. Some feminist critics have protested against increasingly graphic portrayals of sexual violence against women, which they fear will lead some male viewers to carry out real acts of violent abuse outside the cinema. Scorsese's films generally contain a high degree of graphic violence, directed at both men and women, which certainly lays them open to such criticism. Yet the explicit violence in his films is rarely gratuitous. Rather, it is presented as the direct result of a social system that uses violence to maintain corrupt hierarchies and power relations which destroy human aspirations and ideals. It is also a kind of inchoate expression of anger at forces of oppression, providing an outlet for justifiable anger against social abuse. In Scorsese's world, violence is self-destructive. It spirals out of control, playing an integral part in the tragic downfall of his characters. But it can also be a force of redemption, as through violence they learn something about their place in the world. Scorsese's anti-heroes often rediscover their lost innocence through suffering, which, coupled with those strategies outlined above that invite audience identification with them, could be seen as a way of excusing their violent behaviour, and releasing them from responsibility for their actions. At the same time, the infantilisation of these macho characters raises complex questions of masculinity, power and identification. Scorsese's work may be difficult to come to terms with, particularly when it comes to sexual politics, but the challenges it presents have been central to debates about gender and representation in contemporary cinema.

The articles in this section engage with these issues of memory, nostalgia and masculinity in Scorsese's films, navigating a path between the aesthetic and emotional pleasures they offer and their apparent disregard for contemporary sexual politics. The essays try to steer clear of a puritanical rejection of problematic images of sexual violence – indeed, they argue that it is precisely the use of such images that has enabled Scorsese to expose the darker aspects of modern heterosexual masculinity, and to challenge gender boundaries. At the same time, the misogynist aspects of his work, and his inability to move beyond a male-centred perspective (albeit consciously damaged and flawed), come under interrogation as symptomatic responses to postfeminism and its perceived impact on male–female power relations. The first piece on *Raging Bull*, 'Masculinity in crisis?' (1982), reflected current debates about the deconstruction of masculinity and the pleasure offered to female viewers by images of passive, emasculated men who were, in a sense, feminised by being portrayed as disempowered, a position traditionally reserved for women. With their bodies put on display, such characters were the object of an erotic gaze which was not specific to either gender, suggesting that identification in cinema may be more fluid and unpredictable than previously thought – a situation that challenged the assumptions about gender on which much film theory depended.

Raging Bull is a profoundly nostalgic film. As already noted, it was made in black and white as a tribute to classic Hollywood, but also as a protest against the deterioration of colour values. It is replete with visual and aural references to cinema history, drawing the audience in to the pleasures of remembrance, while also using a punchy, visceral style to suggest the experience of 'being there', inside the time and place the film reconstructs. Crucially, there are more reflective sequences, which keep the audience at a distance, creating the impression of being inside and outside history at the same time, and reinforcing the sense of loss of the past. Perhaps the film's most nostalgic element is its depiction of its brutal and brutalised hero, boxer Jake La Motta, whose rise to fame is accomplished at the expense of family and loved ones, and who ends up losing everything. In his final, faltering attempts at reconciliation, he regains some humanity through glimmers of self-realisation.

Raging Bull has a minimal storyline, and is held together by its network of allusions. It is more like a moving photograph album than a conventional biopic, touching only briefly on the facts of Jake La Motta's life and social history. It depends on digression and delay, and on extended sequences in which contemplation of poetic images, or of virtuoso performances on the part of the actors, appears to be an end in itself. Such attenuated narratives, in which meaning is elusive, are characteristic of postclassical cinema, but they are also typical of Scorsese's style, and his attachment to an aesthetic that could be described as masochistic, in contrast to the more goal-oriented narratives identified with classical Hollywood cinema. If masochism depends on enjoyment of pain and the deferral of pleasure, then many of Scorsese's films fit the bill. In movies such as *Raging Bull* and *Cape Fear* (1992), the audience suffers assault on the visual and auditory nerves, and also struggles to interpret meaning, at the mercy of digressive narrative structures. The masochistic central characters of *Raging Bull* and *The Last Temptation of Christ* (1988) have much in common: both are psychologically damaged, addicted to pain and suffering, and ambivalent about heterosexual desire and union, tendencies that form a central aspect of their rebellion against normal society. There are similarities here with Newland Archer, the hero of *The Age of Innocence* (1993), who is unable to break with the past and marry the woman he loves, and perversely seems to prefer to remain in a state of perpetual deferral of desire. These are all characters who resist the processes of socialisation, choosing to mourn what they have lost rather than move forward. They are not conventional, nor necessarily sympathetic rebel heroes, but they are complex figures through whom Scorsese is able to project a searching and occasionally revolutionary exploration of the construction of masculinity in contemporary cinema and society.

Further reading

Christie, Ian and Thompson, David (eds), *Scorsese on Scorsese* (London: Faber and Faber, 1990).

Cook, Pam and Dodd, Philip (eds), *Women and Film: A Sight and Sound Reader* (London: Scarlet Press, 1993).

Kellman, Steven G. (ed.), *Perspectives on Raging Bull* (New York: G.K.Hall, 1994).

Kelly, Mary Pat, *Martin Scorsese: The First Decade* (New York: Redgrave Publishing Company, 1980).

Neale, Steve and Smith, Murray (eds), *Contemporary Hollywood Cinema* (London and New York: Routledge, 1998).

Nicholls, Mark, *Scorsese's Men: Melancholia and the Mob* (Melbourne: Pluto Press, 2004).

Pye, Michael and Myles, Linda, *The Movie Brats: How the Film Generation Took Over Hollywood* (London: Holt, Rinehart and Winston, 1984).

Sangster, Jim, *Scorsese* (London: Virgin Publishing, 2002).

Stern, Lesley, *The Scorsese Connection* (Bloomington: Indiana University Press, 1996).

Taubin, Amy, *Taxi Driver* (London: BFI Modern Classics, 2000).

PART FOUR

Further viewing

The Age of Innocence (Martin Scorsese, USA, 1993)
Cape Fear (Martin Scorsese, USA, 1992)
The Last Temptation of Christ (Martin Scorsese, USA/Canada, 1988)
Raging Bull (Martin Scorsese, USA, 1980)
Taxi Driver (Martin Scorsese, USA, 1976)

Chapter 11

MASCULINITY IN CRISIS?
Tragedy and identification in *Raging Bull*

A great deal has been written about *Raging Bull*. It has found a place as one of the classics of New Hollywood cinema, and if that sounds like a contradiction in terms, we have only to think of the number of films in Hollywood's 'New Wave' that consciously trade on their own past, calling up classic Hollywood's golden moments as a way of getting us into the cinema; no mean feat, these days. With the traditional system of production, distribution and exhibition of films in rapid decline, nostalgia and anxiety about the past from New Hollywood is understandable, though not inevitable. Looking back is fundamental to *Raging Bull*, and to the disturbing pleasures it offers. The decline and fall of its hero, Jake La Motta, provide a pretext for the playing out of a number of anxieties about the irrecoverability of the past. His collapse into impotence is the mainspring of a scenario that evokes profound loss: loss of a great classic cinema, of community values, of family life, of individual energy ... A tragic scenario in which the hero's suffering teaches us something about our own life, and how to accept its terms.

My own cinéphiliac obsession with the film is far from exhausted, and probably never will be. These notes are not an attempt to exorcise my pleasure, or anybody else's, as much left criticism of Hollywood does, nor do I simply want to confirm it. What interests me is the film's appeal to some feminists, who have seen in its explicit representation of violence as a masculine social disease a radical critique of masculinity. While I agree that *Raging Bull* puts masculinity in crisis, I don't think it offers a radical critique of either masculinity or violence, even though it is profoundly disturbing. The film's attitude to violence is ambiguous. On one hand, it is validated as an essential component of masculinity, making possible resistance to a corrupt and repressive social system. On this level violence is seen as inseparable from desire, and is celebrated. On the other, the tragic scenario of *Raging Bull* demands that the hero be shown to be the guilty victim of his

173

transgressive desires: his violence is so excessive, so self-destructive that it has to be condemned. This moralism, combined with the film's nostalgia for traditional family values, produces a condemnation of violence that comes close to that of the Right. Moreover, I would argue that the tragic structure of *Raging Bull* has consequences for its view of masculinity: masculinity is put into crisis so that we can mourn its loss. I believe my pleasures in the film are traditional, and I want to mobilise some of them in the interests of contributing to feminist debate. Must we always justify our pleasure, our fantasies, as 'progressive', or condemn them as 'reactionary'? I'd rather see them non-moralistically as fertile ground for discussion of the more difficult and painful aspects of our desires in relation to our politics. *Raging Bull* propels us into that arena.

Pleasure: cinéphilia

Like all New Hollywood cinema, *Raging Bull* is directed at a relatively new audience of knowledgeable cinemagoers. TV has given wide exposure to cinema's history, creating a large popular audience clued-up to the pleasures of recognising authorship, genre, and so on. This audience coincides with an influx of producers and directors into the Hollywood industry who have college educations in cinema studies. One of the characteristics of New Hollywood that marks it off from classic Hollywood is that it is produced and consumed by knowledgeable intellectuals. It sells itself on the basis of its reflexivity, calling up classic Hollywood in order to differentiate itself from it. The 'modernity' of New Hollywood lies in the way it plays on the known conventions of a past Hollywood to displace it, while retaining the pleasures of homage to the past. *Raging Bull* is a good example of New Hollywood's retrospective impulse. Director Martin Scorsese is known as a cinéphile. His anxiety about preserving the cinema's past is manifested in his preservation of his work in the Scorsese Archives, and one of his reasons for filming *Raging Bull* in black and white (besides as a conscious reference to Warner Bros films of the 1940s) was as a protest against the deterioration of colour values. The film, which has a minimal storyline, is a complex tapestry of allusions in image and sound to a lost popular culture. It offers a challenge to the curiosity and the critical acumen of the cinéphile spectator, a come-on to those of us who are hooked on cinema. Jake La Motta's life brushes against the history of cinema and popular music at certain moments, drawing us in like a puzzle to a game we can never win.

(Losing the game is crucial to *Raging Bull*: Scorsese has said that he wanted to differentiate the film from contemporary boxing pics in which the hero

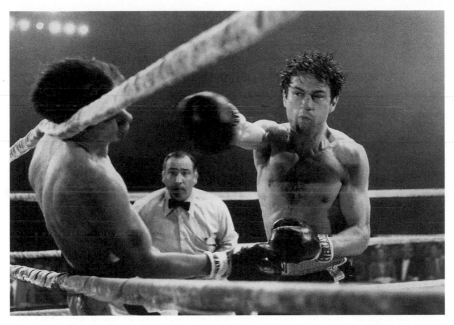

Figure 11.1 In search of redemption: Robert De Niro in *Raging Bull* (1980). Courtesy United Artists and the Kobal Collection.

wins through (such as *Rocky II*) by presenting a hero who loses everything, who redeems himself through loss, recalling the 1940s version of the genre, and returning obsessively to *On the Waterfront*, to Brando's performance as the reluctant working-class hero who becomes, *in spite of himself*, an icon of working-class struggle.)

Then there is the film's visual pleasure: the excitement of a *mise-en-scène* that alternates between long, reflective shots allowing us to contemplate the scene in safety, at a distance, and explosions of rapid montage that assault our eyes and ears, bringing us right into the ring with the fighters. Sometimes we almost literally get a punch in the eye. I don't like boxing; but the illusion of 'being there', the risk involved, is a real turn-on. The film moves and excites by making the past immediately present, by making us present in history. For women, perhaps, this illusion of presence is doubly exciting, since we are generally represented as outside history. But the price of that pleasure is an identification with masculinity on its terms rather than our own.

Pleasure: the body

Hollywood films about sport generally centre on the male body (though not always: *Pat and Mike*, or Ida Lupino's *Hard, Fast and Beautiful*, for example) as object of desire. If, as feminist film theory has argued, classic Hollywood is dedicated to the playing out of male Oedipal anxieties across the woman's body, object of the 'male' gaze, what does it mean to place the male body at the centre?

The classic Hollywood boxing pic has a 'rise-and-fall' structure, an analogy for male sexuality itself. The working-class hero battles his way towards success against opposition from a corrupt, hostile society and his own self-doubts (John Garfield in *Body and Soul*). The Championship is rarely an end in itself: it represents winning the game against society, becoming a man against all the odds. Of course, the hero can lose, and he must recognise this fact in order to become a real man. The hero of boxing films, who is often too sensitive to succeed, travels a painful Oedipal journey, challenging the power of the Father, punished for the attempt. His body becomes the focus for this struggle: the desire to win, followed by punishment and loss. The boxing pic has often been used as a vehicle for left-wing ideas, and the virile working-class hero is a prevailing image in the iconography of socialist politics. For many political women it has a powerful and complex appeal: as an object of desire, as a focus for identification, and as the fulfilment of a sadistic wish to see it destroyed, to make space for our own fantasies of power, activating the desire of the mother for her child.

Raging Bull plays out this problem of class and male sexuality across the body of Robert De Niro. Much has been made of De Niro's virtuoso performance, which involved the donning of a false nose and gaining a vast amount of weight to depict Jake La Motta's decline. I suspect that the actual transformation of De Niro's body is crucial: for those of us turned on by De Niro, the 'real' loss of his beautiful body as an object for contemplation is disturbing, and undermines the sadistic desire to see that body punished and mutilated that the film activates. The loss of the actor's body, known and desired before the film existed, drawing us to the film with the promise of the pleasure of seeing it, implicates us deeply in the tragic hero's decline. Whatever power we may have thought we had, through our sadistic gaze at the bruised and battered male body, we lose through identification with the hero's loss. The pain of our loss motivates us to look back, to seek again the perfect body in all its power and beauty, as the film itself looks back nostalgically to a time when pure animal energy formed the basis of resistance to oppression and exploitation, identifying that energy with masculine virility.

This ambiguity around the male body is not quite the same as that which surrounds the woman's body in classic Hollywood, where the active desire of the woman represents a problem that the film sets out to resolve, finally replacing her as feminine, apparently confirming the security of the power of the 'male' spectator (as in *The Revolt of Mamie Stover*). *Raging Bull*, like its predecessors in the boxing genre, presents the powerful male body as an object of desire and identification, but moving towards the loss of male power. This loss activates the desire to call it up once more: we mourn the loss, so the founding image of male power, the phallus, is centred yet again. The space for desire that the tragedy promises to open up – the celebration of the overthrow of the phallus – is closed off in the search for the lost object.

This fixation on the male body as object of desire has consequences for the representation of the woman's body in the film. The spectator's look at De Niro/Jake is direct, unmediated desire, but our access to Vickie/Cathy Moriarty is mediated through Jake's desire for her. We see Vickie entirely through Jake's eyes, literally, as the expression of his desire for her is a prolonged eroticised gaze cut in with reverse shots of him looking at her. The effect is to deflect the spectator's access to the woman's body, confirming identification with the male hero as simultaneously desiring subject and object of desire. Vickie's body is marked out as maternal (even though she is only fifteen) in its mature fullness, and by the fact that when Jake first sees and desires her she is with a group of the mob's henchmen, the godfathers against whom he will increasingly turn his aggression. Later in the film, a kiss exchanged between Tommy, head of the mob, and Vickie provokes Jake into a jealous rage that is as much an expression of his desire for Tommy as for her. So the film acts out a scenario in which male desire for the mother's body coincides with the wish to kill the father. Moreover, the anxieties aroused by this double transgression are displaced into male homosexual desire and the impulse to punish the mother who initiated the forbidden desire. The film constantly defers and delays Jake's sexual encounters with Vickie. The scene of their first coupling, after a long, protracted sequence, takes place in his parents' bed after they have kissed in front of a photograph of Jake and his brother Joey playfully boxing. Vickie's body is framed by Jake's look, by Joey's look, by the look of the camera in the home-movie sequence, placing her further and further at a distance, until finally she is eliminated altogether. But the maternal body returns in the film, in the language Jake uses to insult other men ('Fuck your mother', 'Your mother takes it up the ass'...), curses that are homosexually turned against his opponents (Jake threatens to 'fuck the ass' of one of them).

The sexual confusion at the heart of *Raging Bull* does, I think, put masculinity in crisis, raising the question of what it takes to be a man, and what the alternatives to macho male sexuality might be. But precisely because it is a masculine crisis defined entirely in terms of male Oedipal anxieties, desire circulates always around the phallus, returning to it obsessively, blocking off other avenues, alternative expressions of male desire, in its stress on the tragic inevitability of the male Oedipal scenario.

Pleasure: tragedy

The tragic structure of *Raging Bull* is, I think, fundamental to the way the film resolves the hero's crisis. Tragedy is an ancient dramatic form going back at least as far as Greek antiquity. History has radically transformed it since then, but it seems to retain a certain continuity of form and function: through a process of emotional release or catharsis brought about by identification with the suffering of the tragic protagonists, tragedy teaches us something about the world and our place in it. The function of tragedy remains important today, or takes on even more importance because we are living through times of great social unrest and change. Tragedy siphons off the pain and contradictions that are the consequences of that change, teaching us that when things change something may be gained, but we inevitably lose, and we should mourn that loss. Tragedy resists the progress of history, giving us a perspective on how it affects the lives of human beings caught up in it, and enabling us to see certain truths about our own lives. This means it can be mobilised politically, to ask questions about the 'positive' aspects of progress, but it can also be used to confirm our feeling that human beings are inevitably the victims of social forces, over which they can never exert control.

As Raymond Williams points out in *Modern Tragedy*, the Christian tradition of tragedy differs from its secular forbears in two important ways. It lacks the background of a social context against which the action is played out, and it centres the dramatic struggle in an individual tragic hero rather than in ruling families or collective groups. The Christian tradition suggests that the outcome of the struggle, and the suffering of the tragic hero, are inevitable, and that our attitude to this inevitability should be one of pity for the hero who suffered in our place. Tragedy moves us to tears, rather than anger or thought. The tragic hero (sometimes, but not often, a heroine: Williams' sole example is Anna Karenina) is compelled by internal and external forces outside his control to act in a way that transgresses social or moral codes, for which he is punished. Punishment and suffering are built into the tragic structure: the hero batters against his fate until he finally redeems himself by accepting it. The notion of the tragic hero suffering in our place is clearly very important to Christian mythology, and without going into the religious symbolism of Scorsese's work, the Christian version of tragedy seems relevant to *Raging Bull*: the rise and fall of Jake La Motta (a traditional narrative structure in classical Hollywood cinema) is close to that of tragedy, which deals with the fall from grace of successful, powerful men and women. However, Jake's fall is not simply a punishment for some unknown crime or guilt, which is the explanation he offers in the film at one point. He comes from the Italian-American immigrant community, and therefore has the misfortune to

178

be caught up in the American Dream, which offered success and power at the same time as it insisted on the innate inferiority of the Italian immigrants, locating them as a source of crime and corruption, and of many other un-American activities, such as political unrest. The history of the Italian immigrant community in America is littered with the martyrs of this victimisation: perhaps the most memorable examples are Sacco and Vanzetti. In this context, Jake La Motta appears as another victim-hero caught between his desire to change the conditions of his existence by becoming a champion boxer, and his powerlessness in the face of those who control those conditions. Jake's violence and animal energy are the source of both his drive for success and his resistance to exploitation, and as such they are validated. But in the tragic scenario of *Raging Bull* their social context and motivation is displaced, so that we are left with the private pain of a single individual whose suffering is caused by his innate guilt. Jake reaches rock bottom when, totally isolated from family and friends and unable to gather support from any source, he is thrown into prison on a charge of allowing teenage prostitution in his club. In prison he finally rejects the guilty self that motivated him to violence and social transgression ('I'm not that guy...'), and when we next see him he is indeed a changed man: humbler, resigned, but you might also say an empty husk.

Jake's story is about the breakdown of one man and the emergence of another. But as in all tragedy, whatever the positive value placed on change, and Scorsese has insisted that at the end of the film La Motta has redeemed himself, the breakdown involves loss and that loss is mourned. Jake's anger and his animal violence stood for something: a resistance to exploitation, a desire for freedom. Once the anger is gone and resignation takes its place, Jake becomes a pathetic creature, a lumbering animal looking for forgiveness. In the tragic resolution of the film we're asked to look with pity on this shell of a man who has lost all the attributes necessary to masculinity. Some of us might want to celebrate that loss (*schadenfreude*, pleasure in another's misfortunes, is built into tragedy), and there is, I think, a sadistic pleasure in the spectator's pitying look at Jake at the end of *Raging Bull*, partly explained by the space opened up for female desire when the powerful male is brought low. But, as the sister of tragedy, melodrama, tells us, there is no desire without the phallus (think of the endings of *Written on the Wind* and *All That Heaven Allows*, where the heroines are caught in the consequences of their desire to overthrow the phallus) and though we may take it up we can only do so at the expense of male castration. So where does it leave us? Our desire is folded in with man's desire for himself, and, like him, we mourn the loss of masculinity.

For Scorsese, it seems, the assimilation of the Italian immigrants into American society is a negative blessing involving the loss of the integrity and the unity of that community, and the breakdown of the traditional Italian family. The film looks back to a time when those values were current, a mythic past when primitive animal instinct formed the basis of resistance to oppression and exploitation, pure energy as a principle of change. In identifying that energy with masculine virility, and in continuing to locate feminine sexuality in its traditional place within the family, as entirely maternal, it seems to me to be far from progressive, bypassing the question of female desire, denying the value of many of the changes that have taken place in the area of sexual politics, retreating into retrograde romanticism and anti-intellectualism. But it does raise crucial questions of desire, of the desires of feminist politics in relation to male desires and masculine politics, of the mobilisation of aggression and desire in the interests of politics.

Chapter 12

THE LAST TEMPTATION OF CHRIST

Synopsis

Jesus of Nazareth, a carpenter, makes the crosses on which the Romans crucify seditious Jews, carrying them to Golgotha on his back. When Judas, a Zealot, accuses him of being a collaborator, Jesus responds that he has a destiny, though he is unsure what it is. He visits prostitute Mary Magdalene, a childhood friend, who also reviles him for cowardice; when she softens and asks him to stay, he refuses. Next, he travels to a monastery whose aged leader recognises him, then dies. Jesus learns that the old man actually died before their encounter; that night, he is visited by Satan in the form of snakes. Another monk tells him that he is now purified and should relay God's message to the people. Judas has orders from the Zealots to kill Jesus, but decides instead to travel with him until he understands. Jesus prevents Mary Magdalene from being stoned, and delivers the Sermon on the Mount, after which he gathers together a group of disciples. Judas, suspecting that Jesus may be the Messiah, suggests they visit John the Baptist in Judaea. John is not convinced by Jesus' message of love, saying that God demands anger, and sends him into the desert to ask God directly. After surviving forty days and nights of testing, Jesus is visited by John, covered in blood, who tells him that he must take up the axe and deliver God's message. Wandering through the desert, Jesus comes across Mary and Martha, who urge him to look for God in a home and family. Learning that John the Baptist has been killed by Herod, Jesus returns to his disciples, declaring war on the devil. He performs a number of miracles, curing a blind man, turning water into wine at Canaan's wedding, and raising Lazarus from the dead. After Jesus throws the money changers from the temple, the Zealots, led by Saul, afraid of his growing power, kill Lazarus, his greatest miracle. Jesus triumphantly rides into Jerusalem on a donkey, and the Jews rally round him for an assault on the temple. Jesus asks God for a sign as to what he should do next, and collapses as bleeding stigmata appear on his hands. Escaping the fray with Judas' help, Jesus tells him that he must help him fulfil his destiny by betraying him to the Romans so that he will be crucified and return as a martyr. After saying farewell to his disciples at a last supper, Jesus goes with them to the Garden of Gethsemane, where Judas brings the Roman soldiers, identifying Jesus with a kiss. Jesus is brought before Pontius Pilate, who tells him that he is more dangerous to them than the Zealots because he wants to change the way people think. Crucified at Golgotha, Jesus is visited by a guardian angel who tells him that God has spared him and that he can now lead a normal life. He marries Mary Magdalene, who becomes pregnant. When she dies, the angel leads him to Mary and Martha, with whom he lives happily for many years and has many children. One day, he hears Saul, now Paul, preaching the story of his crucifixion and resurrection. When Jesus confronts him, Paul insists that the truth is irrelevant: only the myth is important in giving people hope. As Jerusalem burns, Jesus is visited on his deathbed by his disciples and Judas angrily accuses him of betraying the cause. Finally accepting his destiny, Jesus begs God to forgive him and returns to martyrdom on the cross.

Review

The fundamentalist furore surrounding *The Last Temptation of Christ* (1988) is somewhat surprising; the film, after all, declares itself from the first to be an exploration of Nikos Kazantzakis' fictional account of Jesus' life rather than an interpretation of the gospels. And there have been numerous fictionalised versions of the New Testament that have received nothing like the same attention. In a sense, Scorsese's project, which gestated for many years and was subject to endless delays, finally found its historical moment, in much the same way as Kazantzakis' Christ, procrastinator *par excellence*, finally achieves his destiny. Coinciding with the rise of a reactionary, often racist, religious Right, the film stirred up issues of censorship, democratic debate and the politics of religion to an unprecedented degree for a (relatively) mainstream movie. Threats of a boycott in the USA were echoed in the UK in the Church's advice to practising Christians not to see it, thus neatly exonerating them from having to think about it at all.

The objections on the grounds of sex were clearly a red herring; of the two sex scenes, one shows Jesus as a non-participant observer in Mary

Magdalene's brothel, followed by his refusal of her invitation to stay, while the other, in which he makes love to and impregnates Mary Magdalene during his reverie on the cross, takes place after their marriage and is directly tied to procreation. Whatever else this Jesus may be after, it is not sex. Those who, sight unseen, cried blasphemy nevertheless got it right. Scorsese and Paul Schrader produced a deeply transgressive view of religion that at the very least opens it up for general discussion beyond the protective confines of the Church, and at the most unmasks the perverse and contradictory impulses at the heart of Christian faith. In theological terms, the film decisively breaks with dogma in both form and content. Much of it is discursive, consisting of scenes of open-ended debate between Jesus and a host of interlocutors (the disciples, Judas, John the Baptist, Mary and Martha, Pontius Pilate, the Devil, and so on) around questions of knowledge and truth, the relationship between love and vengeance, passive and active resistance, the role of martyrdom in political struggle, and whether revolution should begin with the mind or the body. The world represented is one in the throes of political and ideological turmoil, with Jesus at the centre of a change from an old to a new order, a contradictory, almost schizoid Messiah who will somehow transcend contradiction to unify the Jews.

The crux of the new order is a paradox of faith founded on doubt: this Jesus, up to the very last moment, resists God's plans for him, to the extent of evading his fate through a daydream on the cross in which he leads a 'normal', albeit polygamous, life as a married man with a family. During the daydream, he learns from a conversation with the convert Paul that the truth is immaterial: what matters is that people should believe in the miracle of resurrection enough to be prepared to die for God. Faith consists not in knowledge but in disavowal, the willing suspension of disbelief that is also at work in the fictionalising processes of myth or, indeed, literature and cinema. This perspective is clearly controversial, though not entirely new. There are echoes of Nicholas Ray's militant Jesus in *King of Kings*, and a distinct homage to Pasolini's man of the people in the striving for ethnic authenticity (engagingly overlaid with an urban American flavour to the dialogue), the shots of peasant faces, and a lyrical emphasis on movement. The film's real transgression, and the secret of its fascination, lies not so much in its approach to religion, nor even in its attempt to humanise Christ, but rather in its psychological portrait of a man caught in an identity crisis. This emphasis, deliberately inviting secular analysis, allows Scorsese and Schrader to develop more explicitly than ever before their complex view of masculinity. In this context, Judas' question, 'What kind of a man are you?', takes on a new meaning.

Scorsese has described his Jesus as neurotic, often psychotic: he sees visions, hears voices, has persecutory hallucinations and fainting fits, all of

Figure 12.1   Outcast: Willem Dafoe in *The Last Temptation of Christ* (1988). Courtesy Universal and the Kobal Collection.

which are inseparable from his religion. He vacillates between extremes of fasting and self-immolation and hedonism, between violent anger and docile passivity. Above all, he exhibits classic masochistic symptoms: seeking submission, pursuing pleasure through suffering, and finally, with the aid of his closest friend, setting up his own death. But the film-makers' object is not to dismiss him as deranged. Their characterisation is more in line with recent attempts to reassess masochism as a way of disavowing the power of the punitive, castrating father via a return to a non-genital, pre-Oedipal sexuality.[1] The masochist's rebellion, involving continual postponement of sexual gratification, has an aesthetic dimension: it involves digression through game-playing, the staging of theatrical tableaux, and a repetitive, cyclical (rather than linear, goal-oriented) fantasy structure.

The Last Temptation of Christ matches its masochistic hero's resistance to the law of the father with a non-linear (anti-Oedipal) journey narrative, which wanders back and forth and in which arrival at a final destination seems unimportant. Some scenes, such as the one in the brothel, are staged almost like *tableaux vivants*, while others (the Sermon on the Mount, the raising of Lazarus, Jesus displaying his bleeding heart to the disciples, or the temptation in the desert) have a stylised, theatrical quality, also reflected in Willem

Dafoe's performance, as though Jesus were an actor looking for a role. Much is also made of digression and delay on the visual level, through the use of slow motion and dissolves that set up a tension between movement and stasis, mirroring a similar tension within Jesus himself.

The apotheosis of this masochistic aesthetic is the crucifixion itself, an exquisite spectacle of slow-motion suffering culminating in last-minute deferral as Jesus' reverie breaks the rules of narrative closure by launching into an alternative scenario. The most extensive and elaborate of all the film's digressions, it is actually one of the least convincing, presenting the domesticated Jesus as a lacklustre, inert figure, and failing to explore what his immersion in the traditionally maternal world of the family might mean. The filmmakers are clearly more interested in the final orgasmic reunion with God: crawling on his belly back to Golgotha, Jesus cries out, 'I want to be crucified', on the cross once more, ecstatic, he whispers, 'It is accomplished'.

Predictably, the film's primary concern is with relationships between men, particularly Jesus' friendship with Judas, who is deeply implicated in the masochistic drama. At first a critical, punitive figure, constantly reminding Jesus of his duty, Judas becomes a devoted follower and finally the loving agent of his master's death, all of which gives an interesting complexion to male/buddy relationships. Mary Magdalene is sadly underdeveloped, relegated like Jesus' mother Mary and Martha and Mary to a parenthesis to the main business. Nevertheless, Scorsese and Schrader have taken the exploration of masculinity in crisis begun in *Taxi Driver* and *Raging Bull* to new extremes here. And it might not be too fanciful to see in Scorsese's obsessional devotion to this project an identification with Kazantzakis' visionary outsider, on one level a misunderstood artist figure, a sacrificial victim, on another a supreme showman and magician. Not for nothing does the director's epitaph to his film, 'And finally, I can say that I have done it', echo Jesus' last words on the cross.

Note

1   For example, Gilles Deleuze developed by Gaylyn Studlar in *In the Realm of Pleasure* (Chicago: University of Illinois, 1988).

Chapter 13

SCORSESE'S MASQUERADE

A deafening silence surrounds the sexual politics of Scorsese's *Cape Fear* (1992). Here we have a violent rape movie in which women apparently collude in their own punishment at the hands of a rapist. Yet for the most part critics, even when shocked by the film's brutality, prefer to discuss it in formal and/or moral terms – as 'cinema' or as a treatise on good and evil. Feminists too have been conspicuously quiet. This is not the first occasion on which Scorsese has thrown down a gauntlet to the women's movement. The challenge, it seems, has worn thin. In the face of this general reticence, some male commentators have shown a willingness to speak up on behalf of oppressed womankind. For instance, Jeremy Campbell, the Washington correspondent of the *Evening Standard*, opened his vitriolic review with a poignant anecdote: 'At one particularly horrible moment in ... *Cape Fear*, a woman in the audience put her hand to her face and half sobbed: "Oh, no!" I like to think the woman was protesting, not just at the scene, a sexual assault on a little girl, but at the appalling realisation that here were we, supposedly civilised adults, paying to see what the most debauched and degenerate Roman emperors might have gagged over.'

Again in the *Standard*, in one of the few reviews explicitly to take account of sexual politics, Alexander Walker wrote: 'Feminists will squirm as, under the convict's smiling provocation, she [Lori Davis] proceeds to act out every seductive wile and wink that a promiscuous woman can invent. She certainly "asks for it" – though not, of course, in the form in which it soon comes.'

Such gallantry is surprising when it is considered that almost everybody is victimised in *Cape Fear*. A quick body count reveals that of those who are assaulted, threatened, raped or killed six (including Cady) are male, four female and one canine, while of the final survivors, two are female and one male. Yet, against all the evidence, this espousal of the female cause by the critics quoted above designates women as the natural and obvious victims of

Scorsese's movie. These male writers seem to be motivated by a desire to exorcise their own feelings of victimisation, to put them where they belong, with the 'weaker sex'. That such defensive action should be necessary suggests that *Cape Fear* indulges in some disturbing gender bending.

It's no secret that, in a bid for commercial success, Scorsese decided to remake J. Lee Thompson's taut black-and-white thriller as a horror movie. The end result is no arty, up-market revamp. For, despite its $30 million budget, *Cape Fear* owes everything to low-budget horror movies – Abel Ferrara's 1980 *Ms .45* (*Angel of Vengeance*), for instance. It is a rape-revenge movie in reverse, with an avenging hero instead of heroine. This is a genre in which psychosexual anxieties, the coupling of sexual desire with aggression and the playing out of sadomasochistic power relationships are the narrative mainspring. A contract exists between film-makers and spectators in which the former undertake to 'do over' the latter; to frighten them, precisely, out of their wits. The audience for 'low' horror is one that pays to be hurt, to be assaulted in much the same way as the film's characters. This experience is about arousing the viewer's base instincts – it has nothing whatever to do with the 'uplifting' or purifying qualities of 'high' art.

Scorsese has taken this remit seriously. We cringe as the camera is used like a battering ram, lunging at the actors, glancing off De Niro's chin, or burying itself in Nick Nolte's abdomen, while the pounding soundtrack hammers away at the auditory nerves. We suffer exquisite torture as we wait with bated breath for Max Cady to penetrate the primitive defences of the Bowden house. We scream in terror when Cady leaps from the shadows to garotte private investigator Kersek, and our stomachs lurch in disgust at the sight of Sam Bowden slipping and sliding around in a pool of Kersek's thickening blood. Thus Scorsese makes masochists of us all.

Cinematic masochism offers a host of guilty pleasures, not confined to the terror tactics of the horror film, but nevertheless played out there in particularly blatant form. The suffering of the characters mirrors our own humiliation as we wait – literally 'held in suspense' – to discover their fate. We shift anxiously in our seats as we are drawn into games of disguise and pursuit which postpone the final resolution. And we revel squeamishly in scenes of ritualistic punishment and death. Scorsese, of course, has already proved himself a master of the masochistic aesthetic, in *Raging Bull* (1980), for example, and most elaborately in *The Last Temptation of Christ* (1988). In *Cape Fear* it is no longer subtext, but overt message.

It is well known that Freud thought that masochism was essentially 'feminine'. Fantasies of being beaten, violated and defiled, while common to both sexes, were 'natural' to women but signified 'perversion' (a receptive homosexuality) in men. Horror film-makers would seem to agree. Abject fear is coded as feminine as, in movie after movie, female victims with terrified expressions – wide eyes and gaping mouths – are stalked with evil intent by male aggressors. Yet, as Carol Clover argues in her provocative book *Men, Women and Chainsaws*,[1] this is certainly not the whole story. Horror movies can also be characterised by role reversals in which victims turn the tables on their aggressors. Here, the slasher/rapist, frequently a sexually impaired figure, usually ends up slashed, maimed or killed, often by an axe- or knife-wielding heroine. The female victim-turned-avenger takes on the aggressor role and is thereby 'masculinised', while the slasher/rapist becomes the victim and meets as nasty an end as any masochist could wish for. While victimisation is still regarded as an essentially 'feminine' state, men – at least as often as women – find themselves in it.

Horror's gender disturbances are given several more turns of the screw by Scorsese. From the beginning, his rapist is designated as a victim. Max Cady is victimised by a corrupt legal system which sends him to prison for fourteen years on manipulated evidence. Not only is he sodomised in jail, but he loses his home and family as well. As he tells Sam Bowden, the lawyer whose actions put him away, he is now 'looking for his feminine side' – a bizarre assertion coming from a violent underclass ex-con, but entirely logical in the film's terms. Cady's sense of loss links him with the women characters, all of them 'done over' in some way by Bowden, whose resemblance to Cady the dialogue repeatedly stresses.

Cady's savage sexual (and vampiric) assault on Sam Bowden's mistress, Lori Davis, is both a mirror for Bowden's carelessly cruel treatment of her and, as her refusal to testify makes explicit, an indictment of the legal system that would heap further humiliation on her – as, indeed, it does on Cady, who is subsequently arrested on a trumped-up charge and submitted to a full body search because Bowden suspects him of intending to rape his wife, Leigh. In the vertiginous final sequence, Cady does threaten to rape Leigh, but not before she has pleaded with him not to attack her daughter Danielle in a speech that emphasises their common experience of loss (his years in prison, her years of marriage). Cady's feminine side scandalously surfaces in the brief instant in which, dressed in the clothes of the Bowden family's maid, Graciella, he garottes Kersek in their kitchen. This scene has been much discussed as an obligatory, and therefore easily dismissable, reference to Hitchcock's *Psycho*. Yet De Niro's drag, in the class, ethnic and gender connections it makes between Cady and Graciella, is surely more than this.

Cape Fear's complex pattern of refracted images makes it plain that avenging angel Cady is acting on behalf of victimised women. In this light, the female characters' apparent collusion in their own humiliation – the fact that they are attracted to the rapist – takes on a different hue. They could be said

Figure 13.1   Avenging angel: Robert De Niro in *Cape Fear* (1992). Courtesy Universal and the Kobal Collection.

to be drawn not only to his violent sexuality, but also to the distorted picture he reflects back at them of their own rage and pain, and of their desire for revenge. Scorsese's most controversial move in this respect is to bracket the main action with the narrative voice of Danielle telling the audience that the film is her reminiscence. This ruse shifts the bases considerably. If Cady is conjured up by Danielle, then the threat to the American family comes, not from an intruder, but from within. Problem child Danielle calls up Cady as a defence against her incestuous desire for Sam, and as a wish to find an escape route out of the claustrophobic confines of the Bowden family nexus.

Even more disquieting than the idea that the movie represents a teenage girl's fantasy is the notion that Scorsese, in the time-honoured tradition of storytelling, uses one of his characters as a mask for his own violent sexual fantasies, which include the seduction and rape of a fifteen-year-old girl. But what exactly is going on in this masquerade? Without speculating about his desire for a sexual awakening at the hands of De Niro's Cady, the director's delegation of the narrator's role to Danielle suggests at the very least strong feelings of affinity with this most receptive, most susceptible, of all the film's characters. An attempt by Scorsese to recover his lost innocence, perhaps?

Except that Danielle is far from innocent. She is the one who forms an alliance with Cady and, in a sense, 'employs' him to violate her mother and

189

destroy her father. She is the one who sets fire to Cady in the final sequence and, as the narrator, sees to it that he is devoured by that familiar feminine trope, the swirling black vortex of Cape Fear river. (Indeed, the infamous scene in which Danielle and Cady meet in the school theatre, when he probes her mouth with his finger, can be read as a threat as much to him as to her – an intimation of his eventual 'swallowing up'.) And, of course, in the film's closing moments, it is Danielle's voice that reminds us that, through her dreams, she can raise Cady from the dead.

It would seem, then, that for Scorsese femininity is two-faced, embodying both suffering passivity and monstrous destructive power. Horror's bisexual games enable him to confront us with some unpalatable truths – that there is a victim, and aggressor, in all of us, for example. But in spite of all the gender juggling Scorsese still adheres to a negative notion of the feminine. The real horror in *Cape Fear* is feminisation: the contamination of positive 'masculine' values (heroism, integrity, honour and so forth) by 'feminine' values of weakness, prevarication and moral laxity, typified by the ambivalent figure of antihero Sam Bowden. Scorsese has produced his most overtly femino-phobic movie. We can hardly admire him for that. At the most, we can thank him for laying on the line with blistering clarity the way our culture devalues femininity as an alibi for male fears and desires.

Note

1   Carol J. Clover, *Men, Women and Chainsaws: Gender in the Modern Horror Film* (London: BFI Publishing, 1992).

Chapter 14

THE AGE OF INNOCENCE

Synopsis

New York City, the 1870s. Lawyer Newland Archer is engaged to May Welland of the powerful Mingott family. He is anxious to announce the engagement at the Beauforts' annual ball, partly to deflect the gossips' attention from May's cousin Ellen Olenska, who has returned from Europe after the failure of her scandalous marriage to Count Olenski. Archer wants an early wedding, but May is under pressure from her mother to observe the proprieties. Meanwhile, the rumours about Ellen's past proliferate, much to Archer's annoyance. After New York society snubs Ellen by refusing to attend a dinner given in her honour by May's grandmother Mrs Mingott, Archer asks the influential Van der Luydens to intervene. Ellen is invited to dinner at the Van der Luydens', where she asks Archer to visit her at home. Ellen arrives late for their appointment and Archer is disconcerted to see her with Julius Beaufort, a notorious womaniser. Afterwards, Archer orders the usual bouquet of lilies of the valley for May and sends yellow roses anonymously to Ellen.

Archer's boss Mr Letterblair asks him on behalf of the Mingott family to dissuade Ellen from going ahead with her divorce. Ellen is upset, but accepts Archer's advice that the scandal would be too damaging. Archer is increasingly drawn to Ellen and, when May goes away on holiday with her family, responds to a letter Ellen sends him from the Van der Luydens' by visiting her there. Before he can declare his feelings, they are interrupted by Julius Beaufort and Archer leaves angrily. He goes to see May and pressurises her to bring forward the wedding. May is suspicious of his reasons, but Archer assures her there is no one else. When he hears that the count wants Ellen back, Archer visits Ellen to persuade her not to return to her husband. He finally tells her he loves her, but Ellen, who returns his love, refuses him on the grounds that she could never hurt May. A letter arrives from May telling Ellen that her mother has agreed to the wedding being brought forward.

Eighteen months after the wedding, Archer, still obsessed with Ellen, hears that she is visiting Boston and invents an excuse to go there. Ellen explains that she is meeting Rivière, the count's secretary, who is trying to persuade her to return to her husband. Archer begs her not to go back to Europe, and she agrees to refuse the count's offer of recompense. Meanwhile, Beaufort's business collapses and Ellen loses her investments. After Mrs Mingott has a stroke, the impoverished Ellen returns to New York to take care of her. Archer and Ellen decide to meet and make love, but before the rendezvous takes place, May breaks the news to Archer that Ellen is leaving for Europe. Archer is devastated, and realises that May's family and friends, believing that he and Ellen are lovers, have conspired to keep them apart. Feeling trapped, he tries to tell May about his feelings and wish to travel, but she forestalls him with the news that she is pregnant. She reveals that she told Ellen about her pregnancy two weeks earlier. Archer finally accepts his fate. Many years later, after May's death, the 57-year-old Archer accompanies his son Ted on a business trip to Paris. Ted has arranged a surprise visit to Countess Olenska, but Archer sends him on ahead, and turns and walks away.

Review

Scorsese's *The Age of Innocence* (1993) might have been subtitled *The Man Who Could Not Love Women*. The poet of impotence has translated Edith Wharton's acerbic scrutiny of the suffocating codes and customs of late nineteenth-century New York into melodrama, centred on a tragic hero incapable of breaking through the social ties that bind. On the face of it the film is a faithful adaptation of Wharton's book, even allowing the writer herself a voice in Joanne Woodward's narration. The minutiae of the novel's descriptions of décor and fashion have been lovingly recreated, as the matching of image and voice-over testifies. This is a meeting not only of minds but of compulsions: the obsessional film-maker has found a fellow fetishist in Wharton, whose fascination with fine detail takes social realism to excess. And, of course, they are both artists who study their society with outsiders' eyes.

The shift that takes place in the adaptation is subtle – as delicate as Wharton's découpage. Newland Archer, with his cultural aspirations and dreams of leaving, is as much the centre of the novel as the film and Wharton, who was herself an exile in Europe, was clearly in sympathy with her hero's longing to escape. Yet the secret of her success in depicting Archer's psyche is the distance she takes on his attitude to women. For Wharton, Archer is a flawed, contradictory character, as much at the mercy of his own condescending view of the society women who surround him as of society itself. Scorsese has softened the novel's satire of Archer, reserving it instead, through the use of voice-over, for the manners and morals of fashionable New York. For Scorsese, Archer is pure victim – of his background, the claustrophobic matriarchal culture he inhabits – whereas for Wharton his incapacity plays a key role in the victimisation of Ellen, whose own tragedy as social outcast is given more weight in the novel.

Such distance as Scorsese does take on Archer is realised, characteristically, partly as a problem of vision. His film is literally an art movie in which characters are judged according to their taste and the audience is tested on how many paintings and *objets d'art* it can identify. The camera follows Archer's gaze as he travels from room to room examining acquisition after acquisition. But the connoisseur's eye that sets him apart from most of his peers is also his downfall. Archer's approach to life and love is that of an aesthete – he would rather look than act. To him, May's niceness is a curtain hiding her basic emptiness, but it is his own inability to see beyond surfaces that separates him from the woman he professes to love. His first sight of Ellen after his marriage is from afar as he watches her on the seashore gazing out over the ocean. He promises himself that if she turns round, he will go to meet her, but she does not move and the moment is lost. The scene of Ellen on the shore is reminiscent of an Impressionist painting, with sparkling sunlight and soft colours creating a highly romanticised vista in which the static figure of a woman acts as a kind of guarantee of order and harmony.

Ellen's immobility in this sequence is the mirror image of Archer's passivity and resistance to change. The seashore scene is poignantly replayed at the end of the movie, when Archer, now 57, sits outside Ellen's flat in Paris trying to decide whether to go in to see her. As her manservant closes the window, the image dissolves into a thousand particles of light and Ellen is safely locked away as a memory. But then, she was never real, nor did Archer want her to be, in spite of his token defence of women's rights. Archer's aestheticisation of Ellen is reflected in the portraits of women, which figure prolifically in the film, as well as in the painterly poses the characters take up from time to time. And it is there in Archer's fetishism, his fixation on Ellen's shoe, her pink parasol, the whisper of her skirts, revealing that the emptiness or lack he so despises in May is actually at the heart of masculinity. Once again, Scorsese creates a dark, pessimistic vision of male desire in which woman is never more than an alibi.

Figure 14.1 Locked in the past: Daniel Day-Lewis and Michelle Pfeiffer in *The Age of Innocence* (1993). Courtesy Colombia/Phillip Caruso and the Kobal Collection.

But what if the woman should move? In 1920, when Wharton wrote *The Age of Innocence*, women were certainly on the move, and the novel registers, in the outcast figure of Countess Olenska, the social anxieties attendant on their economic and sexual emancipation. This clearly struck a chord with Scorsese, whose Archer is both dismayed by Ellen's unconventional behaviour and panic-stricken by May's single-mindedness. In the crucial scene in which his wife tells him she is pregnant, dashing for good his hopes of following Ellen to Europe, she rises from her chair and towers over him, causing him to recoil. Scorsese films her gesture twice, the second time focusing on the bustle-encased lower half of her body and heightening the rustle of her skirt. It is a powerful image of male terror in the face of the maternal body.

Scorsese seems unexpectedly at home with period drama, taking more than one cue from that other saga of social change and doomed love, *The Magnificent Ambersons* (1942). As in Welles' film, the tension between tradition and modernity is signalled by the use of irises and masking, which looks back to silent cinema while at the same time acting as harbinger of the new medium about to take the late nineteenth century by storm. *The Magnificent Ambersons* is melancholic, treating its characters swept up in the tide of history with sympathy and projecting a sense of loss at what is sacrificed in the name of progress. At first glance, Scorsese's movie is less nostalgic, ending on a hopeful note, which recognises that Archer's children will achieve the happiness he denied himself. For Scorsese, as for Wharton, Archer's final decision to walk away from love is the last nail in the coffin of the past in which he is entombed. Yet it is clear that the film-maker, more than the novelist, identifies with Archer's desire to live in his memories rather than face reality. Scorsese's *Age of Innocence* is suffused with fear of loss, most notably in its striving for period authenticity (always a lost cause) and in its obsession with faithfully reproducing the novel.

This lends the film a static, stultified quality, which is entirely appropriate to Daniel Day-Lewis' frozen stiffness as Archer, but does less justice to the freewheeling body language of more unconventional characters, such as Julius Beaufort, played with vulgar verve by Stuart Wilson, or Michelle Pfeiffer's Ellen, who strides out with an appealing mannish swagger. All the performances are excellent, and the production is a visual *tour de force*; but it really is time to lift the shroud of despair.

Reinventing history

Costume and identity

INTRODUCTION

The focus of this book is on the questions and challenges presented by the preoccupation with memory, history and nostalgia in contemporary cinema. I have tried to navigate a path between opposing positions: those which mourn the loss of authentic histories, seeing in the growth of irony and pastiche a decline in our access to the truth, and those which celebrate the value of dissolving boundaries between truth and fiction, and between gender, race and ethnic identities. The former seems too attached to traditional notions of authenticity (needless to say, 'authenticity' is generally constructed according to individual agendas) and the authority of historians, while the latter runs the risk of losing sight of the aims and objects of historical enquiry altogether. As with any period of transition, the most productive site for investigation seems to be the nature of the transition itself, the conflicts and conundrums thrown up by the breakthroughs and blind alleys of heated debate. In such circumstances, we are unlikely to reach definitive conclusions – indeed, we are more likely to find our cherished belief systems thrown into disarray. But even if many hard-won intellectual and political achievements seem to have been lost, there is something to be said for being aware that nothing can be taken for granted, and that history requires us to constantly reassess priorities and positions.

One aspect of the process of reassessment engendered by the current moment is the need to think again about how history is to be approached and presented. In many ways, it is liberating to acknowledge that the truth of history lies in the eye of the beholder; on the other hand, this can lead to the anarchy of relativism, in which all accounts of the past are accorded equal value. One way out of such impasses is to view history as an activity of deciphering historical accounts, treating them as representations which can reveal the whys and wherefores of reconstruction and reinvention, and the complex emotional, psychological and ideological investments that contribute to

199

making histories. This involves quite a radical shift of emphasis away from major events and leading figures to the day-to-day business of consuming and engaging with cultural images and artefacts. The interpretation of such everyday encounters is generally the responsibility of cultural historians, who look at material objects and images as evidence of social history, shedding light on their context and the reasons for their existence. However, the matters of aesthetic judgement, formal analysis and creative response are usually the province of disciplines such as literature, philosophy, archaeology, art and film studies, all of which look at texts or objects as forms of representation. These analyses often pay more attention to subjective response, whether of cultural producers or consumers, seeing such responses as linked to broader social and cultural developments. The most productive set out to illuminate the interplay between text and context, demonstrating the way each transforms the other. However, this is not easy to accomplish and remains relatively rare – more often than not, text and context are brought together as transparent reflections of one another, with the text viewed as a vehicle for recording social events.

The first piece in this section, 'Fashion and sexual display in 1950s Hollywood' (1995), tackles issues raised by the relationship between text and context, beginning with the way the 1950s have been characterised by historians as culturally and ideologically repressive, particularly with respect to women. It surveys a range of conflicting discourses about gender, sexuality and consumerism to show that the 1950s was in fact a turbulent era in which many different ideas about tradition and modernity were in circulation, creating a climate in which many conservative ideas were under pressure. The article reveals that far from being passive victims or sexual objects, women were perceived as having an active role to play in the postwar consumer economy, which paradoxically endowed them with social power both inside and outside the home. Rather than losing the sexual and economic independence they had gained during the Second World War, women found their emancipated status channelled in different directions, through home and family, consumerism and part-time office work. At the same time, contemporary studies revealed that their sexuality was not necessarily satisfied by their role as domestic goddess. This context suggests that the white, middle-class, heterosexual couple and monogamous family so often identified as the cornerstone of 1950s society was far less stable than has been previously presented. Looking closely at the change in female body shape manifested in the shift from Utility-inspired fashions of the 1940s to the flamboyant New Look designs of the 1950s, which gave rise to huge controversy, the article suggests that the prevailing view of the 1950s, and of women's social position during the decade, deserves to be rethought.

Turning to the relationship between this unstable context and the films of the period, 'Fashion and sexual display in 1950s Hollywood' argues that analysis of those films has tended to reflect post-1970s feminist concerns around female sexuality, voyeurism and fetishism, and to produce a rather puritanical, negative critique as a result. By looking at the way those films engage with and comment upon social discourses of the time, it suggests that a more complex picture of the relationship of cultural artefacts to social context, and of the position of women in society, emerges. Popular films are often perceived as imbued with and confirming prevailing ideologies, a perception that neglects the extent to which they can offer the opportunity to escape, or indeed challenge, socially imposed identities. The second piece, 'Replicating the past: memory and history in *Dance With a Stranger*' (1997), explores the extent to which identities can be transformed by encounters with the past in period fiction films. It reassesses the cultural value of popular historical fictions, which are frequently condemned as vehicles for 'vulgar', commodified versions of national history that package conservative images for sale in world markets. While accepting that period costume dramas do not necessarily offer 'authentic' histories, the article claims that they provide other kinds of experience by drawing attention, through self-conscious use of costume, production design and performance, to the processes of historical reconstruction. Through films such as *Dance With a Stranger* (1985), which is set in the 1950s and tells the story of Ruth Ellis, the last woman to be hanged in Britain, audiences are invited to engage in a number of activities, from exercising their aesthetic and critical judgement on the success or otherwise of the reconstruction, to debating the pros and cons of arguments about capital punishment circulating at the time the film was made. Those critiques which condemn popular historical fictions for their failure to project accurate versions of the past seem to miss the point: such films are by definition creative reinventions, and they have much to tell about the aesthetic, emotional and imaginative dimensions of historical reconstruction, whether by film-makers, audiences or historians.

One of the aspects of popular historical films that has been extensively criticised is their proclivity for putting on display an array of period artefacts, almost like a museum, to satisfy the audience's desire to consume, rather than engage critically with history. The essay explores the way such replicas can enable viewers to construct different identities for themselves, imagining themselves in other times and places. It suggests that while spectators may on some level be aware that they are involved in an illusion, they can at the same time make imaginative leaps through which they can participate in the process of reconstructing the past, and become historians of a kind themselves. These issues are explored in more depth in the book's opening chapter, 'Rethinking nostalgia'.

The final piece in this section, 'Fictions of identity: style, mimicry and gender in the films of Kathryn Bigelow' (1996), takes these ideas about the fluidity of identity further, using Bigelow's work to explore cross-gender identification in contemporary cinema. Although Bigelow's films are not historical fictions, they use pastiche extensively, quoting from other movies and mixing genres and styles, often from male-oriented action films. Like many postclassical film-makers (for example, Martin Scorsese, discussed in Part Four), Bigelow appropriates the work of other film-makers, past and present, in order to produce her own, distinctive style. She has cultivated a reputation as a maverick director, one who is unwilling to accept categorisation of her work in traditional gender or generic terms. She emulates the visceral style of high-profile action directors such as James Cameron, Sam Peckinpah and Oliver Stone, refusing to be restricted to 'women's material'. Her play with gender roles extends to the construction of her public persona and sartorial style, which is deliberately androgynous, cool and ironic. The essay explores the extent to which this tactic of pastiche and mimicry, which amounts to 'film-making in disguise', has enabled Bigelow to retain a clear identity and voice in mainstream Hollywood, or whether she has lost her way as a result.

Bigelow's relationship to cinema history is rather different from that of male contemporaries such as Scorsese. As this book has demonstrated, the preoccupation with the cinematic past often results in a melancholy nostalgia, as the loss of authentic identities is mourned. While there is an element of nostalgic homage in films such as *The Loveless* (1982), rather than a desire to recover a yearned-for past, the intention seems to be to raid its images in order to rewrite history from a contemporary perspective. Quotations from other film-makers' work suggest a desire for continuity with a canonical tradition of radical, maverick cinema, but Bigelow uses those images and styles in an ironic manner, so that they appear like lexicons that can be mobilised to create new meanings. This process of selection and reassembly of the past in the present resembles the activity of historians; however, Bigelow's approach is deliberately iconoclastic, motivated by a desire to overturn accepted wisdom and create new, exciting possibilities in the arena of gender and representation.

It is often argued that the predilection for pastiche and irony in contemporary cinema disconnects it from history, collapsing the past into a perpetual present in which style and image are privileged over content and context, with a consequent diminishing of emotional affect. It is true that the emphasis on style in Bigelow's films can create an ironic distance, as the audience is invited to engage in a game of recognising the references, without necessarily remembering their context. While this may result in a loss of historical understanding, it could be said to facilitate different kinds of awareness – of the role played by images in accessing the past, for example, or of the way images create meaning by reference to other images, rather than by referring to a fixed content. Appropriately enough, since it appears at the conclusion of this book, Bigelow's work raises fundamental questions of how the past is approached, understood, deconstructed and reconstructed in cinema.

Further reading

Bruzzi, Stella, *Undressing Cinema: Clothing and Identity in the Movies* (London and New York: Routledge, 1997).

Higson, Andrew, 'Re-presenting the national past: nostalgia and pastiche in the heritage film', in Friedman, Lester (ed.), *British Cinema and Thatcherism: Fires Were Started* (London: University College London Press, 1993).

Jermyn, Deborah and Redmond, Sean (eds), *The Cinema of Kathryn Bigelow: Hollywood Transgressor* (London: Wallflower Press, 2002).

Landy, Marcia, '"You remember Diana Dors, don't you?": history, femininity and the law in 1950s and 1980s British cinema', in *Cinematic Uses of the Past* (Minneapolis: University of Minnesota Press, 1996).

Monk, Claire, and Sargeant, Amy (eds), *British Historical Cinema* (London and New York: Routledge, 2002).

Moseley, Rachel, *Growing Up With Audrey Hepburn: Text, Audience, Resonance* (Manchester: Manchester University Press, 2003).

Neale, Steve, and Smith, Murray (eds), *Contemporary Hollywood Cinema* (London and New York: Routledge, 1998).

Tasker, Yvonne, *Spectacular Bodies: Gender, Genre and the Action Cinema* (London and New York: Routledge, 1993).

Further viewing

Aliens (James Cameron, USA, 1986)

Blue Steel (Kathryn Bigelow, USA, 1990)

Dance With a Stranger (Mike Newell, UK, 1985)

Funny Face (Stanley Donen, USA, 1957)

Gentlemen Prefer Blondes (Howard Hawks, USA, 1953)

How to Marry a Millionaire (Jean Negulesco, USA, 1953)

The Krays (Peter Medak, UK, 1990)

The Loveless (Kathryn Bigelow and Monty Montgomery, USA, 1982)

Near Dark (Kathryn Bigelow, USA, 1987)

Peeping Tom (Michael Powell, UK, 1960)
Point Break (Kathryn Bigelow, USA, 1991)
Rear Window (Alfred Hitchcock, USA, 1954)
Ruby Gentry (King Vidor, USA, 1952)
Scorpio Rising (Kenneth Anger, USA, 1964)
The Silence of the Lambs (Jonathan Demme, USA, 1990)
Strange Days (Kathryn Bigelow, USA, 1995)
Terminator 2: Judgment Day (James Cameron, USA, 1993)
The Girl Can't Help It (Frank Tashlin, USA, 1956)
Thelma & Louise (Ridley Scott, USA, 1991)
Vertigo (Alfred Hitchcock, USA, 1958)
Weekend (Jean-Luc Godard, France, 1967)
The Wild One (László Benedek, USA, 1953)
Written on the Wind (Douglas Sirk, USA, 1956)

Chapter 15

FASHION AND SEXUAL DISPLAY
IN 1950s HOLLYWOOD

Contemporary feminism has looked at the 1950s with some suspicion. Often the decade is seen as a period in which women were expected to retreat into domesticity, relinquishing the gains they had made during the Second World War. The sexual and economic emancipation achieved by women during the 1940s, when they were in the position of standing in on the home front for men who were away at war (the Rosie the Riveter phenomenon), is said to have deteriorated as the postwar consumer economy relocated them as wives and mothers whose primary responsibility was the home and family. From this perspective, the 1950s are seen as an ideologically repressive era, presided over in the USA by the conservative president Dwight Eisenhower, in sharp contrast both to the 1940s and to the more liberated 1960s. However, this conception does not entirely stand up to scrutiny – and, indeed, some feminists have begun to characterise the 1950s as a turbulent decade, in which prevailing notions of femininity came under pressure from conflicting ideological currents.[1] This was a period, for example, when female sexual display was as much in evidence as images of respectable, buttoned-up housewives, and although this cannot necessarily be seen as progressive, it is at least evidence that there were a number of contradictory notions of femininity (and by implication, masculinity) in circulation. This appears to have been a time when women's position at the centre of the family and the consumer economy endowed them with a certain power. While from our post-1970s viewpoint we may regard that power as flawed, or illusory, and may see the overt display of the female body as a retrograde step, we should perhaps ask ourselves whether such a censorious position is not equally repressive. If we take a more historical view, we may discover a different map of the social and cultural position of women during a period when gender and other social roles were the subject of heated debate.

Figure 15.1   Size matters: Jayne Mansfield and Tom Ewell in *The Girl Can't Help It* (1956).
Courtesy Twentieth Century Fox and the Kobal Collection.

I shall approach this issue by looking at the role of costume in 1950s Hollywood films, focusing on the changes in female body shape between the 1940s
and 1950s and exploring the ideological implications of that transformation.
These developments have been widely discussed by feminist writers,[2] not all
of whom see the shift as undermining women's place in society. I shall focus
on the female body, but it should be pointed out that the male body also
underwent a transformation during this period, and participated in the general
ethos of physical display. Little has been written about male screen costume,
partly because consumerism and fashion are still mainly (and mistakenly) associated with femininity. Suffice it to say here that the tall, muscular, well-built
body shape of 1950s stars such as Marlon Brando and Rock Hudson contrasted
vividly with the slighter proportions of leading male stars of the 1940s such as
Humphrey Bogart. In 1950s Hollywood, to be a small man often meant that
your sexuality was in question – as with James Dean, for example, or Montgomery Clift. Hollywood explored this masculinity crisis in a variety of genres
– in comedies such as Frank Tashlin's *The Girl Can't Help It* (1956) or *Will
Success Spoil Rock Hunter?* (1957) the 1950s preoccupation with body image is

mercilessly satirised, and we should not forget the outbreak of biblical and historical epics featuring muscular male bodies rendered vulnerable by the skimpiest of costumes. The male physique in Hollywood cinema has been comprehensively covered elsewhere,[3] so I shall leave this tantalising train of thought here. However, it is important to note that body size, as well as shape, was a significant factor in depictions of both femininity and masculinity.

To return to the transition in the female form from the 1940s to the 1950s, a shift has been detected from the broad-shouldered, tailored suits and dresses inspired by wartime Utility fashions, to the extravagantly feminised, hour-glass shape of Christian Dior's New Look, launched in 1947, which became the dominant body image during the 1950s. The minimalist, simple lines of Utility designs, which were often based on military uniforms, gave way to soft folds and pleats. The broad, square shoulders became curved. The breasts, waists and hips that had all but disappeared during the war years were now emphasised with the help of uplift bras, whalebone corsets and stiff petticoats. Sensible footwear was replaced by high-heeled, pointed court shoes. Cheaper, functional fabrics were replaced by expensive ones that fell beautifully, again emphasising softness and curves rather than sharp angles. The New Look, in all its manifestations, projected a spectacular, sexualised vision of femininity that was consistent with commodity fetishism, recognising the power of women as consumers. However, the transition from old to new was not pain-less, and was not achieved overnight.

The New Look's projection of modern femininity was complex, articu-lating the contradictions facing postwar women. While women's role in the family was high on the social and cultural agenda, there were other, conflicting discourses in circulation too. The results of the two Kinsey Reports in 1948 and 1953 indicated that the sexual preferences and habits of both male and female Americans were more aberrant than had previously been thought, and that the family was hardly a cornerstone of Christian morality. The Kinsey reports had a huge impact on postwar culture, provoking intense discussion about sexuality. The influence of the Second World War, during which large numbers of women became sexually and economically emancipated, cannot be overestimated. The relationship between the genders was radically transformed, and this, combined with postwar manpower shortages, meant that women could not simply be relo-cated within the family after the war. At the same time as they were perceived to be crucial to postwar drives to replenish the falling birth rate, they were needed in certain jobs in the expanding economy. They had a dual role – as wives and mothers, but also as workers. This dual role was reflected in consumer discourses around labour-saving devices in the home, which would enable women to work and look after the family. It was also reflected in fashion. As well as the full-skirted, ultra-feminine version of the New Look, a slimline, tailored variant more suitable for office work emerged a few years later. Another outfit that was popular during the 1950s was jeans and check shirt, indicating that women had not entirely given up their aspirations as manual workers either.

The controversy surrounding the New Look when it was launched in the late 1940s illuminates many of the debates around female sexuality in the 1950s. Dior's New Look had been mooted as early as 1938, but its progress had been interrupted by the war. The war accelerated the democratisation of class and gender relationships that was already taking place during the 1930s. The wartime ethos was characterised by a discourse of social egalitarianism, manifested in Utility clothing designed to iron out class and gender differences. The Utility movement was introduced in Britain in 1941 as part of a programme to manage and control consumerism in the context of wartime shortages, but it also aimed to use available resources to produce quality goods at reasonable prices that would be accessible to everyone, regardless of social status. The simple, tailored lines of Utility clothing designs were often based on military uniforms – dressed in uniform, everyone looked the same. Many women felt empowered by their apparent equality with men in the public sphere, and looked forward to a postwar world in which they would continue to be equal members of society.

To these women, the New Look represented a retrograde step. The long, full skirt was completely unsuitable for manual labour, unlike the dungarees and slacks fashionable during the war. It was also expensive, and beyond the reach of most women, so it was perceived as reconstituting outmoded class barriers. Above all, it was sexy – an eye-catching distraction from the serious business of postwar reconstruction. Some feminists at the time described the New Look as reminiscent of 'caged bird' attitudes towards women prevalent before the war, a view shared by some feminists today.[4] The contemporary responses to the dramatic change in female body shape signalled by the New Look indicate an understandable unwillingness to relinquish the freedoms that many women had gained as a result of the war. But it also articulates a commonly held perception that the masculinised androgyny typified by wartime Utility clothing represents freedom, progress and modernity, while the feminine erotic display embodied in the New Look connotes restriction and regression. From this perspective, we can only assume that the women who embraced the New Look in the 1950s, when it became mass-produced and available ready-to-wear, did so in bad faith, duped by advertising campaigns into accepting a powerless, domestic role once more.

However, if we look more closely at the New Look in the context of the multiple discourses around femininity circulating in the late 1940s and 1950s, a different picture emerges. To take the consumer discourses first, it is well documented that the family was at the centre of postwar consumerism, with advertising focused on women in the home. Women as housewives, mothers and workers represented a powerful market for domestic appliances, so it is hardly surprising that they featured prominently as the addressees of advertising campaigns. As Lynn Spigel and others have revealed,[5] in these discourses, the home is presented as women's realm. The figure of woman is foregrounded, while fathers and children often remain in the background. This female figure is often glamorised, stylishly dressed to match the elegant décor of the home. Woman and home are put on display as if in a shop window.

Yet though these discourses clearly do commodify women and the home, something else seems to be going on too. The home, and women's place within it, are professionalised. The woman's role is akin to that of a manager: she manages her domestic work efficiently in order to manage the family better, helped by labour-saving devices such as washing machines and refrigerators. Although women still perform domestic tasks, they spend less time on them, which frees them to spend more leisure time with the family and to take on part-time work. It also frees them, of course, to do more shopping, not just for the home, but for themselves. The abundance of leisure time also enables them to seek pleasure in other directions, too – perhaps outside the heterosexual, monogamous family. In many advertisements of the period, women dressed in designer outfits compete with the television set for their husband's attention, the implication being that their sexual needs are in danger of being ignored.

In these consumer discourses, centred on the home, women are a powerful presence as managers and as sexual beings. This is hardly a traditional view of women's domestic role. It suggests a model of the family as a significant arena for work and play, for visual pleasure and sexuality, for romance and spectacle – a theatrical space with woman at the centre, as protagonist, but also as responsible to a large extent for the *mise-en-scène*. If the female manager/consumer depicted in these discourses was presented as powerful, then the women addressed by them were encouraged to perceive themselves as powerful too. While such images were consonant with contemporary capitalism, and were designed to encourage women to 'spend, spend, spend', they also had a cultural dimension. They mobilised ideas and debates circulating at the time that did not always fold in neatly with prevailing ideologies.

This brings me to discourses around female sexuality in the late 1940s and 1950s. I have already suggested that fears about the falling birth rate focused

on the postwar maternal role of women. This was a period of intense scient-
ific investigation of sexuality. The pioneering reports by Alfred Kinsey, one
on male sexuality published in 1948 and another on female sexuality in 1953,
unveiled some shocking, little-known facts. Kinsey's controversial research
revealed that male and female sexual desires were not exactly compatible.
While men's sexual peak occurred early in life, women's sexual potential
increased later on, in their 30s. What is more, women's sexual needs were
not satisfied by heterosexual intercourse, and were far more demanding and
diverse than had previously been considered. Far from underwriting the
ideology of the patriarchal family, Kinsey's findings shattered the self-esteem
of the American male and undermined his authority within the family.

In the light of these conflicting discourses, it is possible to see the 1950s
female body, corseted and padded to produce an exaggerated version of femininity, as a complex cultural phenomenon encapsulating a number of social
anxieties revolving around the figure of woman. At the same time, this body
represented possibilities for women. While it did display female sexuality for
consumption, it also presented the body as active and mobile. The very ex-
hibitionism of the sexualised body image demanded attention and satisfaction
in excess of what could be achieved. The visual pleasure it offered was also a
challenge – certainly to the male viewer, but perhaps to the female viewer
too. King Vidor's 1952 melodrama *Ruby Gentry* can be seen as commenting
directly on a number of these issues. Ruby, played by the wonderfully excessive Jennifer Jones, lives with her family on the edge of a swamp and is def-
initely from the wrong side of the tracks. She uses her sexuality to move up
the social ladder, marrying into the local gentry, but she is never accepted by
the respectable community, nor does she get what she really wants – the man
she loves, played by Charlton Heston, who regards her with suspicion, guilt
and fear, though he desires her sexually. At the end of the film, Ruby gives up
the power and wealth she has acquired, remaining a social outcast.

We first see Ruby outlined in silhouette in the doorway of her father's
hunting lodge. She is wearing jeans and tight sweater, clothes normally associated with blue-collar work, which, far from masculinising or deglamorising
her, emphasise her feminine curves. Yet she is a curiously androgynous figure.
She is the object of the doctor's and Jim Gentry's gaze, but she is also in
control of the look, and manipulates the gaze in the scene with a torch, when
she torments her upper-class lover by fixing him in the beam of light. When
she first appears in the doorway, Ruby is on the boundary between interior
(domestic) and exterior (public) space, and she moves freely in both those
spaces. She performs domestic tasks, such as serving food to the men gathered
in the lodge, and she also handles a gun with confidence – indeed, she is a
more accomplished hunter than many of the men. In the course of the film,

Figure 15.2   Out of the swamp: Jennifer Jones in *Ruby Gentry* (1952). Courtesy Twentieth Century Fox and the Kobal Collection.

she becomes a successful businesswoman, only to discover that money and power cannot buy her the man she loves. She gives it all up and returns to running a fishing boat. The narrative of upward mobility is also told by the visual codes of costume. As Ruby moves up the social ladder, she exchanges trousers for New Look designer dresses, until at the end she returns to sweater, trousers and cap on the fishing boat.

Ruby is presented as a destructive force. It is precisely her mobility in class and gender terms that is so threatening. Yet even though the narrative punishes her, making sure that she does not get what she really wants, which is depicted in highly sexual terms, she remains mobile to the very end. We see her steer the fishing boat out of the harbour as the voice-over of the liberal-minded doctor who is in love with her condemns society's treatment of her. Characters such as Ruby Gentry are everywhere in 1950s Hollywood cinema. They are restless and dissatisfied, challenging patriarchal authority and social norms. They are troublemakers, and although the narrative attempts to neutralise their threat by disempowering them, their transgressive impulses remain a powerful focus for identification. Their body image,

211

characterised by ample curves, with large breasts and hips, suggests a mature, fertile sexuality, but it is not really a maternal body. In fact, such figures are generally demonised in comparison to more compliant female characters who represent traditional maternity. Yet even these more conventional maternal characters are rarely simply the embodiment of traditional values; they seem to function more as victims of social pressures.

The 1950s female body image can be interpreted in different ways. It can be seen as a sign of the re-feminisation of women after their wartime emancipation, relocating them as sexual objects rather than active subjects. Some feminists perceive the spectacularisation of the female body during this period as linked to pornography, and the constricting padding and whalebone necessary to achieve the New Look shape as evocative of fetishism and bondage.[6] This pornographic body is then seen as a retrograde phenomenon, locking women into a femininity coded as biologically female. But there is surely more to it than that. This body pressed so emphatically into a female shape is mobile and active, and it can be a sign of transgression and power. In so far as it connotes bondage, it may also signify active female sexual pleasure, or it can operate as a kind of commentary on the tension between sexual desire and social containment or repression.

During the 1950s, melodrama was a key genre for articulating the contradictory pressures affecting the lives and experiences of women. In Douglas Sirk's *Written on the Wind* (1956), which tells the story of the disintegration of a wealthy, dysfunctional patriarchal family, those contradictions are literally embodied in the character of Marylee Hadley, whose wilful and promiscuous behaviour results in her father's death from a heart attack. In the scene in which this happens, Marylee is brought home by the police after picking up a petrol pump attendant for casual sex. Unrepentant, she goes upstairs to her room, where she plays loud music and indulges in a manic dance, dressed in a revealing basque and scarlet negligee. This would seem to be a clear example of pornographic display, but the sequence is more contradictory than it may appear at first sight. On one hand, the *mise-en-scène* emphasises restraint and restriction: characters are often framed looking out through windows, for example. Yet Marylee's defiant progress across the hallway and up the stairs to her bedroom, wearing a very tight dress, is accomplished with skill and confidence. Her body movements are exaggerated but fluid, and she moves freely in three-dimensional space.

In her room, she again moves freely and confidently in a space littered with expensive commodities, which she somehow manages not to break as her dance becomes increasingly frenzied. Her body in the red negligee does break the edges of the frame, however, giving the impression that the cinema screen is too small to accommodate this excessive female body. The *mise-en-scène* is

Figure 15.3   Exhibitionist: Dorothy Malone and Rock Hudson in *Written on the Wind* (1956). Courtesy Universal and the Kobal Collection.

consciously colour-coded, with the red associated with Marylee connoting danger, while the more respectable Lucy is dressed first in off-white for her horrified reaction to Jasper Hadley's death, and then later, framed by a window, in a green dress that seems to suggest that the future of the family rests on her fertility. The orgiastic dance sequence, in which Marylee strips down to her underwear, is voyeuristic, yet in its visual and auditory excess it moves beyond the security that has been associated with cinematic voyeurism. It seems to assault the viewers' senses, addressing them as voyeurs, so that the situation in which they can watch in safety without being found out is destabilised. This aggressive assault on the spectator has been identified as one of the strategies of horror, and it may be that these destructive 1950s viragos have something in common with the monstrous castrating women populating the horror film.[7] At the end of the film, Marylee is redeemed. With her father and brother dead, she takes over as head of the family oil business – but she still has not found the love she wants so desperately. As with Ruby Gentry, true satisfaction continues to elude her.

So far, I've focused on a particular female body image circulating in the 1950s, an extravagantly feminine one shaped by the New Look, characterised

213

by abundant curves. I have tried to demonstrate that this body image, while clearly imbued with commodity fetishism, could also connote female power and mobility. Despite efforts to contain the excess embodied in such images of restless feminine desire, they were sometimes difficult to manage, and the transgressive impulses they evoked could have a threatening or destabilising effect. However, there were a number of other body images available to women in the 1950s. This was also the era of the tomboy dressed in jeans, or, like Audrey Hepburn in *Funny Face* (1957), decked out in simple black sweater and pants. Hepburn's body image was gamine, pre-sexual rather than sexually mature, linked to youth culture and the burgeoning counter-culture movements. Nevertheless, her star persona was also characterised by mobility – of class and gender, and, through her connection to continental Europe, of national identity.

Hepburn's slim, elegant body shape was associated not only with the beatnik movement, but also with Parisian haute couture. Her costumes for the screen and in her private life were designed by French couturier Givenchy, with whom she had a long-standing professional relationship, and this link played an important part in constructing her image. In many of her films she could almost be seen as a fashion plate, or as a model on the catwalk, put on display like any other commodity. Many famous fashion designers worked for Hollywood studios during the 1950s, which is an indication of the degree to which fashion became a significant factor in cinema of the period – indeed, this was an era in which haute couture designs became more widely available through mass production. Yet although stars such as Audrey Hepburn bore the signature of the designers who dressed them, and apparently styled them to fit their own conceptions of femininity, they did not necessarily entirely conform to those conceptions, and their performance both on and off screen could often be at odds with their costume, or vice versa. Similarly, though the glamorous designer clothes worn by Hepburn were no doubt intended to promote identification and inspire the desire for shopping sprees in members of the audience, they had an aesthetic, cultural dimension too.

The relationship between cinema and fashion, and between stars and fashion designers, did not start in the 1950s. In his magisterial, influential study of consumer tie-ins between the cinema and fashion industries in 1930s Hollywood,[8] Charles Eckert argues that cinema acts as a shop window for product placement. Focusing on the female consumer's assumed identification with female stars such as Bette Davis, Eckert argues that this film fan is led to purchase the clothes and accessories that she hopes will make her resemble the admired star. According to Eckert, through this process of identification the female viewer participates in the circulation of commodities that sustains the capitalist economy, whether she realises it or not (and he strongly implies that she does not, and that she is duped by the system).

There is no doubt that Eckert puts his finger on something important – that is, the desire to imitate that is at the heart of commodity fetishism. We acquire possessions and clothes partly in order to construct imaginary identities for ourselves, forged from the identities of others, especially idealised others such as stars or celebrities. There is a strong element of masquerade in the process of selecting what to wear, or how to decorate a house or room. By dressing up we may make a statement about ourselves, but we may also disguise ourselves, and fashion offers a multiplicity of disguises for us to try on and discard. It is precisely this element of masquerade in fashion, which implies a certain phoneyness, or a slipperiness of identity, that arouses ambivalence in some cultural critics, and has contributed, I would suggest, to the marginalisation of debates around screen costume in film studies until recently.[9]

Partly because of the connection between the film and fashion industries, the image of woman in cinema has been perceived as corrupted by commodity fetishism, and by the duplicity associated with costume and masquerade. It has often been argued that the female images with which women viewers are said to identify are fashioned in the interests of capitalism and patriarchy, and that they do not reflect the needs and desires of women themselves. The films of Alfred Hitchcock have been seen as employing a particularly fetishistic female image – and it is interesting that it is mostly titles from the 1950s, such as *Rear Window* (1954) and *Vertigo* (1958), that are cited in this respect. While some claim that in such films the spectacular female star is cut to the measure of male desire,[10] others have suggested that such figures are not simply passive objects, and that it is possible to read Hitchcock's deployment of images of women as presenting a threat to emasculated male characters, who are rarely powerful or dominant.[11] While their voyeurism is a strategy to control and manage the troublesome female image, they are not usually successful in their aim.

It is interesting in this respect that Hitchcock's films often betray a deep suspicion of female fashion. In *Vertigo*, for example, James Stewart plays a character obsessed with a woman (played by Kim Novak) who resembles someone he once loved, whom he believes to be dead. He tries to recreate his dead lover, Madeleine, by making the lookalike, Judy, dress and behave like her, but he is deceived by his own attempt to make a female fetish object, as it is revealed that Madeleine and Judy are one and the same, and he has been set up by Madeleine's husband, his friend. He tracks Judy down with the intention of exacting revenge, and she dies accidentally, so that he loses everything. There could hardly be a clearer statement of the vulnerabilty of heterosexual male desire, and the danger represented by the feminine image. *Rear Window* expresses a similar distrust of the fashion industry, and of fashion's power to deceive. The hero, Jeff, once again played by James Stewart, is a photographer who covers dangerous news assignments. He is confined to his apartment with a broken leg following an accident in which his camera was also smashed. He spends his time spying on his neighbours and speculating about their private lives — he is a classic Peeping Tom.

Jeff's girlfriend Lisa, played by Grace Kelly, is very glamorous and works in the fashion industry — one of the reasons why Jeff seems unable to take their relationship seriously. Lisa is introduced as a dominant, controlling woman who takes charge of Jeff's life, and does her best to persuade him to give up his dangerous occupation and become a fashion photographer, something he is unwilling to do, since he perceives such work as trivial and demeaning. He only begins to take Lisa seriously when she enters into his fantasy about a murder that he suspects has taken place in the apartment opposite, and she stands in for the immobile Jeff, investigating the murder and putting herself at considerable risk, all the while dressed in exotic New Look designer clothes. Like many of the 1950s Hollywood heroines discussed above, Lisa proves herself the better man, and by the end of the film she has exchanged her exquisite New Look dresses for a chic pair of slacks and a shirt.

Both *Vertigo* and *Rear Window* focus on male desire and fantasy, exploring the vulnerability of masculinity by projecting femininity as deceptive, and as a threat to patriarchal authority. Ironically, this very focus seems to open up space for female fantasies of mobility and empowerment, through identification with stars who are both spectacular and active protagonists, and who manage to evade the control of the male hero. These female figures oscillate between masculine and feminine positions in the narrative, articulated through visual codes of costume, an oscillation that is not necessarily settled by the ending. In a sense, all the films I have looked at here, through the ambivalence they display towards male and female sexuality, heterosexual desire, and fashion and consumerism, embody the contradictions facing women in the 1950s, as their role in society and culture was being debated. I hope I have demonstrated that this role offered possibilities as well as constraints, and that the multiple images of femininity in circulation allowed women to conceive of themselves as active protagonists with the power to move between different identities — a process in which fashion and the spectacular female body played a vital part, one that cannot necessarily be regarded as retrograde.

216

Notes

1 See, for example, Birmingham Feminist History Group, 'Feminism as femininity in the nineteen-fifties?', *Feminist Review* 3 (1979), pp. 48–65; Barbara Klinger, 'Selling melodrama: sex, affluence and *Written on the Wind*', in *Melodrama and Meaning: History, Culture and the Films of Douglas Sirk* (Bloomington and Indianapolis: Indiana University Press, 1994), pp. 36–68.

2 For example, Maureen Turim, 'Designing women: the emergence of the new Sweetheart Line', in Jane Gaines and Charlotte Herzog (eds), *Fabrications: Costume and the Female Body* (London and New York: Routledge, 1990), pp. 212–28; Elizabeth Wilson, *Adorned in Dreams: Fashion and Modernity* (London: Virago, 1985); Pam Cook, *Fashioning the Nation: Costume and Identity in British Cinema* (London: BFI Publishing, 1996).

3 For example, by Steven Cohan and Ina Rae Hark (eds), *Screening the Male: Exploring Masculinities in Hollywood Cinema* (London and New York: Routledge, 1994).

4 Maureen Turim, 'Designing women', refers to the Sweetheart Line as a form of 'guilded bondage' [sic]. These debates around the New Look are described in more detail in Cook, *Fashioning the Nation*.

5 Lynn Spigel in Denise Mann and Lynn Spigel (eds), *Private Screenings: Television and the Female Consumer* (Minneapolis: University of Minnesota Press, 1992).

6 See Turim, 'Designing women'.

7 See Carol J. Clover, *Men, Women and Chainsaws: Gender in the Modern Horror Film* (London: BFI Publishing, 1992); Barbara Creed, *The Monstrous-Feminine: Film, Feminism, Psychoanalysis* (London and New York: Routledge, 1993).

8 Charles Eckert, 'The Carole Lombard in Macy's window', in Christine Gledhill (ed.), *Stardom: Industry of Desire* (London and New York: Routledge, 1991), pp. 30–9.

9 For further discussion of this point, see Pam Cook, 'Changing places: costume and identity', in *Fashioning the Nation*, pp. 41–63.

10 The phrase is Laura Mulvey's in 'Visual pleasure and narrative cinema', in *Visual and Other Pleasures* (Basingstoke and London: Macmillan, 1989), pp. 14–26. This article, which criticises Hitchcock's work as one example of classic Hollywood cinema's drive to present women as passive objects and men as active subjects through a particular regime of looking, became feminist orthodoxy in the late 1970s and 1980s.

11 See, for example, Tania Modleski's analysis of *Rear Window* and *Vertigo*, in *The Women Who Knew Too Much: Hitchcock and Feminist Theory* (London and New York: Methuen, 1988).

Chapter 16

REPLICATING THE PAST

Memory and history in *Dance With a Stranger*

*D*ance *With a Stranger* (1985), set in the 1950s, is an example of a contemporary film that recreates a relatively recent period in the British past. These are not normally perceived as historical films or costume dramas in the sense of those that reconstruct the more distant past, and they are not usually as flamboyantly spectacular. But such movies adopt similar stylistic strategies and perform the same function as a heritage film or a Jane Austen adaptation. These latter examples are different in so far as they are literary adaptations, which means that the question of the film's relationship to the source text comes into play as well as their representation of period. But the films about the 1950s that I discuss here – that is, those based on 'true life stories' – produce similarly bowdlerised versions, or travesties of history. Using cinematic conventions of visual display, together with sound and music, they invite nostalgic encounters with the past perceived as imaginary, as an arena for fantasy, and as an opportunity to explore the process of historical reconstruction itself.

Although historical films may contain an element of social commentary – in other words, they do connect on some level with social reality – and they are frequently interpreted in these terms, this is not generally their only, nor even their primary, concern. Rather, they use the cinematic medium self-consciously to explore our imaginary relationship with past events, presenting history as a collection of mementoes, as fragmented and partial, accessible only through the mediation of personal perceptions and emotional responses. In doing so, these films contribute to debates about the status of historical truth and objectivity.

While I would argue that period films cannot be viewed as 'authentic' histories, I do not intend to diminish their power and significance as historical fictions. Indeed, the questions that historical films raise about the representation of the past are extremely important. I shall explore some of those questions by focusing on *Dance With a Stranger*, which formed part of a cycle of British films produced in the 1980s that recalled the 1950s. I shall also touch briefly on *The Krays*, which deals with the notorious East End gangster brothers, and was released at the end of the decade in 1990. These films, like others made in the 80s, have been discussed primarily in the context of Thatcherism, for the ways in which they engage with Conservative policies and ideologies of the time.[1] In other words, what the films have to say about 1980s Britain is usually privileged over their relationship to the past, a fairly common approach to historical films.[2] However, as many commentators agree, it is often difficult, if not impossible, to construct a coherent social message or identifiable political position in period fiction films. At most, what tends to be offered is a vaguely liberal position which touches on a range of contemporary issues while intentionally keeping its options open.

Dance With a Stranger, which takes as its subject Ruth Ellis' hanging in 1955 for the murder of her lover David Blakely, can be read as an intervention in debates about capital punishment circulating during the 1980s, and as a deliberation on Thatcherite rhetoric about a classless society, as well as a discourse on gender, class and sexuality – but it is not easy to identify what the film-makers are actually saying about these issues. By her own account, Shelagh Delaney, who wrote the script, saw Ruth Ellis and David Blakely as victims of a snobbish and class-conscious society, and *Dance With a Stranger* could be interpreted in that light. However, the film presents its protagonists as deeply flawed individuals drawn together by sadomasochistic obsession, so that on one level we are encouraged to think that their tragic downfall was more the result of individual psychology than social forces. Similarly, while *The Krays* can be seen as commenting on 1980s Thatcherite notions of family values and free enterprise, among other things, its message about those issues is obscure. It is not at all clear whether the film-makers see the villainous Kray twins as a symptom of social forces such as the matriarchal working-class family, or as the offspring of a particularly deranged version of that family, from which no general conclusions can be drawn.

But if these two films do not make definitive statements about the state of the nation, they do make statements of another kind, as I hope to show when I look at *Dance With a Stranger* in more detail. Those approaches that concentrate on what historical fictions have to say about the present tend to retrieve the contemporary social message from behind the trappings of historical reconstruction, which are rarely discussed in their own right. If they are discussed, they are often perceived in negative terms as carriers of ideological messages contaminated by consumerism. The images themselves are seen as commodities – selling 'us' (the British) to 'them' (primarily the American market).[3] Without denying the validity of such approaches, I would claim that historical films are far more complex and interesting than is allowed by those critiques which focus on their appeal as commodities for consumption. I hope to demonstrate that *Dance With a Stranger* has only a tenuous connection with social reality, past or present, but that it has much to tell us about the process of historical reconstruction. But first I shall give a brief account of the historical moment which this film reinvents.

The year in which *Dance With a Stranger* was released theatrically in the UK, 1985, was the thirtieth anniversary of Ruth Ellis' death. Ellis' story appears to be emblematic of a particular moment in British history. Her death sentence was perceived by many at the time to be barbaric, and as reflecting badly on Britain's claim to be a civilised nation. It also brought the country's legal system into question, since certain evidence that might have proved mitigating circumstances was not submitted, and the fact that the murder was clearly a crime of passion was deemed irrelevant in British law. Ellis was the last woman to be hanged in Britain, and her death provoked a fierce controversy in the press. Leading liberals, such as Raymond Chandler, wrote to the papers condemning the savagery of the sentence, while the same year writer Arthur Koestler and publisher Victor Gollancz launched a campaign to abolish capital punishment, which was already under public scrutiny. This was not the only area in which liberalism was rearing its head. The 1950s have often been represented as a period of social repression, particularly when it came to female sexuality, with respectability the order of the day. However, on closer inspection the decade is revealed as one of intense cultural conflict, in which traditional social structures such as the monogamous nuclear family were under pressure from new ideas about the sexual preferences and behaviour of both men and women. Although there were attempts by official agencies to control this move towards sexual liberation by containing it within a discourse that emphasised sex within marriage, the evidence was that a sexual revolution was shaking the foundations of British society. Increasingly, women were seen as more than wives and mothers, as workers too, as sexual beings outside their reproductive role, and as consumers, not only of household appliances, but also of fashion and cosmetics. There was also a class revolution in progress. With full employment, working-class people had more to spend and aspirations to upward class mobility. Such aspirations were often expressed in terms of material wealth and acquisition of consumer goods.

This is clearly a schematic outline that presents a particular view of the 1950s. It may be woefully inadequate to describe the complexities of the period, but it captures, in shorthand, the way in which cracks were beginning to appear in the fabric of society. Other accounts have stressed the repressiveness of the time, and the official attempts to relocate women within the family after the Second World War. Some have focused more on the rise of youth cultures and teenage rebellion. There is also the influence of popular American culture to be considered, and the question of race and ethnicity. As more people could afford to take European holidays, the impact of European cultures needs to be addressed. The list of social factors and events necessary to provide a complete picture of 1950s Britain is almost endless, and all accounts necessarily leave something out.

My point may seem obvious: historical reconstruction is a highly selective process, subject to different agendas, and also to fashion. Cultural historians, museum curators and archivists alike cut a slice out of all that is available and re-present selected material as historical evidence for the scrutiny of others. Priorities — that is, what is considered suitable for selection — change according to the demands of the current moment. A gap in the historical record is identified, which the historian or curator attempts to fill. This process is often justified in the name of completism, involving the collection of more and more data in order to fill such perceived gaps. But my own experience of working on a cinema journal of historical record,[4] and as a feminist historian, suggests that such completism is equally subject to criteria that reflect specific cultural and ideological choices. Thus I would argue that history is not so much a matter of producing definitive versions or explanations of past events, as of producing contested interpretations by different interest groups, which are usually in conflict. The 'truth' or validity of any interpretation can only be determined by a process of contestation, which may eventually produce a consensus. However, it is perfectly possible to believe in an interpretation that lies outside the consensus.[5]

A less obvious point, perhaps, is that the activity of historical investigation and reconstruction, whether it is carried out by an eminent historian, a novelist or a film-maker, is a matter of cut and paste, of cutting out bits and pieces of historical record and pasting them together to create new texts, interpretations and meanings. I am not suggesting that all histories are therefore equally valid, but I would claim that historians are consumers as well as producers, in that we collect objects and materials that arouse our curiosity, which we invest with special meaning and power. We cut these objects and materials out of the wider fabric of history and reassemble them to produce new objects and materials. This process of collection and reassembly is not that different from the way a film is put together, or the way a fan responds to their favourite star. To my mind, historical investigation is as much a part of the process of commodity production and consumption as any other form of cultural activity, but the historian's implication in this process is rarely recognised. The pleasures and perils of historical research itself have hardly been addressed, despite the fact that history itself is a fiercely contested and debated discipline.

If the historian participates in the process of commodity production and consumption, it can also be argued that cultural commodities such as historical films contribute to the process of making history. It is now quite widely accepted that historical fictions feed into popular conceptions of history, where they mingle with and inflect other kinds of history, such as the official histories we learn at school, or our own private recollections of the past.[6] Part of the pleasure in such fictions is deciding how their interpretations of events match up to those official and personal versions.

Although I have no means of knowing what actually takes place in the minds of audiences, I would argue that the spectacular display of images of the past offered by historical fiction films invites more than passive consumption on the part of the viewer. Indeed, I would claim that consumption is never simply passive, since it involves skills, knowledge, negotiation and discrimination. Confronted with an image of the past, a spectator may appreciate its beauty, or contest its accuracy, or want to acquire a copy of it. The first requires an aesthetic judgement, the second historical knowledge, while the third may involve considerable persistence in obtaining a satisfactory facsimile. A case in point are my own attempts to track down a copy of the earrings worn by Phyllis Calvert in *Madonna of the Seven Moons* (1944), which have been continually frustrated.

If I were lucky enough to find and wear those facsimile earrings, I would have collected a highly prized memento that would connect me with someone else in another time and place, thus closing the gap between myself and the past, and I would have retrieved a little piece of exotica that might magically transform my own environment, endowing me with the rebellious spirit of its original wearer. Both of these involve an element of disguise and masquerade, and an element of pastiche, since the gypsy earrings would probably be worn with clothes and accessories of a different style. In this play with history, I would be making a statement about my special knowledge of the past, as well as consuming a particular image of it. This fascination with images of the past is, of course, deeply imbued with consumerist impulses, but those impulses do not seem so very far removed from those motivating historical research, which must also involve an imaginative leap across time and place.

This digression into the contaminated pleasures of history is by way of introducing my detailed analysis of *Dance With a Stranger*. I shall look at the opening of the film to explore some of the questions about reconstructing history that I have discussed. The opening scenes of any film are clearly important in establishing time and place, in introducing the main characters, and in setting up the direction of the narrative. Since this film is dealing with a fairly notorious incident, the film-makers can expect a certain amount of knowledge in the audience about the story, but they can also expect that

Figure 16.1 Historical connections: Rupert Everett and Miranda Richardson in *Dance With a Stranger* (1985). Courtesy First Film/Goldcrest/Film 4/NFFC and the Kobal Collection.

knowledge to be hazy in many cases. Most people know that Ruth Ellis killed her lover and was hanged for the crime, but they may not know much more than that. Others may not even know that, and may be drawn to the film as a tragic love story, or a women's picture.

As a piece of historical reconstruction, then, *Dance With a Stranger* needs to provide some background information. However, as the production notes repeatedly stressed, this is not a documentary. It is fiction, an imaginative interpretation. Rather than embarking on a search for truth, analysis or explanation, the film invites the audience to enter a fantasy world. This is clearly marked in the opening credits, over which a woman's voice is heard singing a popular love song from the 1950s, a song that asserts the power of fantasy over reality. The song also suggests the power of love to overcome obstacles, but at the same time its mournful rendition implies that these sentiments may be misguided. At the end of the credits, the interior, subjective mode of the song continues as a title appears stating that this is London in Spring 1954 and the camera focuses on a 1950s-style car driven by Ian Holm as Desmond Cussen, leading a group of wild young things to the club managed by Ruth. There is no dialogue or other sound until Desmond and his group of friends reach the inside door of the club. The subjective mode of the song is overlaid

223

on the exterior, objective mode of the title, which seems to suggest that what we are about to see, although based on reality, should be regarded as fiction. The presence of the title itself tells us that this is a fictional reconstruction of the past. It is this tension between fiction and reality that seems to lie at the heart of the historical film, and I shall return to this later.

A great deal of work is done by the visual codes of costume, make-up and décor in this sequence. As well as reconstructing period, costume and make-up give us information about character. Desmond's tight pinstripe suit, short back and sides and thin moustache contrast with the more dishevelled, though no less expensive, appearance of Blakely and his cronies. The difference is one of class as much as personality. Desmond is newly rich, and this shows in his uneasiness with his clothes – he is always adjusting his tie, for instance. Blakely, in contrast, is confident and relaxed in what he wears, a confidence that we assume emanates from his middle-class background, and perhaps his youthfulness. In photographs of the period, while the real Desmond looks very similar to his 1985 lookalike, the real David Blakely is more conventionally dressed and coiffed than his 1980s counterpart. Contemporary factors therefore play a significant part in the process of reconstruction. The film-makers' desire to stress class differences, together with the need to take into account Rupert Everett's star appeal to 1980s audiences, have resulted in a retro-chic look for David Blakely that has as much to do with 1980s style as with any attempt at faithful reconstruction of the 1950s.

Miranda Richardson's costume also serves more than one function. In the opening sequence, and throughout the film, Ruth Ellis wears different versions of the New Look. The New Look, launched by French designer Christian Dior in 1947, was a style that stressed extravagance and excess in contrast to the more austere Utility clothing of the war years. In its later, tailored version, the New Look projected an elegant, professional working woman image, while the long, full skirts, tight waists and padded busts of the more flamboyant versions presented a romantic, luxurious and eroticised vision of postwar femininity. Because of its abundance, the New Look connoted wealth and consumerism, and because of its haute couture origins, it was a middle-class image. By the early 1950s it had gone into mass production and was available to a wider range of people. It could be seen, then, as an aspirational style worn by working-class, or lower-middle-class women who wanted to rise up the social ladder. By all accounts, Ruth Ellis was such a person, and the film presents her in those terms.[7]

The elegant New Look gown worn by Miranda Richardson in the opening sequence defines Ruth Ellis' character and motivations as well as setting period. Her carefully permed, peroxide blonde hair and heavy make-up, however, betray her lower-class origins – as one of David's friends comments later about

Ruth's unsuitability as a match for him: 'You only have to look at her.' Neither Ruth nor Desmond is 'the real thing' in terms of class, nor, it is suggested, could they ever be. Later in the film, when Ruth loses her job at the club and moves in with Desmond, there is a scene in which Desmond asks her why she does not let her hair revert to its natural colour. Ruth teases him about whether she is 'the real thing' or not, sticking her false eyelashes on his eyelids and asking him if she can shave off his moustache, creating a grotesque parody of her lover David. This poignant moment seems to comment not only on the images of the two characters, but on the image-making process itself.

Costume and make-up are an essential part of creating images that resemble the real people the actors are impersonating, yet the resemblance is only ever approximate. These impersonations are doubles or replicas that we accept as stand-ins for the real thing, even though we know they are fake. The fascination of these lookalikes seems to lie in the extent to which they resemble the real thing. We may suspend our disbelief in order to enjoy the film, but we are also invited to make judgements about the quality and credibility of the actor's performance. Costume, make-up, décor and performance act as recognition points, as shorthand signs to trigger collective memories of the past. They are complex, multilayered images that serve a variety of functions. They offer visual pleasure, give narrative and other kinds of information, or they can be used to comment ironically on the proceedings.

The period costume film uses images in a self-conscious and self-referential fashion to involve the audience in a sophisticated play with the process of historical reconstruction, a play which depends on aesthetic judgements and historical knowledge, but also on a sense of history as partial and incomplete, available only in fragments and imperfect memories. There is an element of masquerade in the accumulation of period detail with which they represent the past, which can tip over into irony. This irony is evident in the scene where Ruth and her boss Morrie Conley, played by Stratford Johns, discuss her suggestions for improving the club.

The scene begins with a tightly framed two-shot of Ruth and Morrie in the corner of the room, sitting at a table. As they tot up the night's takings and talk about the cost of hiring a pianist, Ruth gets up to go to the mantelpiece to pick up a very 1950s heart-shaped dish containing books of matches given away by other clubs. The camera follows her, panning round the room to reveal a sideboard with lamp, before settling on the mantelpiece with its clock and a mirror hung over it, all in 1950s style. Incidentally, this enables the audience to view the back of Ruth's New Look outfit as she turns to go towards the mantelpiece, a movement which is repeated twice more in the scene, once when she goes to the sideboard to make a drink, and again when she goes to switch on the radio to obliterate the sound of the couple having sex in the room above. Miranda Richardson's performance is arch and brittle, and she plays with her glasses in an affected manner. A little later, Morrie gets up from his chair and moves from left to centre frame, where he remains for some time, so that we get a good look at his tie, which is, in 1950s fashion, wide and short. The film cuts to Ruth switching on the radio, a shot that reveals the rest of the room, evidently her bedroom, furnished with yet more 1950s-style furniture.

In this scene, everything, including the actors' body movements, seems to be built around the business of displaying period objects and costume. Although the décor is relatively sparse, the period objects are all carefully placed in the set, which looks more like a museum reproduction than a room in which someone lives. This has the slightly uncanny effect of drawing attention to the fact that these objects, and indeed, these actors, are replicas, and that what we are watching is a reconstruction. Miranda Richardson's brilliantly twitchy performance, however authentic it is meant to be, simply has the effect of underlining the sense of masquerade.

There is another way in which *Dance With a Stranger* plays on the idea of doubles, replicas and masquerade. The film draws on American popular culture, particularly in its use of music. The music soundtrack is compiled from jazz numbers and 1950s American ballads, among them Mari Wilson's hit 'Dance With a Stranger', and, significantly, 'Diamonds Are a Girl's Best Friend' from Howard Hawks' 1953 film *Gentlemen Prefer Blondes*, starring Marilyn Monroe and Jane Russell. There are other references to Marilyn Monroe too. Ruth constantly plays with her glasses, and when asked why she does not wear them, she replies, 'Men don't make passes at girls who wear glasses', a direct reference to Monroe's role in *How to Marry a Millionaire* (1953), where, although extremely short-sighted, she refuses to wear glasses, believing that they will spoil her chances of marrying a rich man. On one level, this is simply a self-reflexive joke for the benefit of film buffs in the audience, and a further piece of period detail. But on another, it has the effect of providing yet another layer of replication. A peroxided Miranda Richardson masquerades as a peroxided Ruth Ellis, who models herself on a peroxided Marilyn Monroe. During the opening sequence, David Blakely asks if the drink he is offered is the 'real thing'. Through such self-conscious references, *Dance With a Stranger* seems to imply that there is no 'real thing' when it comes to reconstructing history, just an endless series of replicas. One might expect this ironic play to distance us from the characters, and perhaps to some extent it does. But it is also quite touching, as though we are watching children dressed up and pretending to be adults.

I have suggested that the historical costume film is a sophisticated form that has the potential to comment on the process of historical reconstruction itself, and that when it does so, it draws on a wide range of skills, knowledge and pleasures in the audience, who are not addressed simply as passive consumers, but are drawn into a complex and self-conscious engagement with history. I have also argued that we might learn something about the historian's relationship with the past from these historical fictions, in so far as they deal with questions such as representation of the past, and the nature of our emotional investment in images of the past. While the activity of historical investigation is not precisely the same as that of making a historical fiction film, or the pleasures involved in viewing a period drama, there are considerable areas of overlap. Historical objects or documents are already images when they are captured, whether by historians, film-makers or audiences, and as images, they have the status of commodities as well as cultural artefacts – a multi-layered identity in which the different functions cannot necessarily easily be separated out. The power of period films such as *Dance With a Stranger* is that, rather than offering us historical 'truth' or knowledge, they enable us to understand the complex pleasures of those processes of historical reconstruction that are fundamental to any engagement with the past.

Notes

1 See, for example, many of the contributions in Lester Friedman (ed.), *British Cinema and Thatcherism: Fires Were Started* (London: University College London Press, 1993).

2 Pierre Sorlin's argument in *The Film in History: Restaging the Past* (Oxford: Blackwell, 1980) that historical films reflect current preoccupations rather than past events has been very influential on film studies.

3 This is Thomas Elsaesser's argument in 'Images for sale: the "new" British cinema', in Friedman (ed.), *British Cinema and Thatcherism*, pp. 52–69.

4 Between 1985 and 1991 on the British Film Institute publication *Monthly Film Bulletin*, later absorbed into *Sight and Sound*

5 An expanded version of these debates about history can be found in my introductory chapter in Pam Cook (ed.), *Gainsborough Pictures* (London and Washington: Cassell, 1997), pp. 1–12.

6 See Sorlin, *The Film in History* and Alison Light's discussion of the relationship between popular historical fictions and official histories, in '"Young Bess": historical novels and growing up', *Feminist Review*, 33 (autumn 1988), pp. 57–71.

7 For a more extended discussion of the historical and cultural significance of the New Look, see Maureen Turim, 'Designing women: the emergence of the new Sweetheart Line', in Jane Gaines and Charlotte Herzog (eds), *Fabrications: Costume and the Female Body* (London and New York: Routledge, 1990), pp. 212–28; and Pam Cook, 'Changing places: costume and identity', in *Fashioning the Nation: Costume and Identity in British Cinema* (London: BFI Publishing, 1996), pp. 42–63.

Chapter 17

FICTIONS OF IDENTITY

Style, mimicry and gender in the films of Kathryn Bigelow

Kathryn Bigelow is one of a few women directors who have moved into mainstream film-making since the early 1980s, and have managed to retain a distinctive style and voice. She appears to be a postfeminist, postmodern phenomenon, in that while she is clearly inspired by a feminist agenda, she does not allow herself to be constrained by political correctness – indeed, she is more concerned with pushing back the edges of the envelope when it comes to political issues. Her work challenges the boundaries of representation, particularly when it comes to graphic depictions of violence, a prominent feature of all her films. She has said in interviews that she is interested in provoking debate, and her reputation as a serious film-maker rests on her willingness to take risks with form and content. Most of her films appropriate established genres, often producing hybrid forms, such as the vampire western *Near Dark* (1987) or the rape-revenge cop movie *Blue Steel* (1990), both of which explore the violent underside of heterosexual desire. She continued to court controversy with the futuristic action movie *Strange Days* (1995), which dealt with the less salubrious aspects of virtual reality, exploring the possibility of cross-gender identification, among other things. In a notorious sequence, the audience was invited to share a rapist's point-of-view, and the point-of-view of his victim as she experienced her own rape and murder. This daring investigation of cinematic voyeurism was also the subject of Michael Powell's 1960 film *Peeping Tom*, one of many to which *Strange Days* paid homage. Indeed, it seemed that the element of pastiche and mimicry in *Strange Days*, the 'quoting' from other films and film-makers, had taken over to such an extent that what remained was a series of borrowed set pieces lacking a coherent identity. The two central characters played by Angela Bassett and Ralph Fiennes were not strong enough in themselves, nor was their relationship convincing enough to hold the film together or to give it a moral centre.

A similar problem occurred with *Point Break* (1991), the surfing action movie Bigelow directed after *Near Dark*. The confident direction of complex action sequences, the visceral, edgy style and the dramatic use of light to create stunning, seductive images were impressive, but it was difficult to detect a difference between Bigelow's film and any other buddy action movie with a homoerotic subtext. *Point Break* looked and felt rather like a James Cameron movie, and the fact that Cameron was executive producer on the film and claims to have ghost-written the script seemed to bear this out.[1] Cameron is a superlative action director himself, and is also responsible for some of contemporary Hollywood's most successful and interesting feminist-influenced movies. Indeed, it is something of an irony that *Aliens* (1986), *Terminator 2: Judgment Day* (1993) and *Titanic* (1997) appear to contain more overt feminist content than *Point Break*. We tend to assume that it is possible to decipher an identifiable female discourse in films directed by women. When films directed by men, such as Hollywood women's pictures, also display this recognisable female element, or specific address to women, more often than not it is put down to female scriptwriters, stars or other women who may have had input. The feminist elements in many of Cameron's films could be attributed to the influence of producer Gale Ann Hurd, for example. Apart from the difficulties inherent in giving ideas an individual source or origin, particularly in a collaborative enterprise such as film-making, the notion that the gender of the director is reflected in a film's style or content is clearly problematic, despite our desire to see women film-makers and audiences adequately represented, and given a voice in Hollywood. It is entirely possible for a male director to make feminist or feminist-influenced movies, such as Ridley Scott's *Thelma & Louise* (1991) or Jonathan Demme's *The Silence of the Lambs* (1990), and for a woman director to film a macho action epic that focuses on male sexuality.

In the light of such gender fluidity, we may well ask what is the point of women working in the mainstream, since men are able to do the feminist thing just as well. But the question needs to be put another way. Since Kathryn Bigelow, among others, has proved that a woman director can handle action epics at least as well as her male counterparts, why is it that women directors working in Hollywood are generally assigned to women's picture material, and find it difficult to break out of this genre? It seems that when it comes to the gender divide, there is a double standard at work. Bigelow's films challenge that double standard, but they also create a conundrum. When women film-makers move outside the female ghetto into the male arena, how should they proceed? Should they disguise themselves as men, or should they keep their female identity and produce films that comfortably fit traditional notions of femininity and feminist creativity? It could be argued that both *Point*

229

Break and *Strange Days* are films made in disguise — that is, Kathryn Bigelow chose to assume a male identity in making both of them. She did so very successfully, since both films more than match the efforts of her acknowledged mentors such as Martin Scorsese, Sam Peckinpah, Michael Powell and Alfred Hitchcock, all of whom used action genres to investigate the dark side of human sexuality.

I want to explore this question of film-making in disguise, beginning with Bigelow's image or public persona. The significance of the star image in feeding into the promotion and reception of a film has been widely discussed,[2] but the role of the director in this process can be equally important. Like Alfred Hitchcock, who excelled at self-publicity and successfully created an image of himself which encouraged the belief that he was the sole author of his work,[3] Bigelow has carefully constructed her persona in press and television interviews. This persona partly depends on the way she looks — her clothes, make-up, hairstyle and so on — partly on her manner, and partly on what she says about her own work. She has long hair and wears make-up, at the same time as dressing in masculine-style, dark tailored suits with simple white shirt or T-shirt. Occasionally, she has been photographed wearing more casual sports gear with baseball cap. This is an androgynous look, but it is not the androgyny associated with cross-dressing or gay and lesbian identity. There is, I would suggest, no vocabulary for this particular style, though it may be related to the power-dressing phenomenon of the 1980s, when women making their way up the corporate ladder to the boardroom adopted masculine-style tailored clothing with exaggerated padded shoulders. But Bigelow's is an artier, more relaxed version. What is interesting about her fashionable designer suits is that, unlike cross-dressing and drag, they do not seem to suggest a crisis or parody of gender or sexuality. Rather, they project a stylish heterosexual woman who is at ease in male clothing. At the same time, there is an element of performance, or a hint of masquerade about many of her publicity shots, which suggest a self-conscious play with gender roles.

This is exemplified by the widely circulated image in which she is shown wearing a dark jacket over a white shirt, leaning back slightly, with hands in pockets, looking coolly into camera, almost as if this were a fashion shot. A camera eyepiece is worn as a necklace — a touch of irony which comments on both her gender and her professional status. Many of Bigelow's publicity photographs have her posing for the camera dressed like this. It is a style statement that evokes androgynous, postmodern movie heroines such as Sarah Connor dressed in combat gear in *Terminator 2: Judgment Day*, Megan Turner sporting cop's uniform in *Blue Steel*, or Ripley decked out in metal terminator hardware in *Aliens*. These are women who take on male armour in order to survive, but also in order to change the course of history. They challenge the

230

Figure 17.1   Cool customer: Kathryn Bigelow. Courtesy the Kobal Collection.

notion that biology is destiny, though in all cases they suffer for their temerity. They are all driven characters, completely focused on their respective missions, and looking for power and control. Bigelow's image shares many of these characteristics. In interviews she has described herself as a highly organised film-maker who plans everything down to the last detail before shooting begins (incidentally, this was a feature of Hitchcock's working methods too). By all accounts, she is rather cool and reserved in interview, frustrating the interviewers' desire to get behind the image and to discover more about the real Kathryn Bigelow.[4] This may be a deliberate strategy, suggesting that the image is all there is, that perhaps there is nothing behind it.

This short detour through Bigelow's personal style is not entirely a digression. I would suggest that her public persona corresponds closely to the kinds of films she makes. In other words, like Megan Turner in *Blue Steel*, Bigelow takes on the trappings of masculine identity and risks losing her own identity in the process. On one level, all her films are about identity crisis, featuring characters who form dangerous liaisons that threaten to engulf or obliterate them. Before looking at those films in more detail, it might be useful to provide some biographical background. Bigelow trained as a painter at the San Francisco Art Institute and in the late 1970s became involved with a group of conceptual artists called Art and Language, who were concerned with finding new forms of artistic expression. This early experience in performance art and painting has been seen by many as accounting for the painterly quality of Bigelow's films, her preoccupation with light and concern with composition. The performance side of her artistic training is rarely used to explain the films, but once looked at from this perspective, a self-conscious element of performance can be detected in all of them. This focus on performance and identity links Bigelow with Judith Butler's work, where she maintains that gender is a matter of external performance rather than the expression of an interior, essential identity.[5] My approach here is influenced by Butler's ideas, and by the writing of costume and art historian Anne Hollander, who argues that identity is a surface phenomenon, and that there is no essential or preexisting body, only the outer representation of different bodies.[6] I shall explore these ideas in relation to Bigelow's films, but first I want to focus on the way she is perceived by others, since this provides insight into the way her work is received.

As already indicated, press and television interviews provide a rich source of material for looking at the circulation of images of Bigelow as a director. A biographical item made by BBC2's cinema programme *Moving Pictures* at the time of *Blue Steel*'s release in Britain includes coverage of Bigelow's formative experiences in the 1970s. In the interview with her, Bigelow appears reticent about her personal background, which may help to explain why there is so much material featuring other people talking about her and her work. In an early section, her ex-comrade from Art and Language, Mel Ramsden, talks rather disparagingly about her work, and about her success as a commercial film-maker. This section includes some rare archive footage from the 1970s of Bigelow performing in an experimental video. One of the most interesting aspects of the programme is the different ways in which Bigelow and her work are described by other contributors. Such descriptions deserve more extended analysis than I have space for here, because not only are they revealing of attitudes and expectations, they also feed into to the construction of the Bigelow image. In this particular case, the interviewer sets the scene by describing Bigelow as a 'control freak', and this is taken up by Mel Ramsden, who claims not to recognise the woman he knew in the 1970s as an incompetent film-maker in the control freak that is Bigelow today.

The programme also features a number of shots of Bigelow directing on the set of *Blue Steel* in a masterful manner. The implication is that she has undergone some kind of transformation, and that what she is today bears little relationship to what she was then, which seems unlikely to be the case. There also seems to be an underlying suggestion that she is something of a fraud. The idea put forward by her ex-tutor, film theorist Peter Wollen, that she has abandoned the formalist concerns of her performance art years for narrative cinema ignores the fact that performance clearly remains an important element in her films. A history is constructed for her that goes against the grain of the evidence included in the programme itself. I am not suggesting a conspiracy, but it is interesting that the Bigelow persona constructed by the programme is largely made up of pastiche – a mixture of anecdotes and critical judgements from other people that tells you more about them and their attitudes than about Bigelow herself.

The other aspect of Bigelow's formative experiences mentioned by this programme is collaborative work. Art and Language was a collective dedicated to group discussion and to non-hierarchical ways of working. This was seen as a political statement against the divisions of labour imposed by capitalism and patriarchy, and such collectives mushroomed in the 1970s. Apart from a brief flash of titles giving the dictionary definition of the word 'collective', the programme does not really take this seriously – in fact, in the light of the video clip and Mel Ramsden's comments, it becomes a bit of a joke. Yet Bigelow's feature films are all characterised by collaboration, particularly collaboration with men. *The Loveless* (1982) was directed and scripted with Monty Montgomery, she collaborated with Eric Red on the scripts of *Near Dark* and *Blue Steel*, and with James Cameron on *Point Break* and *Strange Days*. In addition, as noted earlier, she claims to have been influenced exclusively by male film-makers. Susan Sontag is the only woman I have come across who has been cited as having an impact on Bigelow's thinking. Film-making is, of course, a collaborative process, despite the fact that films are usually identi-fied by the director's name, as though the director were the sole author. This is a literary model of authorship, which sees the work as an extension of an individual vision or psyche. Even in those cases where the director seems to exert total control, their role is mainly supervisory – she or he organises and interacts with all the different creative contributions that go to make up the film. The significance of those other contributions is often overlooked, and the director is privileged as the primary source of meaning.[7]

Although the auteurist discourse can be an advantage for women directors working in Hollywood, enabling those few who succeed to get proper recogni-tion, it can also be a double-edged sword, especially when women directors are evaluated according to the traditional values of the male directors' canon. Bigelow has been accorded the status of auteur by critics, and it is interesting that she does not play down the element of collaboration and influence, even if those who write about her do. When talking about her work, she does present it as the projection of her own interests and preoccupations, but at the same time she emphasises the pastiche factor, the borrowing of styles that challenges the very idea of individual vision or identity. The idea of collaboration, which I would argue is a carry-over from her experiences in the 1970s, is important in attempting to establish what might constitute the Bigelow style. Is there such a thing, or does it amount to little more than a mixed bag of ideas and images appropriated from the work of others? And if the latter is the case, what are the implications for the situation of women directors working in the mainstream? There are different ways of answering this question. Some would argue that in white, male-dominated Hollywood, Bigelow's work manifests the compromises women inevitably have to make if they are to survive. Certainly, as with any Hollywood director, considerable negotiation and the help of powerful male supporters[8] are necessary in order to make the films she wants to make. While this could be seen as evidence of compromise, it also enables her to challenge the preconceptions of the Hollywood community, and of audiences, about what constitutes women's, or feminist, film-making.

I'd like to explore this question of influence and identity in relation to *The Loveless*. The film is based on an original screenplay by Monty Montgomery and Bigelow, but the plot itself is scarcely original. A group of bikers drive into a small town, where their arrival triggers a catastrophe. *The Loveless* is a 1980s update of the 1950s black-and-white Marlon Brando biker movie *The Wild One* (1953), and it reflects the earlier film's preoccupation with subcultural style, the intricate language of the bikers' clothes, the fetishisation of black leather and shiny chrome, and the homoerotic relationships of the male group. It is also a self-conscious reconstruction of the small-town melodramas popular in the

1950s. But the film also borrows from sources outside the mainstream, from avant-garde film-maker Kenneth Anger's poetic, erotic celebration of male biker culture in the 1964 film *Scorpio Rising*, for example, and from French New Wave director Jean-Luc Godard's dramatic use of colour in the late 1960s and 1970s. On one level, *The Loveless* can be seen, as Bigelow has said, simply as a nostalgic homage to films and film-makers of the past, and perhaps it should not be seen as much more than that. But there is something so excessive about the film's emphasis on the composition of the images and the actors' performances that it bears closer examination.

The Loveless seems to put everything in quotation marks. The sequence in the garage in which the bikers gather to work on their machines refers to *Scorpio Rising*, in which romantic popular music is played over images of leather clad boys posing with their bikes, while the moment when the young woman and her car enter the scene recalls Godard's apocalyptic road movie *Weekend* (1967), where a weekend in the country turns into a disaster (at one point in Bigelow's film, Willem Dafoe even refers sarcastically to a weekend in the country). *The Loveless* has the look of a 1950s Hollywood studio melo-drama – the young girl's red car is reminiscent of Marylee Hadley's in Douglas Sirk's 1956 *Written on the Wind*, in which a daughter is also respon-sible for killing her father, though by a more indirect route than in *The Love-less*. This pastiche of quotes from movies of the 1950s and 1960s creates a kind of time warp in which nothing is real – rather, we are witnessing a celebration of image and style. This is underlined by the extremely mannered perform-ances of the actors, their stylised delivery of the clichéd dialogue, and the way they seem to be posing all the time.

While all this could be seen as rather laboured homage, it is surely signific-ant that the films quoted are all subversive in some way. *The Wild One* is a relatively radical exploration of male heterosexuality, *Scorpio Rising* is a cele-bration of gay sexuality as well as being formally experimental, *Weekend* is a devastating indictment of bourgeois French society, and *Written on the Wind* is highly critical of the patriarchal family. Most of these films feature a cata-clysmic element of violence which threatens to overturn the existing social order. As in *Written on the Wind*, in *The Loveless* the daughter's sexual rebellion leads to the death of her father and the end of his tyranny, an event that is viewed in apocalyptic terms as a necessary act of violent destruction, rather than as a positive political statement. It is as if the film were saying that beneath the stylish veneer simmers a volcano waiting to erupt. The bikers act as a catalyst, and at the end they move on, perhaps to destroy another community – rather like the vampire gang in *Near Dark*.

The Loveless seems to celebrate the subversive potential of subcultural style, but also the power of the male biker group to inspire desire and

Figure 17.2   Pastiche: Willem Dafoe in *The Loveless* (1982). Courtesy Pioneer Films and the Kobal Collection.

identification in the female characters – the woman who is part of the group, the waitress, and the daughter. The group's mobility, freedom and amorality is aspired to by women who feel trapped by dead-end jobs, family and narrow social codes. This cross-gender identification is central to all Bigelow's work, and it is always given this apocalyptic edge, as though it were capable of destroying everything. Another theme that figures prominently in *The Loveless* is the relationship between the individual and the group, something that recurs in later films. It may not be too speculative to suggest that Bigelow's experiences of collective group activity in the 1970s contributed to the sense of the revolutionary potential of the group that occurs in *The Loveless* and *Near Dark*.

The vampire western *Near Dark*, co-scripted by Bigelow and Eric Red, is an extreme statement of this preoccupation with subversive subcultural groups. A group of sadistic vampires, looking like rejects from a Sam Peckinpah or Walter Hill western, roam across the American landscape picking off the population to satisfy their boodlust. There is a high degree of graphic violence in *Near Dark*, executed with gleeful perversity by the vampires. There is also a strong element of quotation, and a fascination with visual style. However, in contrast to *The Loveless*, in *Near Dark* it is the demonic subcultural group that appears to be destroyed. Because this is a horror film, the narrative resolution, in which normality is restored, the good family reconstituted and the heterosexual couple apparently united, is not straightforward. In horror films the monster is never destroyed, only repressed, and what is repressed always returns.[9] In *Near Dark*, the threat of the return of the repressed is, appropriately enough, signified by an item of clothing, or more precisely, an accessory. During the film, the young hero's homoerotic relationship with Severin, a particularly violent and sadistic member of the vampire gang, is sealed by his wearing the vampire's spur. When he finally manages to destroy Severin, who is in a way his double, our hero is still wearing the spur. The suggestion is that the threat to normality, and to stable sexual identity, has only temporarily been overcome. The hero's identification with his demonic other self is still there, waiting for an opportunity to surface again.

This idea of the destructive power of transgressive identification recurs in *Blue Steel*, Bigelow's next film, again co-scripted by her and Eric Red, and with the involvement as producer of maverick Hollywood film-maker Oliver Stone. *Blue Steel* also uses clothes and accessories (in this case, guns) to explore the instability of gender identity. In this film, rookie cop Megan Turner, played by Jamie Lee Curtis, becomes sexually involved with a serial killer, a commodities broker played by Ron Silver, whose gun fetish mirrors her own. Like *Near Dark*, *Blue Steel* plays on the identification between an apparently normal character and their monstrous double, a demonic figure who threatens to destroy them and their world, and has to be overcome. As in *Near Dark*, the encounter with the demon involves a risk, not only to life, but to the self. In *Blue Steel*, the struggle to defeat the demonic double results in a loss of identity for the heroine Megan, and despite the fact that she manages to kill Eugene, the film ends on a pessimistic note. The final sequence depicts a prolonged, bloody shoot-out between Megan and her adversary, which leaves her in a state of catatonic collapse as her gun falls from her hand.

The sequence is deeply melancholic, pervaded with a sense of loss, as though Megan's achievement in destroying the killer Eugene, her victory and revenge, are seen as a defeat. Considering that it was directed by a woman who has succeeded in a male-dominated world, *Blue Steel* is remarkably pessimistic about the consequences of women aspiring to enter that world, and of their ability to survive. Indeed, entry to that world is seen as a dangerous risk, almost a flirtation with death, with death being the ultimate loss of identity in oblivion. This flirtation with death and oblivion of the self is a common theme in Bigelow's films, but it is not unique to those films, any more than her visual style is unique. Visual and thematic echoes of James Cameron's 1986 film *Aliens* can be found in *Blue Steel*, and Ripley certainly has much in common with Megan Turner. For both these warrior women, survival is almost a military exercise, with Megan's cop uniform and the articulated metal hardware outfit in which Ripley defeats the alien nothing less than suits of armour.

The sense of appropriating the armour of masculinity in order to survive is there in *Aliens* and *Blue Steel*, as are the death-defying risks that both women take in their struggle for power and authority. According to these films, survival in the male world is a painful and potentially lethal business. *Aliens* is more optimistic about the chances for survival,[10] but Ripley remains isolated, an outsider. Both films seem to question the value, or even the possibility, of assimilation. If cross-gender identification seems to promise the end of socially imposed gender divisions and hierarchies, then these films seem to be asking where that actually leads, as Ripley ends up in deep space in *Aliens*, and Megan is left in a catatonic stupor in *Blue Steel*. The use of predominantly blue light underlines the overall sense of melancholy, suggesting that something is lost in the process of crossing over into the male domain. It is as though heroines such as Megan and Ripley, through their acquisition of the trappings of masculinity, become displaced persons, condemned to wander the borders of identity. As action heroines, they have been seen as feminist role models, yet at the same time they manifest a deep ambivalence towards the male ambience in which they operate, which could also be interpreted as a critique of feminist aspirations to equality in a man's world. *Blue Steel* is equally pessimistic about the possibility of heterosexual love in such a world, where violence and alienation predominate. At the end of *Strange Days*, which is set in Los Angeles on the eve of the millennium, the hero and heroine do affirm their love, kissing on the stroke of midnight amid a frenzied explosion of celebratory noise and fireworks whose very excessiveness imbues their union with irony.

Through my analysis of Kathryn Bigelow's films, I have suggested an equivalence between their exploration of gender and her persona projected in

Figure 17.3   Ironic excess: *Strange Days* (1995). Courtesy Lightstorm Entertainment/Merie W. Wallace and the Kobal Collection.

publicity material and interviews. This persona seems to embody the predicament of many of her protagonists as they find themselves in the grip of identity crisis in a world where gender roles are destabilised – a dilemma that characterises her own position as a woman film-maker working in the Hollywood industry. Unlike many of her colleagues, Bigelow presents herself as image, and there is an element of performance in her self-presentation which implies that it is a conscious fiction, fabricated from a variety of sources. This makes it difficult to find essential truths and meaning, feminist or otherwise, behind such images, as well as challenging the premises behind accepted notions of cinematic authorship and the search for origin and intention. Bigelow's work implies that feminist discourse must be constructed by film-makers and audiences from the available cinematic vocabulary. Thus feminist cinema is seen as a dynamic process of appropriation and exploitation of existing languages, from which new, critical meanings can be created. Through strategies of mimicry and pastiche, prevailing ideologies can be lampooned or overturned.

This also raises questions about the relevance of gender in film production. Bigelow has asserted in interview that she does not consider the film-making process to be gender specific in any respect, and that she sees no reason why female directors should be confined to women's pictures, or men to hardware

239

action movies.[11] However, she also acknowledges that the Hollywood industry categorises film-makers along gender lines. While she and other women film-makers aspire to transcend gender, they cannot escape it altogether, with the result that they are in a position of constantly struggling against the way they are perceived – like the heroines in the movies discussed earlier. Bigelow dramatises this struggle in films such as *Blue Steel* and *Strange Days*, and also through the performance of her public persona, with its ironic take on gendered images.

Notes

1 See Cameron's testimony in his introduction to the published script of *Strange Days* (New York: Penguin Books, 1996).

2 See Richard Dyer in *Stars* (London: BFI Publishing, 1978), and John Ellis in *Visible Fictions* (London and New York: Routledge, 1982).

3 See Robert E. Kapsis, *Hitchcock: The Making of a Reputation* (Chicago: Chicago University Press, 1992), for a detailed account of Hitchcock's strategies for constructing himself as an auteur.

4 This was apparently the case with two documentaries in which Bigelow appeared: an item on her career filmed for BBC2's *Moving Pictures* programme (discussed on p. 232), and a Channel 4 programme on women working in contemporary Hollywood, *Reel Women*.

5 Judith Butler, *Gender Trouble: Feminism and the Subversion of Identity* (New York: Routledge, 1999).

6 Anne Hollander, *Seeing Through Clothes* (Berkeley: University of California Press, 1993).

7 The auteur debate has a long history in film studies – see Pam Cook and Mieke Berninck (eds), *The Cinema Book* (London: BFI Publishing, 1999) for a full account. See also Yvonne Tasker, *50 Contemporary Filmmakers* (London and New York: Routledge, 2002).

8 James Cameron, and also Oliver Stone, who was instrumental in getting *Blue Steel* made.

9 See Robin Wood, 'The American nightmare: horror in the 70s', in *Hollywood from Vietnam to Reagan* (New York: Columbia University Press, 1986), pp. 70–94.

10 Unlike David Fincher's sequel, *Alien³* (1992), in which Ripley dies at the end in an act of heroic self-sacrifice. However, in Jeunet's *Alien Resurrection* (1997) she is brought back to life.

11 Bigelow interviewed in Jim Hillier, *The New Hollywood* (London: Studio Vista, 1992), p. 127.

Index

Page numbers in **bold type** indicate an illustration

INDEX

INDEX

INDEX